D1612929

BORDERS, MIGRATION AND CLASS IN AN AGE OF CRISIS

Producing Workers and Immigrants

Tom Vickers

BRISTOL
UNIVERSITY
PRESS

First published in Great Britain in 2019 by

Bristol University Press
University of Bristol
1-9 Old Park Hill
Bristol
BS2 8BB
UK
t: +44 (0)117 954 5940
www.bristoluniversitypress.co.uk

North America office:
Policy Press
c/o The University of Chicago Press
1427 East 60th Street
Chicago, IL 60637, USA
t: +1 773 702 7700
f: +1 773-702-9756
sales@press.uchicago.edu
www.press.uchicago.edu

© Bristol University Press 2019

British Library Cataloguing in Publication Data
A catalogue record for this book is available from the British Library

Library of Congress Cataloging-in-Publication Data
A catalog record for this book has been requested

ISBN 978-1-5292-0181-9 hardcover
ISBN 978-1-5292-0185-7 ePub
ISBN 978-1-5292-0186-4 Mobi
ISBN 978-1-5292-0183-3 ePdf

Cover design by Andrew Corbett
Front cover image: Shutterstock
Printed and bound in Great Britain by CPI Group (UK) Ltd,
Croydon, CR0 4YY
Bristol University Press uses environmentally responsible print partners

In memory of Stephen Thompson

GLOBAL MIGRATION AND SOCIAL CHANGE

This series showcases original research that looks at the nexus between migration, citizenship and social change. It advances new scholarship in migration and refugee studies and fosters cross- and inter-disciplinary dialogue in this field. The series includes research-based monographs and edited collections, informed by a range of qualitative and quantitative research methods.

Series editors:

Nando Sigona, University of Birmingham, UK
n.sigona@bham.ac.uk

Alan Gamlen, Monash University, Australia
alan.gamlen@monash.edu

Forthcoming:

Belonging in Translation
Reiko Shindo, Aug 2019

Negotiating Migration in the Context of Climate Change
Sarah Nash, Oct 2019

Out now in the series:

 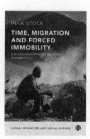  

Contents

List of Figures and Tables

Figures

Tables

Acknowledgements

Many people have contributed to this book, and have my heartfelt thanks. They include: participants in the various research projects that inform the book, for their time and energy; my research collaborators, including John Clayton, Michal Chantkowski, Georgina Fletcher, Hilary Davison, Lucinda Hudson, Maria Aurora Cañadas Romero, Paul Biddle, Sara Lilley, Herbert Dirahu, Daniel Krzyszak and Annie Rutter (some of these collaborators also co-authored articles with myself, which inform Chapters 5 and 6); Advisory Board members for one of the projects, including Andrew Collins, Ian Fitzgerald, Maggie O'Neill, Irene Hardill and Karen Kavivi Harrison; funders, including the British Academy and Leverhulme Trust (grant SG132753), Northumbria University, and Nottingham Trent University; the Sociology Department at Nottingham Trent University, for allowing me time during the final stages of writing, as well as the colleagues who have been an invaluable source of support; the Editorial Board of *Fight Racism! Fight Imperialism!*, who provided discipline and guidance to my writing for that newspaper, which contributes to parts of Chapters 3 and 4; all those who read and/or listened to me talk about this research at various stages and commented (the names are too numerous to list but I am very grateful to you all); and my family, in particular, Annie, Ellen, Rowan, Lyrrie and Rob, for your unstinting support and interest. Any shortcomings are, of course, my responsibility.

Series Preface

Crises of Migration within Crises of Capitalism

We are delighted to bring to you Tom Vickers' insightful and detailed new contribution to this book series on *Global Migration and Social Change*.

The aim of the book series is to launch new interdisciplinary debates by showcasing migration and refugee studies scholarship that is both academically rich and innovative as well as engaged with public debates, policy and practice.

The idea for the series began during the 2016 'migration crisis' that was unfolding in Europe in the wake of the Eurozone crisis and, not long before that, the global financial crisis. In this context we felt it timely to ask questions such as: how does the so-called migration crisis fit into the broader and longer-term unfolding structural pattern of global migration? How do the current flows to Europe interact with and alter flows of migrants and refugees in other regions? How are these interactions on the global scale mediated by the economics, politics and policies emanating from Europe? Are the current population movements in and around Europe, and the crises of cooperation surrounding them, fundamentally changing broader global patterns of people on the move?

The perception of crisis around migration has not subsided since then, but has intensified and moved to the centre of politics and economics across the US and Europe, and particularly in Britain, which is the focus of this book. It is more relevant than ever today to look at the role of migration within the broader political economy capitalism, and to highlight the connections between this system's endemic financial crises and its less-remarked-upon periodic migration crises.

In this book, Tom Vickers admirably addresses these kinds of broad, structural questions and provides a thoroughgoing analysis of the unfolding crises. At heart it is a powerful Marxist critique of the options facing Britain – one that is at times scathingly pessimistic, but never fails to provide thought-provoking insight.

Among its strengths is one of the most lucid and up-to-date summaries of Marxian views of migration – and of Marxist theory more generally – that a student of migration and border studies could hope to find today. The book covers many themes, but perhaps speaks clearest (at least to this reader) when discussing the 'mutability' of class, and writing about the increasing relevance but also complexity – and 'irreducible heterogeneity' – of this social category at the present, under conditions of global migration and superdiversity. Throughout, Vickers highlights the crucial point that welfare and borders, today as never quite before, form part of the same process of inclusion and exclusion.

The book is also not short on fruitful provocation. Full of epigraphic insights, in a few parts it may read to some like Marxist scriptural exegesis rather than argument from first principles. In the classic Marxist tradition, there are moments of glibness about 'liberation' from capitalism that abstain from offering a feasible alternative. The rise of populist nationalism globally has been one of the most obvious outcomes of similar calls to revolution against capitalism for years – and reflecting on the way migration is depicted in political speech today, this suggests it pays to be careful what one wishes for.

Such provocations and controversies are strong reasons to read the book. We can think of few titles or topics more central to the themes of the current book series than this one – *Borders, Migration and Class in an Age of Crisis: Producing Workers and Immigrants*.

Alan Gamlen
Melbourne, 2019

1

Introduction

Today, we are immersed in narratives of crisis, from speeches of politicians, to media headlines, to broader public discussion. Campesi (2018: 197) defines crisis as:

> a situation that breaks with routine and calls for immediate action. The occurrence of a crisis calls for immediate judgement and decision making, but in circumstances with limited room for manoeuvre.... By labelling a situation as a 'crisis' one creates alarm, suggesting the existence of a threat to the ordinary lives of the populace.... The political response ... may point to the conservation and consolidation of the legal and political order ... or it may open a space for political change.

Indeed, the etymology of crisis is 'decision', in the sense of a judgement, from the Greek '*krisis*'. The word first entered the English language as a medical term denoting the turning point in a disease, to be followed by recovery or death.[1] Today's sense of crisis takes forms that are economic, social and political, and are often mutually reinforcing (Castells et al, 2018). Reflecting this, Britain's Conservative Party gained the largest number of votes in the 2010 general election – though not a majority – campaigning on the slogan of 'Broken Britain', and won the 2017 general election promising 'strength' and 'stability'. Europe's 'migrant crisis' or 'refugee crisis' has been presented as the responsibility of those on the move and an existential problem for European societies. Britain's housing system, National Health Service (NHS), social care system and benefits system are also said to be in crisis.

For hooks (2014: 19), the contemporary sense of crisis is located in systems of domination and dehumanisation:

> We live in a world in crisis – a world governed by politics of domination, one in which the belief in a notion of superior and inferior, and its concomitant ideology – that the superior should rule over the inferior – effects the lives of all people everywhere.... Systematic dehumanization, worldwide famine, ecological devastation, industrial contamination, and the possibility of nuclear destruction are realities which remind us daily that we are in crisis.

Crawley et al (2018: 131, 130) point to the way in which crisis narratives run together, suggesting that the migration crisis 'was symptomatic of, and became shorthand for, a range of economic, political, foreign policy and humanitarian crises taking place at the national, regional and global scales' as part of a process 'beginning back in 2008 with a global financial crisis which triggered the European financial and debt crisis associated with far-reaching austerity policies'. Dines et al (2018: 440) note that 'Human mobility has long been associated with the idea of crisis', and argue that over the last ten years, the connections between migration and multiple forms of crisis have become more pronounced while the sense of crisis has become more protracted. Crises of immigration and welfare spending have been presented as an explanation for the daily problems of poverty, precarious work, declining services and housing that face large parts of Britain's population (Shafique, 2018). Paraphrasing C. Wright Mills (2000 [1959]), it is the ruling classes[2] that have been most successful in making 'personal troubles' into 'public issues', but in a way that mobilises collective action in concert with the state against oppressed sections of the working class. The absence of any significant independent working-class movement has given such interventions free rein. The central aim of this book is to identify points of division, connection and commonality among the working class as a basis for deepening solidarity and resistance, and struggling towards an alternative.

While other crisis narratives have proliferated, the financial crisis that erupted over the course of 2007–08 has quickly been forgotten and replaced by a narrative of crisis in public sector finances caused by excessive welfare spending. The deep-rooted crisis of the international economic system rarely reaches further into the public domain than the elite pages of the *Financial Times*. It has found expression, however, in a crisis of parliamentary democracy, with none of the major parties able to make a sufficiently persuasive argument that they could address voters' problems to win a convincing majority in the 2010, 2015 or 2017 general elections.[3] This political crisis has played out in different ways in Britain's two largest parties: Conservative and Labour. For the Conservative Party, long-running divisions over Britain's membership of the European Union (EU) were amplified by the growing popularity of the UK Independence Party (UKIP), leading the Conservative government to call a referendum on EU membership in 2016. The political crisis was further demonstrated and intensified by the outcome of the referendum, with a majority voting 'No' to continued membership despite both the Labour and Conservative Party leaderships and most of the mainstream media backing a 'Yes' vote. For the Labour Party, the crisis manifested through the surprise election of Jeremy Corbyn as leader in 2015. Corbyn's connection to social movements and a parliamentary record that is significantly to the left of most Labour MPs and councillors have created deep divisions, and Corbyn has struggled to keep the fundamentally opposed wings of the party together.

Writing in an earlier period of capitalist crisis but, as this book will argue, one closely connected to the present, Stuart Hall et al (1978) point out that representations of crisis are powerful political tools, shaping people's fears and consequently their (re)actions against perceived problems. Representations of crisis also play a role in setting the limits of what people consider possible. It follows from this that developing a more critical perspective requires the articulation of alternative understandings of crisis. The crisis also presents opportunities, as Lenin (2000 [1916]; emphasis in original) argues: 'Every crisis discards the conventionalities, tears away the outer wrappings, *sweeps* away the obsolete and reveals the underlying springs and forces'. This book aims to contribute to realising these opportunities.

Aims of the book

As mentioned already, immigration plays a prominent role in contemporary discussions of crisis. In the wake of the 'Brexit referendum' and facing an uncertain future, debate rages as to whether immigration is good or bad for British society, both in cultural and economic terms. Within the political mainstream, both sides in this debate share the assumptions that categories based on nationality, citizenship and country of origin are fixed, legitimate and appropriate for assessing social change, measuring benefit and harm, and allocating resources. Likewise, both sides of the debate limit their options to what is possible within capitalism, which Fleming (2015: 2) describes as 'the ultimate ontological horizon of social life'. The idea of 'illegal' migration marks the limits of acceptability and is rarely called into question, providing a 'common-sense' bottom line against which the value and rights of other categories of migrants are judged (Karakayali and Rigo, 2010: 125). Given the long history of migration to and from

Britain (Craig, 2012), and the historically recent development of ideas of nation and citizenship (Jones, 2016), it is necessary to ask how and why these ideas have become so widely accepted, to the point that they appear as a natural division of humanity. Perhaps more importantly, what role do these ideas play in shaping responses to crisis, and what are the alternatives?

Contemporary discussions of migration often take the nation state for granted; indeed, Anderson (2013) argues that the construction of migrants as outsiders plays a fundamental role in defining the nation, suggesting that migration and the nation are interdependent. On the other hand, many recent academic studies adopt a transnational frame that presents nation states as far less important than previously (eg Faist et al, 2013; Hillmann et al, 2018). This book aims to move beyond the limitations of both approaches by applying a theoretical method that integrates elements of classical Marxism, Lenin's theory of imperialism and critical migration and border studies. It follows the line of questioning pursued by Jones (2016: 5) to dispute 'the idea that borders are a natural part of the human world', arguing that:

> The border creates the economic and jurisdictional discontinuities that have come to be seen as its hallmarks, providing an impetus for the movement of people, goods, drugs, weapons, and money across it. The hardening of the border through new security practices is the source of the violence, not a response to it.

Furthermore, this book questions the wider social context in which borders operate. As Peutz and De Genova (2010: 2) say of deportations, borders need to be understood as not simply legal restrictions on movement, but as 'the expression of a complex sociopolitical regime that manifests and engenders dominant notions of sovereignty, citizenship, public health, national identity, cultural homogeneity, racial purity, and class privilege' (see also Mohanty, 2003: 141). Thus, borders arise from and help to constitute the structure of society. Borders carry implications for all of us, whether or not we have ever crossed a border, as Anderson (2013: 3) points out: 'Judgements about who is needed for the economy, who counts as skilled, what is and isn't work, what is a good marriage, who is suitable for citizenship, and what sort of state-backed enforcement is acceptable against "illegals", affect citizens as well as migrants'. Such acts of differentiation play an important role in regulating human bodies in motion, following traditions established under colonialism.

Taking the global space of capitalism as a starting point, this book considers the role of borders and border struggles in structuring that space and producing categories of labour, focusing on changes following the global capitalist crisis that has been widely acknowledged since 2007. Mobility is situated in relation to class formation and exploitation through the concept of the labour process, which highlights the importance of capitalist control over movement, at a micro and macro scale, to extract surplus value from living human subjects. This draws on Braverman's (1998 [1974]: 39) argument that the drive for capitalists to increase control over workers is ultimately rooted in the indeterminate character of human labour, which enables it to expand its production of value beyond the value of wages, but also carries risk for the capitalist that workers may assert their own priorities. This analysis is tested and developed by drawing on a programme of empirical and theoretical research during 2013–18 concerning patterns of migration and settlement, labour markets, state policy and implementation, the media, and activism.

The book deals with Britain in particular, a national focus that has value given the persistent national organisation of capital and the continuing significance of the nation state in governing citizenship, migration and migrants' rights, as discussed in Chapter 2. This has added importance in the context of the UK referendum vote to leave the EU, which represents an overt turn back towards the nation and is part of a wider international turn towards protectionism and unilateralism supported by populist movements, as also exemplified by the presidency of Donald Trump in the US and the rise of nationalist parties in many European countries (Hanieh, 2018). Yet, despite this 'inward turn', the British economy remains heavily reliant on international investments and the export of services, and key sectors are structurally dependent on migrant labour. Through a detailed analysis of Britain, theoretical insights are developed that have international significance.

Geddes (2011: 203) argues that borders within and between states 'need to be understood not only in relation to borders of territory – the classic site for much analysis of migration – but also to organisational borders of work and welfare and conceptual borders of belonging, entitlement and identity'. Histories of migration are intimately bound up with histories of work and state welfare (Craig, 2007), and this connection continues (Moore and Forkert, 2014). This is not coincidental: immigration control and state welfare describe two dimensions of state intervention that actively structure the operation and reproduction of waged labour that is vital to capitalism. This informs the approach taken here to include the role of immigration controls, and the state more broadly, alongside wider social relations in analysing the condition of the working class. It will be argued that increasingly restrictive border controls and welfare conditionality form two significant elements of the same process, reshaping class relations as successive governments attempt to escape the capitalist crisis within the constraints of capitalism. The rest of this chapter introduces the book's theoretical approach, followed by an outline of its structure.

Applying Marxism today

This book takes a Marxist approach. It aims to historicise contemporary problems, to examine the interplay between discourse, policy and material relations, and to draw connections between differential forms of oppression within international capitalism.

The contemporary relevance of Marx's ideas is widely disputed. For example, Savage et al (2013) point to the apparent defeat of Marxist understandings of class since the 1970s, despite their continued influence, albeit in altered form, within the work of various traditions often called 'post-Marxist'. Outside universities, major defeats for working-class movements that drew on Marxism, including the destruction of the Soviet Union during the 1980s and 1990s, dealt a major blow to Marxism's credibility as a tool to transform the world. Yet, there has also been a resurgence of interest in Marxism since the financial crisis of 2007/08. In April 2018, the Governor of the Bank of England, Mark Carney, spoke about Marxism's continuing relevance and warned that automation could drive a revival of communism.[4] Mass movements guided by Marxism already exist in many underdeveloped countries, from India to Venezuela.

The central premises of Marxism, derived from empirical and historical study, are that: people must produce to satisfy their needs; the satisfaction of these needs leads to further needs; people act to reproduce not only themselves, but also their species; and all this activity is organised socially, depending on the means of production available (Marx and Engels, 1991 [1845]: 48–52). Marxism directs attention to the way in which consciousness is shaped by experience, and how experience is shaped, in turn, by the social organisation of production and reproduction.

Capitalism can be defined as a 'mode of production',[5] which is characterised by: private ownership of the 'means of production', referring to the machinery, raw materials and infrastructure needed to meet society's needs; production for exchange; a social division of labour; and the transformation of 'labour power', referring to the capacity to work, into a commodity that those who lack access to the means of production must sell for wages to buy what they need to live (Yaffe, 2009). Marx (1967 [1890]) argues that monopoly ownership of the means of production by a capitalist class enables it to both direct production and capture what is produced, giving back to workers only what is necessary for them to come back to work the next day. As James (2012 [1983]: 149) puts it: 'Free choice under capitalism is the right to choose between forced labour and destitution.... Doing forced labour is the condition of our survival at the cost of our development'. Today, the process by which this occurs is highly complex, and there are many variations in workers' relationship to capital and social definitions of 'necessities'. Carbonella and Kasmir (2018: 3) suggest that this mutability of class has been neglected, and that an overemphasis on the 'Fordist working class, a specific historical/ geographical formation' has led to the mistaken idea 'that class as a social formation has simply disappeared over the last thirty-odd years'.

At the level of society as a whole, the fundamental division remains between those who own and control the means of production and those who lack access and must sell their labour power to live. This social structure impacts on the general character of society and individuals' subjective experience. It produces differential conditions of work and life according to how gender, race, age, nationality and so on structure people's relationship to the means of production. Attention to these lines of division within the working class and the differential conditions that they produce is necessary for a concrete understanding of the working class in its entirety; they are also a precondition for deep solidarity and liberatory unity (Mohanty, 2003; Grady and Simms, 2018). Specifically, this book follows the empirical focus also adopted by Carmel and Cerami (2011: 1) to explore how differential forms of inclusion are produced through 'the interaction of migration, migration policies and social protection', and sets this within a Marxist analysis of the capitalist crisis. 'Workers' is used throughout this book as shorthand for members of the working class, without implying a uniform experience or suggesting that all workers are in waged employment.

Marx (1971 [1859]: 21) argues that it is not purely contradictions at the material level that determine the development of history, but also 'the legal, political, religious, artistic or philosophic – in short, ideological forms in which men [sic] become conscious of this conflict and fight it out' – which interact dialectically with the material base. Discourse can be loosely defined, within this framework, as systems of ideas that arise from material conditions but impact back upon them. 'Hegemony' was used by Lenin (1978 [1902]) to describe processes of working-class leadership, and was expanded by Gramsci (1982 [1929–35]) to explain the ideological domination by the capitalist class over the whole of society. This book uses hegemony to examine the formation of discourses that are not linear or unitary, but set the boundaries of acceptable ideas. The term 'regime' complements this, drawing on Mezzadra and Neilson (2013: 178–9), being used to refer to systems of power in which the state plays a powerful role but that extend beyond formal measures and involve a multitude of actors.

As Gramsci (1982 [1929–35]) points out, capital penetrates every aspect of society and, vice versa, many forms of unwaged activity impact back on capital. As a consequence, class struggle operates not only within the immediate sphere of waged labour, but also across diverse social domains – an insight that has been applied by radical community workers (Blagg and Derricourt, 1982; see also James, 2012 [1983]). Through most of capitalism's existence, the reproduction of labour power, or the work needed to feed, clean and nurture workers so that they can return to work each day, has been the private responsibility of the family, and most of the necessary labour has been performed on an unpaid basis by women in the home (Engels, 1987 [1887]). Whether this labour is part of the capitalist production process or something outside it, and on which it is nevertheless dependent, has been fiercely contested. Adamson et al (1976) argue:

> Domestic work – child-care, cooking, laundering, cleaning and so on – functions in capitalist society as a whole to produce those use-values which are necessary to the life of the individual. Domestic work is privatised, individual toil. It is concrete labour which lies outside the capitalist production process and therefore cannot produce value or surplus value.

This book follows the line of argument of Strauss and Meehan (2015: 6–11) to reassert the equal weight that Marx and Engels attached to production and reproduction. In recent years, this aspect of capitalism has been analysed within the 'social reproduction perspective', which involves several key propositions that are consistent with the approach taken here:

> sex/gender divisions of labour ... are historically and socially constructed and subject to change.... The activities involved in sustaining and reproducing daily life are ... determined by regional historical, political, economic, and social relations.... These labors are ... socially necessary and central to the production of both subsistence and wealth in any society. In the capitalist economies ... that labor is essential to the process of capital accumulation. (Braedley and Luxton, 2015: vii)

The expansion of state welfare in Britain and some other countries during the 20th century transferred some elements of this work to social labour, paid for through a deduction from surplus value and delivered by the state, but its gendered character largely remained. Today, drastic

8

reductions to state welfare are transferring more of this burden back into the home, performed on an unpaid basis or by paid domestic workers who are often low paid, precarious, lacking basic freedoms and, in many cases, migrants (Strauss, 2015). The feminisation of migration has thus facilitated the continued reproduction of labour power in the context of austerity (Hanieh, 2018). More broadly, 'The costs of the global economic restructuring are increasingly "downloaded" onto daily life' in ways that extend far beyond the workplace (Strauss and Meehan, 2015: 3). This is discussed further in Chapter 2.

Marx (1959 [1844]) argues that transforming the world around us is central to what it means to be human, or, as Trimikliniotis et al (2016: 1037) put it, 'labour is a force or energy propelling us "forward" or "back and forth" that is derived from our vitality-as-existence (survival, pleasure and revolutionary imagination)'. In the process of capitalist production, both the capitalist class and working class are alienated from work, but in very different ways. The capitalist class 'feels happy and confirmed in this self-alienation, it recognises alienation *as its own power*, and has in it the *semblance* of human existence', while the working class 'feels annihilated in its self-alienation; it sees in it its own powerlessness and the reality of an inhuman existence' (Lenin, 1972 [1895–1916]: 26–7; emphases in original). Due to the economic compulsion to sell one's labour power, to be directed according to the needs of capital, capitalism is inherently violent and dehumanising. James (2012 [1983]: 153) argues that this violence often infects relations within the working class:

> We are compelled to sell ourselves – what we are and what we can be – voluntarily, compelled to spend our waking lives in activities which we have not chosen or designed, an alien will imposed on us, directly and through others, from birth. This is the violence that we are forced to endure. We absorb violence from those above and then often let it out on those less powerful than we are.

This violence expresses itself in ways that can be unpredictable, and may be disruptive for capital while also harming individuals and social relationships. The state and other institutions of capital must therefore attempt to manage these unruly side effects where they infringe on the smooth running of capital accumulation, simultaneously with managing capitalism's functional requirements and preventing resistance. This helps to explain the British state's simultaneous racism and promotion of 'race relations' legislation, for example.

The capital accumulation process, and struggles for an alternative, ultimately hinge on the movement of human bodies. The transformation of human potential into labour, producing surplus value, requires people to move in particular ways and for the outcomes of those movements to be captured by the capitalist. Considering capitalism as a material relation involving human bodies in motion opens possibilities to explore the connections between migration – as a state-mediated and socially constructed form of human mobility – and class. Rather than asking whether 'migrants' harm or benefit 'British workers', we might instead ask what kinds of movements are occurring, on what terms and in whose interests. Jones (2016: 166) suggests that 'The conflict over movement is really between what rulers and states categorize as "good" and "bad" movements'. This points towards a further question regarding how and why they are defined as such, which is a central concern throughout this book.

Braverman (1998 [1974]: 176; emphases in original) argues that 'the investigation of the movements of *labor* … are but another form of the investigation of the movements of *value*'. Yet, it is also something more: the movement of living human beings and their social relations, whose totality cannot be captured by value, either individually or collectively. This tension between the logic of capital and the productive essence of humanity is at the heart of many of the struggles that capitalism engenders. It means that capitalist discipline can never be absolute, and workers pose a perpetual latent threat, requiring repeated reinforcement of the terms of waged labour (Braverman, 1998 [1974]: 96).

Reclaiming lost traditions

Agostinone-Wilson (2013: 2) suggests that criticisms of Marxism often boil down to an acceptance of the status quo, and the boundaries this sets on research: 'Marxism … appears to be "dead" because it is often outnumbered by other theoretical paradigms supported by the ruling elites'. However, this is not the whole story. Many people who are concerned with challenging oppression have rejected Marxism as failing to recognise the diverse forms of oppression that people face. However, this neglect is not fundamental to Marxism. James (2012 [1983]), K. Anderson (2010), Brown (2012) and others show that Marx himself devoted considerable attention to 'race', gender and other forms of differentiated oppression, and many Marxists have continued in this tradition. This book argues that Marxism has continuing relevance and utility as a scientific method to analyse the inner workings of capitalism and to inform interventions to influence the direction of social change.

More specifically, this book is located within a Marxist tradition outlined by Young (2001), running through Marx and Engels to Lenin and on to 'Tricontinental Marxism'. This tradition is distinguished by theoretical openness and responsiveness to concrete conditions, attention to divisions within as well as between classes, and recognition that perspectives and priorities necessarily differ according to people's structural location. Exploration of the relationship between class composition and borders has also led to engagements with autonomist Marxism, and the combination of some of its insights with a Leninist analysis of imperialism. While autonomism and Leninism may seem incompatible, for example, in their differing views on questions of spontaneity and leadership, Wright's (2002) history of debates within autonomism shows a more complex relationship. Both traditions emphasise the need to start with a concrete examination of workers' conditions and the ideas they give rise to, and both share a concern with the composition of the working class. Parallels might also be drawn between the autonomist conception of the 'social factory' and Lenin's broad conception of the struggles of the 'working class and oppressed' and recognition of the limitations of trade union struggles (Lenin, 1978 [1902]). These are all central concerns for this book.

Activist scholarship as public sociology

Marxism has arguably been at its most vibrant and innovative when applied within social movements and liberation struggles. There is a rich history on which to draw in the work of activist-scholars immersed in collective struggles and producing 'insurgent knowledge' (Mohanty, 2013: 1970). This includes theorists such as Thomas Sankara, Amilcar Cabral, Claudia Jones, Beverley Bryan, Ernesto 'Che' Guevara, Selma James, Mao Zedong, Fidel Castro, Sylvia Pankhurst, M.N. Roy, Vladimir Illich Lenin and back to Marx and Engels. These intellectuals are so significant because they draw together and embody the insights of political cultures at decisive moments, recognising that 'ideas are always communally wrought, not privately owned' (Mohanty, 2003: 1). As Braverman (1998 [1974]: 21) argues:

> The interpretation of the opinions, feelings, sentiments, and changing moods of the working class is best accomplished by experienced and well-attuned observers and participants.... It is for this reason that the most astute interpreters of the moods of submerged and ordinarily voiceless populations have often

been union organizers, agitators, experienced revolutionaries
– and police spies.

This represents a radical alternative to the model of intellectual production
based on individualised labour in a university, as well as a way of struggling
beyond some of the problems identified by hooks (2014: 29), when she
suggests:

> The academic setting … is not a known site for truthtelling.
> It is not a place where the oppressed gather to talk our way
> out of bondage, to write our way into freedom, publishing
> articles and books that do more than inform, that testify,
> bearing witness to the primacy of struggle, to our collective
> effort to transform. Yet this is our most urgent need, the most
> important of our work – the work of liberation.

It also enables a challenge to what hooks (2014: 37) describes as an
'Anti-theoretical backlash [that] tends to privilege concrete actions and
experiential resistance … however narrowly focussed their impact'. While
hooks is referring to feminism in the US, it is arguably also true of a lot
of anti-racist, migrant rights and welfare rights activism in Britain today.

Connections can be drawn from such activist-theorists to some
approaches under the broad banner of 'public sociology', for example,
Ngai et al (2014) and Jones et al (2017). It is also the approach that this
book strives for by setting academic literature, empirical research and
grass-roots activism in conversation with one another. Many of the
movements discussed here are small, and some were short-lived, but they
carry significance due to their embodiment of radical counter-hegemonic
narratives that this book argues offer important insights, demonstrate
practical applications and could be taken up more widely. They embody
what Tyler (2013: 2) calls 'voices of resistance against the abjectifying logics
of neoliberal governmentality'[6] and combine what Latham et al (2014:
13) describe as 'resistance and alternative framings'. These movements
do not stand above the current conditions of society. As with the activist
perspectives documented by Bassel and Emejulu (2017: 4), they are
'determined by, but also challenging, the particular discursive and material
opportunity structures' of a particular time and place. They thus point to
the possibilities but also the limitations facing the realisation of alternative
conceptualisations in the here and now.

Research methods

This book draws on academic literature and other publications produced by the government, non-governmental organisations (NGOs), campaigners and journalists, together with empirical research conducted by the author during 2013–18, which included:

- 402 survey responses and 40 in-depth interviews about experiences of work and worklessness among people in North-East England who arrived in Britain since 1999;
- in-depth interviews with 12 voluntary and statutory sector practitioners engaged with issues of migration, work and welfare in North-East England;
- in-depth interviews with 17 grass-roots campaigners in Newcastle-upon-Tyne, Nottingham, Birmingham, Worcester and London who were attempting to influence change in various areas of state welfare and immigration policy and practice;
- a discourse analysis of three television documentaries; and
- numerous informal conversations, private correspondence and observations as part of a reflexive activist practice in a range of social and political movements.

All of these data were treated with caution, following Smith's (2016) approach to statistics, treating empirical data as 'traces' of actual social and economic processes, rather than complete representations. Where possible, triangulation was carried out between multiple sources to check for accuracy. Together, these data were used to develop an analysis of trajectories in British society and to inform consideration of possible futures. This responds to Mohanty's (2003: 167–8) proposal to combine empirical examination of concrete conditions with a systemic analysis of international capitalism in order to identify points of commonality and connection as a basis for working-class unity that takes account of differences.

The regional focus of much of the empirical research on North-East England enabled an exploration of how uneven geographies interact with labour and welfare not only across, but also within, national borders. This research focused on migrants from the 'EU10' countries in Eastern and Central Europe that joined the EU in 2004 and 2007,[7] refugees, and asylum seekers, all of whom are included in the definition of 'migrant' adopted by the United Nations Statistics Division (2013). These migrant categories were selected because they have been stigmatised, have had their mobility problematised by significant sections of the media and politicians (Philo et al, 2013; Allen, 2016), and show concentrations in precarious, low-paid work and worklessness (Lewis et al, 2014; Fitzgerald and Smoczynski, 2017). These categories also present significant differences in countries of origin, immigration status and associated rights, and employment patterns. Considering these categories together thus enables a consideration of commonalities and differences between and across categories in order to avoid a priori assumptions that immigration status is the most important factor and to call into question rigid binaries such as free–forced that often dominate discussions of migration (Lewis et al, 2014). Further details on research methods are provided in the Appendix.

Structure of the book

Chapter 2 presents an analysis of contemporary capitalism in order to frame the ensuing discussions of immigration and welfare crisis. This draws on a Leninist analysis of imperialism, engages with other writers and argues that Lenin's approach represents a distinctive contribution to understanding how international movements of capital, commodities and labour interact with national divisions to structure the working class.

Chapter 3 situates British immigration policy and practice in relation to the changing needs of British imperialism since the 1990s. The chapter traces the proliferation of Britain's borders, both internally within many areas of everyday life and externally, including the outsourcing of border management to private organisations and other states. The last part of the chapter considers re-articulations of the 'migrant crisis' through the praxis of social movements and campaigns.

Chapter 4 examines the process by which politicians transformed the narrative about the global financial crisis, and the massive transfer of wealth to financial institutions that followed, into a narrative about high welfare spending as a justification for austerity. Anti-austerity narratives are also critiqued. Changes to state welfare and implications for mobility are discussed, focusing on housing, health care and social care, and benefits. The last part of the chapter explores re-articulations of the welfare crisis through a discussion of social movements and campaigns organising around demands for decent housing and against cuts to local state services.

Chapter 5 draws together the preceding chapters by arguing that the changes to border and welfare practices discussed in previous chapters help create conditions for 'precarity', associated with the growth of various forms of labour-related and social insecurity. This can be understood as an intensification of labour discipline, reducing workers' control over their mobility and often involving enforced patterns of movement or stasis. The second part of this chapter develops these ideas by drawing on empirical data from North-East England to conceptualise multiple 'dynamics of precarity' as ways of understanding differential conditions for exploitation.

Chapter 6 discusses the ways in which state-endorsed divisions within the working class have been reflected and reinforced at a discursive level. The chapter argues that ideological categories position workers in multiple, shifting and often contradictory ways within 'common-sense' narratives that justify and reinforce capitalist exploitation. This is illustrated through an empirical analysis of three British television documentaries. Conclusions are drawn for anti-racist education.

Chapter 7 concludes the book, arguing that on the basis of the analysis presented here, there seem to be two trajectories possible for Britain: remaining within capitalism, with increasingly antagonistic relations around the migrant–native divide that are enforced with increasing violence, legally, physically and discursively, and reduced mobility power for the majority, leading to deepening exploitation; or radically breaking from capitalism to find a social form that can move beyond its inherent crises and divisions, afford people material security, and enable them to realise their creative potential. The third option that has been pursued in the past – of limited concessions to substantial sections of the working class alongside continued exploitation – no longer seems viable given the severity of the crisis.

Notes

1 See: www.etymonline.com/word/crisis
2 'Ruling classes' refers to those sections of society with a dominant relation to the means of production and land, and also, through the state, a dominant relation to political, legal, military, media and educational institutions.
3 In the 2010 general election, no party gained enough seats to form a government, and a coalition was formed between the Conservative and Liberal Democrat Parties. In 2015, the Conservative Party gained a majority but only by 12 seats. In 2017, no party achieved a majority and the Conservative Party formed a minority government with support from the Democratic Unionist Party.
4 See: www.independent.co.uk/news/uk/home-news/mark-carney-marxism-automation-bank-of-england-governor-job-losses-capitalism-a8304706.html
5 Defined by Braverman (1998 [1974]: 15) as 'the manner in which labour processes are organised and carried out'.
6 Tyler (2013) uses 'social abjection' to refer to the production of subjects of violence and exclusion.
7 EU10 includes the EU8/A8 countries of the Czech Republic, Estonia, Hungary, Latvia, Lithuania, Poland, Slovakia and Slovenia, as well as the EU2/A2 countries of Bulgaria and Romania.

2

Imperialism, Migration and Class in the 21st Century

Introduction: capitalism is crisis

This chapter situates Britain within contemporary capitalism, laying the foundation for the analysis of migration crisis, welfare crisis and precarity that follows. The chapter begins by arguing that the economic crisis that has been widely recognised since 2007/08 arose from fundamental contradictions within capitalism and has had far-reaching consequences for society. This is followed by three main sections: the first uses 'imperialism' to describe capitalism's contemporary form as a distinctive organisation of the global space of capital and labour; the second considers migration, focusing on the role of borders and racism in structuring human mobility within imperialism; and the third discusses class, shaped by borders and racism within imperialist Britain.

Today, it is difficult to deny that capitalism is in crisis. We have moved a long way since the triumphalist declarations of the 'end of history' that followed the destruction of the Soviet Union (Fukuyama, 1992), and the 1997 Labour government's promises that it had escaped the 'boom and bust' cycle.[1] These claims rang hollow in 2007 when the subprime mortgage crisis in the US set off a global chain reaction leading to the most severe economic crisis in a century (FRFI, 2011). Imperialist states responded by injecting massive amounts of public money into the banking system, followed by sweeping cuts to state welfare. Since then, the economic recovery has been 'sluggish' at best, and even many pro-capitalist economists predict further crises in the near future.[2] An analysis of what Marx (1991 [1894]) calls the 'laws of motion' of capital accumulation shows that far from being exceptional, or the result of poor regulation, bankers' greed or other moral or policy failings, crisis is intrinsic to capitalism.

Marx (1991 [1894]) argues that capitalism is necessarily expansive because without the promise of a larger return on the amount invested, there is no reason for capitalists to invest. As Grossman (1992 [1929]) demonstrates, a growing mass of accumulated capital requires constantly increasing investment opportunities, which will then return an even greater mass of capital requiring opportunities for investment, and so on. Sooner or later, the mass of accumulated capital cannot find sufficient profitable outlets and the system goes into crisis. Other tendencies may postpone the crisis, but not indefinitely (see also Yaffe and Bullock, 1979). The over-accumulation of capital leads to a crisis of profitability, and this tends to produce reduced investment, falling productivity, reduced production, the destruction of capital through factory closures and increasing numbers of redundant workers. By reducing the stock of capital and forcing down wages, the crisis creates conditions for its resolution, raising profit rates and enabling a fresh round of accumulation – until the next crisis (Marx, 1991 [1894]: 364). While this process is part of capitalism's resilience, the hardships it produces for the working class often breed resistance. The crisis thus represents the limits of control for the capitalist class, imposed by the internal dynamics of the system itself, which may be resolved at the expense of the working class but also opens the possibility for revolutionary transformation.

Marx was not prone to prophecy – he did not predict the specific forms that capitalist crisis would take – yet his analysis of capitalism's internal dynamics remains remarkably effective in explaining the roots of the crisis. The current crisis is part of a long-term capitalist decline in which, 'over the past 100 years, the global rate of growth has, despite a few peaks when the working class has been disciplined by the market, continuously declined. We are moving toward the zero-limit of no growth' (Kyriakides and Torres, 2014: 197). This is rooted in an 'incapacity to absorb all of the surplus capital that [advanced capitalist countries] are generating internally and pulling in from abroad' (Foster et al, 2011: 21–2). Over-accumulation of capital is such that by the autumn of 2014, corporates and private equity firms globally held US$7 trillion in cash for which they could not find a profitable outlet, with £53.5 billion among just the top 100 companies on the British stock exchange (Capita Asset Services, 2014).

Marx's theory of crisis also helps explain capitalism's history. By the early 20th century, a capitalist crisis was driving rivalries between the major capitalist states as they competed internationally for opportunities for profitable investment (Yaffe, 2006). This contributed to the First

World War, an upsurge in anti-colonial resistance in countries including Ireland (Young, 2001), revolutionary movements that came close to taking power in countries including Germany and Italy, and the Russian Revolution (Carr, 1969). This demonstrates the open-ended consequences of capitalist crisis. The First World War did not resolve capitalism's underlying crisis, and so was followed by continuing inter-imperialist rivalries, accompanied in Britain by punitive means-tested welfare, work camps for the unemployed and other measures to increase exploitation and manage resistance in a period of mass unemployment (Hannington, 1973). The Second World War and a period of fascist rule across much of Europe during the 1930s and 1940s eliminated huge amounts of capital, destroyed some of the most powerful workers' organisations in Europe and left the US in an unrivalled position among capitalist states (Yaffe, 2006). This created conditions that were exceptional in the history of capitalism, enabling the 'post-war boom', a period of continuous capitalist expansion internationally. These conditions came to an end by the early 1970s, and the crisis resurfaced (Yaffe and Bullock, 1979).

Prior to the financial crash of 2007/08, the underlying capitalist crisis was already evident in intensifying rivalries between the major capitalist powers, and in the drive to privatise and outsource many previously public services and industries. This reflects two significant ways for capital to find new investment opportunities: by extending its reach internationally to exploit resources and labour in new parts of the world; and by extending its reach socially by commodifying new aspects of human life. These developments are discussed further in Chapters 3 and 4. Neoliberalism can thus be understood as a phase in the capitalist crisis, rather than a mere policy or a new form of capitalism. Credit also played a crucial role in postponing the crisis and enabling the 'long boom' that preceded the financial crisis of 2007/08, but it increased capitalism's instability over the longer term (Kitson et al, 2011: 291). Credit enables continued accumulation, even in the absence of sufficient profitable opportunities, by effectively betting on future profits. Sooner or later, the bets had to be called in, borrowers defaulted and millions of pounds were written off because they lacked any material basis. Understanding the impact of the capitalist crisis on Britain requires a discussion of how capitalism structures space, and Britain's position within this.

Imperialism: structuring the global space of capitalism

Contemporary capitalism is highly interconnected at a global scale, as well as uneven, with regimes of employment, production and exchange differing between and sometimes within countries. Mezzadra and Neilson (2013: 97) suggest that it is consequently easier than ever before to imagine a global working class with interconnected interests, but harder to translate that into the highly varied concrete conditions of labour.

Capitalism structures space in ways that are rarely questioned. Jones' (2016) sweeping historical account shows that walls and boundaries are neither natural nor arbitrary, but have always been ultimately rooted in struggles over material resources. National borders reflect power relations arising from the control and ownership of capital, and stabilise these relations by creating different regimes of accumulation and regulating movement between regimes. Borders create 'pools of exploitable resources, with rules on extraction and access that differ across territories' (Jones, 2016: 143). This spatial differentiation develops according to the underlying dynamics of capitalist accumulation, '*economically mediated* by relations of competition among individual capitals like TNCs [transnational corporations] ... and *politically mediated* by the policies of the nation state' (Charnock and Starosta, 2016: 6; emphases in original). Jones (2016) points out that borders were required to establish the private ownership of land, and traces the production of the English working class through the enclosure of common land in the 17th century, forcing the majority to move to cities as wage labourers. As Marx (1967 [1890]: 668–9) puts it:

> The immediate producer, the labourer, could only dispose of his own person after he had ceased to be attached to the soil ... these new freedmen became sellers of themselves only after they had been robbed of all their own means of production ... the history of this, their expropriation, is written in the annals of mankind in letters of blood and fire.

This expropriation was supplemented by other forms of domination over mobility, including 'mass incarceration of the poor in work and correction houses and "transportation" to the colonies' (Carbonella and Kasmir, 2018: 10). Just as importantly, the creation of the British working class required the massive concentration of wealth through colonialism and the transatlantic slave trade to fund industrialisation. This included the forced transportation of millions of people from West Africa, the seizure of land in the Americas and elsewhere for private ownership, and the forced displacement of native populations, together with many other acts of violence. Seizures of land and forced movements of people according to the needs of capital, including expulsion, exclusion, containment and regulation, have thus been central to capitalist accumulation from the start.

Today, Sassen (2014: 15–16) connects accelerating tendencies to forced displacement in the 'Global South' and incarceration in the 'Global North', using the concepts of dispossession and prison-as-warehousing. Consistent with these developments, many borders have undergone a transformation into 'militarized security spaces' (Jones, 2016: 32), combined with more structural forms of border violence, discussed in later chapters. These developments reflect ongoing national divisions in the control and operation of capital, which are shaping responses to the capitalist crisis.

The material basis of national divisions

Capital ownership has become concentrated in a small number of countries, often described as 'developed' and counterpoised to 'developing', although these terms will be questioned and replaced later in this chapter. Vitali et al (2011) analysed ownership networks among 43,060 TNCs and found that control of global capital was even more concentrated than direct ownership of wealth, primarily within Europe and North America, with a small number of banks exerting huge influence (see also Yaffe, 2006). Mezzadra and Neilson (2013) use the concept of 'frontiers of capital', drawing on Lenin, to express divisions in the control of capital that have a relationship to nations but do not necessarily correspond to a country's geographical boundaries. Frontiers of capital have developed historically, through a process of capital accumulation and export in which national states have intervened to support the activities of that nation's companies.

Stages of production have become increasingly separated on a national basis, although the form that this takes has changed over time: in an earlier period, most pronounced from the late 19th century, raw materials were extracted from developing countries, manufactured into finished goods in developed countries and then divided between domestic consumption and export; since the 1980s, improved technologies of communication and transportation have enabled a new international division of labour in which the most labour-intensive parts of assembly processes are often exported to developing countries, where they are delivered for extremely low wages, while more highly automated stages and often the final stage are performed in developed countries (Charnock and Starosta, 2016).

Foster et al (2011) point to the significance of wage differentials in determining geographical distributions of production. For example, 'labor costs for spinning and weaving in rich countries exceed ... that of the lowest wage countries (Pakistan, Madagascar, Kenya, Indonesia, and China) by a factor of seventy-to-one in straight dollar terms, and ten-to-one ... taking into account the local cost of living' (Foster et al, 2011: 14). In one graphic illustration of the results of such differentiation, 22 per cent of the profit margin for Apple's iPhone relied on the lower wages paid to assembly workers employed by the outsourced company Foxconn in China, compared to US wages. These profits are made at the following costs for workers:

> In Foxconn's Longhu, Shenzhen factory 300,000 to 400,000 workers eat, work, and sleep under horrendous conditions, with workers, who are compelled to do rapid hand movements for long hours for months on end, finding themselves twitching constantly at night. Foxconn workers in 2009 were paid the minimum monthly wage in Shenzhen, or about 83 cents an hour. (Foster et al, 2011: 12–13)

Smith (2016) describes extremes of labour discipline and speed in these Foxconn plants, with precision timing of production-line work and last-minute changes to working patterns. Workers have responded with a mixture of resistance and despair. Foster et al (2011), Jones (2016) and Smith (2016) give many other examples based on other global commodities. These international production processes are strongly racialised and gendered, with informal 'home-based work' often occupying the bottom of global value chains, 80 per cent of which is performed by women (Piper, 2011; see also Mohanty, 2003). However, this is not simply a case of capital moving to where wages are lower. Buyer-driven global value chains actively drive down wages and conditions as suppliers compete to meet buyers' demands for lower costs within profoundly unequal power relations (Smith, 2016: 26).

National concentrations of power and profits operate by various means. Smith (2016: 51–4) explores statistics indicating the rapidly increasing share of world manufacturing exports accounted for by developing nations, totalling more than 40 per cent by 2011. Although this is very uneven, even in those countries whose economies have not shifted towards export manufacturing, there are often export processing zones (EPZs) that are consistent with this general trend and have a major impact on the wider economy. Some of the capital involved in this is directly owned by capitalists based in developed countries. In 2013, foreign direct investment (FDI) into developing countries exceeded that going into developed countries for the first time (Smith, 2016: 72), and this underplays the disparity because a greater proportion of FDI into developed countries is accounted for by mergers and acquisitions rather than 'new' investments (Yaffe, 2006). Portfolio investments, referring to shares in a company of less than 10 per cent, are increasingly significant, together with loans. From 1997 to 2016, the total international debt of low- and middle-income countries grew by 251 per cent, from US$1,962 billion to US$6,877 billion, despite these countries repaying US$9,861 billion over the same period.[3] Smith (2016: 50) examines other diverse forms of outsourcing and offshoring, and the difficulties in capturing this fully with available statistics. Developing countries' priorities are consequently tied to the needs of developed countries, while the flow of surplus value from developing to developed countries is sustained by a complex web of institutions. Indicating the net result of this international exploitation, Kar et al (2016) estimate that, on balance, £12 trillion has been transferred from developing to developed countries since 1980 (see also Curtis, 2016).

These national divisions within the ownership, control and ownership of capital lend importance to a national focus for analysis. While national blocs inevitably interpenetrate one another, socially, culturally and economically, and within-country differences and inequalities are sometimes greater than between-country differences (Sassen, 2014: 31–2), this does not override the significance of the position of countries within capitalism. Unequal relations between countries are obscured by the terms 'developed' and 'developing', which imply different stages of progress along the same path. It is more accurate to see their differences as mutually constituted through relations of oppression and exploitation in which the 'development' of some countries is predicated on the systematic underdevelopment of others. The processes described here are consistent with longer-standing features of capitalism that were conceptualised a century ago by Lenin (1975 [1916]) as 'imperialism'.

Theorising imperialism

'Imperialism' has been used to describe relationships of oppression and exploitation between countries, but with a variety of definitions and explanations (Young, 2001; Day and Gaido, 2012). Academic discussions of imperialism have a long history, and have received renewed attention since the invasion of Afghanistan in 2001 (see, eg, Harvey, 2003; Meiksins Wood, 2005). One understanding reduces imperialism to foreign interference, normally through military means. Smith (2016: 71) cites various writers, including Callinicos and Harman (eg Callinicos et al, 1994), who represent this trend. Imperialism can also be understood as a primarily cultural or ideological system of domination that creates hierarchies between countries and racialised groups (Tomlinson, 1991). Both trends tend to neglect the material basis of imperialism, which lies in the contradictions of capitalist accumulation, and thereby give the illusion that a capitalist future beyond imperialism might be possible.

Lenin (1975 [1916]) defines imperialism as a stage of capitalism characterised by the domination of the economy and society by monopoly finance capital, resulting from intrinsic capitalist tendencies towards expansion and concentration.[4] Finance capital represents the fusion of banking and manufacturing capital into massive multinational companies, whose operations are international but whose ownership and management are concentrated in a handful of countries. 'Imperialist' and 'oppressed' are used in this book as shorthand for countries' relationship to this system. There are significant differences of degree and quality within each category, including whether an oppressed country has political independence, which leads Lenin (1975 [1916]) to sometimes use 'dependent' to refer to 'countries which, politically, are formally independent, but in fact, are enmeshed in the net of financial and diplomatic dependence'. Here, countries' relationship to imperialism is understood as fundamentally rooted in their material relation to global capital, mediated by such other factors.

Imperialism was of central concern for African theorists struggling with the new relations of domination and exploitation that followed formal decolonisation in the second half of the 20th century. Nkrumah (1965) uses the term 'neo-colonialism' to describe the 'sum total of these modern attempts to perpetuate colonialism while at the same time talking about "freedom"', constituting a distinct stage of imperialism in which political independence was accompanied by economic domination. He highlights a diverse array of mechanisms by which the subordination of oppressed countries is reinforced, including the international financial system, debt, the control of shipping, media institutions, religion, non-governmental organisations (NGOs) and international trade union bodies. However, Nkrumah differs from Lenin in arguing that exploitation on a national basis has entirely displaced class struggle within each country and that the entire population of imperialist countries benefit from imperialist exploitation. Some contemporary theorists (eg Smith, 2016) reach similar conclusions. Cabral (1964) offers a different analysis:

> Neocolonialism is at work on two fronts – in Europe as well
> as in the underdeveloped countries. Its current framework in
> the underdeveloped countries is the policy of aid, and one of

the essential aims of this policy is to create a false bourgeoisie to put a brake on the revolution and to enlarge the possibilities of the petty bourgeoisie as a neutraliser of the revolution; at the same time it invests capital in France, Italy, Belgium, England and so on. In our opinion the aim of this is to stimulate the growth of a workers' aristocracy, to enlarge the field of action of the petty bourgeoisie so as to block the revolution. In our opinion it is under this aspect that neocolonialism and the relations between the international working-class movement and our movements must be analysed.

In Cabral's conception, as in Lenin's, imperialism leads to several distinct developments in capitalism's class structure, including the emergence of sections of the working class within imperialist countries who are exploited as waged labour but have greater material security, more autonomy within the labour process and a higher standard of living than the mass of the working class. This provides the material basis for political trends that act as agents of imperialism within the wider working class to restrict the horizons of analysis and action to within limits that allow the continuation of imperialism (see also Foster, 2010; Clough, 2014). These forces encourage other sections of the working class who have nothing to gain from imperialism to accept it in practice. This also creates the material basis for an alliance between the mass of the working class within imperialist countries and the majority of the populations of oppressed countries, but it means that realising this potential requires the development of a leadership that is materially and ideologically independent of those class forces that align themselves with imperialism.

Britain as an imperialist country

Applying the framework discussed in the previous section, Britain has pronounced imperialist characteristics. Britain's economy is reliant on surplus value drawn in from overseas assets and via the financial sector in myriad ways, including returns on loans and the export of financial services (Norfield, 2016). In 2014, Britain's external assets (foreign investments) totalled £10,171.7 billion (ONS, 2015b), more than 5.5 times gross domestic product (GDP). Rates of return from FDI, which accounts for around 10 per cent of Britain's total overseas assets, were 9 per cent from investments in Africa and 13 per cent from investments in Asia, compared to 5 per cent from investments in Britain and the North of Ireland[5] (ONS, 2015b). This represents imperialist super-exploitation.

A large part of Britain's investments abroad takes the form of loans, an example of what Lenin (1975 [1916]) calls a 'gigantic usury capital' that is typical of imperialism. Britain is highly dependent on the import of goods, with a net deficit of £123.7 billion in 2014, and finances this to a great extent through the export of services, with a net surplus of £89.1 billion (ONS, 2015b). A total of 29 per cent of Britain's service exports are accounted for by financial services, the highest for any of the G7 group of wealthy countries. Financial and insurance services employed more than a million people in 2013 and accounted for 6.8 per cent of GDP, again the highest proportion for any G7 country (Banks et al, 2014). Financial services do not produce anything, they simply redistribute wealth produced elsewhere in the global economy into the hands of British finance capitalists. This reliance on the financial sector places the city of London at the heart of British capitalism, making it vital that the city's global position is sustained. Britain's departure from the European Union (EU) threatens its international position, with serious implications for British capitalism (Boleat, 2018).

Bell (2016) argues that Britain's international interests are pursued through a combination of 'hard' and 'soft' power. While military spending has been reduced in recent years, Britain still has considerable capacity to implement 'hard power' around the world, with current deployments of British military in over 80 countries, and it extends its military influence further through its alliances with the US and other countries within the North Atlantic Treaty Organisation (NATO). 'Soft power' includes cultural institutions such as the British Council and increasingly also 'commercial diplomacy' by British corporations. Bell (2016: 77) also argues that 'The role of international development aid provided by the UK's Department for International Development (DfID) is crucial, ensuring much continuity between Conservative-led governments and their New Labour predecessors'. These are just some of the ways in which the state continues to play an important role for capitalist interests.

The state as the executive of the (national) ruling classes

Jones (2016: 155) defines the state as 'a political institution with a bureaucracy, territory, borders, and the sovereign right to create and enforce laws'. He goes on to suggest that 'The state is a boundary-making institution that legitimizes the exclusion of others from land, resources, wealth and opportunity through legal regimes and military power' (Jones, 2016: 164). This is a useful definition because it foregrounds the role of the state in controlling space, producing categories of human beings and using these as a basis for the differential allocation of resources. It is also consistent with Lenin (1972 [1917]: 13–14), who understands the state as an organised system of violence by which an economically dominant class secures political control and uses this control to consolidate their economic domination. Capitalist states have developed through a dialectic of exploitation and resistance to repress the irreconcilable contradictions between classes and create the social peace necessary for capital accumulation. Police, courts and prisons, welfare institutions, and the ideological apparatus of education and the media all play a role. Sovereignty represents a claim to the unique authority to use force within a given territory, and through international institutions that are based on nation states, it provides a basis for claims to legitimate acts of violence beyond a state's territory. The state also represents a unique claim to authority in determining standards regarding things like food safety, environmental protection and minimum wage rates, and it has the final say in the allocation of resources for human benefit, witnessed, for example, in schemes requiring the registration of NGOs or in the criminalisation of non-state actors rescuing people from the Mediterranean, discussed in Chapter 3.

The state's class character becomes most visible at times of intense class conflict; in Britain, these include such examples as the National Unemployed Workers Committee Movement in the 1920s (Hannington, 1973), the 1976–77 Grunwick Strike (Pearson et al, 2010), the 1984–85 Miners Strike (Coulter et al, 1984) and the 1987–90 Poll Tax Movement (Reid, 1990). In these cases, powerful grass-roots movements advancing working-class interests were met by systematic state violence. The class character of the state has also been exposed in periods of capitalist crisis, when capital has been the beneficiary of massive state welfare in the form of bail-outs, while services and welfare provision for the working class have been cut (FRFI, 2011). Its class character is also evident on a day-to-day basis, from the differential treatment of different classes and class fractions by the police, to the role of social welfare institutions in controlling working-class behaviour, as well as in the differential likelihood for class fractions to be on the receiving end of repressive and supportive elements of the state, discussed in Chapter 4 (see also Vickers, 2012). Under imperialism, the class character of the state takes a racialised form in its differential treatment based on nationality, citizenship and racialisation (for a discussion of racialisation as an active process, see Oliveri, 2018).

Today, many states are shifting, hardening their approach to the movement and rights of workers, while new agreements such as the Trans-Pacific Partnership (TPP), Transatlantic Trade and Investment Partnership (TTIP) and the Trade in Services Agreement (TiSA) threaten states' ability to regulate corporations' activities within and across their borders (Jones, 2016: 130–1). States coexist with other types of institution, for example, the EU, International Monetary Fund, World Bank, United Nations (UN) and International Organisation for Migration. Yet, states also play a major role in directing and funding these institutions, which can therefore be seen as mediating the interests of states that are founded on national fractions of capital, rather than standing above national interests.

States of imperialist and oppressed countries often cooperate in the extraction of super-profits. Smith (2016) shows that not only companies, but also imperialist states, benefit financially from low wages in oppressed countries, allowing them to capture a substantial part of the surplus value as commodities cross their borders. For example, in 2013, money taken by the US state through tariffs on the import of textiles from Bangladesh totalled US$809.5 million, exceeding the US$690 million in wages received in total by the workers in Bangladesh who produced those goods (Smith, 2016: 13–14). The repression of super-exploited workers at the bottom of supply chains is usually left to the states of oppressed countries, enabling imperialist states to present themselves as liberal and morally superior. Nkrumah (1965: xi) shows how this affords imperialist countries 'power without responsibility' and 'exploitation without redress', with the governments of oppressed countries considered disposable if they become either too embarrassing or too uncooperative. To give a recent example of the role of oppressed states in defending imperialist profits, in 2010, the Bangladeshi state created a dedicated Industrial Police force, with 2,900 officers, amid a strike wave by textile workers who were producing for export to imperialist multinationals (Smith, 2016: 15). Following the Rana Plaza factory collapse in 2013, when workers organised to demand safer working conditions, the Industrial Police targeted workers' protests, alongside regular police, *ansars* (village militia) and the anti-terrorist Rapid Action Battalion. Smith (2016: 19–21) points to the hypocrisy of many trade unions and NGOs in imperialist countries, who sometimes express concern about 'labour standards' in oppressed countries, blaming employers and governments based there, while rarely taking action against the international institutions, multinationals and imperialist governments that all exert the greatest power in keeping these standards low to keep profits high.

To say that the state consistently represents the interests of capital is not to suggest that it does so perfectly. There are exceptions where capitalist states have appeared to act in ways that are contrary to the general tendencies outlined earlier. In some cases, these represent concessions that have been won through struggle; in some cases, states take actions that may disadvantage one section of the capitalist class but are necessary to protect the general interest of capital; and in others, they simply result from miscalculations on the part of politicians or state officials. Wills et al (2010) argue that rather than state immigration policy directly reflecting employers' needs, Britain's low-waged migrant workforce has emerged from a complex interaction of migration routes, changes in the global economy and the actions of the state. This process is certainly complex, but for the state to act in the interests of the capitalist class as a whole does not require a direct link with specific employers, but rather that the fundamental structures of the state are geared to maintaining conditions for the survival of British capitalism. Contradictions may also exist between the state and the personal values or priorities of some of the individuals it employs. For example, Feldman (2012: 113–14) describes tensions between professional expectations and personal values of some migration officials within the EU, but concludes that, ultimately, 'The sympathy that individual European officials qua individuals express toward migrants cannot override the apparatus's dehumanizing effects'. In some cases, such individuals have contributed to resistance to state practices from within (LEWRG, 1980), but this has almost always required the existence of movements outside the state apparatus with which they can ally.

The character of the contemporary British state is rooted in the imperialist character of British capital and has been shaped by conditions of crisis and a long-term shift in the balance of forces against the working class. Under conditions of crisis, the British state is changing significantly, withdrawing from some areas while extending its reach in other strategic areas, internationally and domestically. Internationally, since the invasion of Iraq in 2003, the British state has increasingly relied on mercenaries and other proxy forces to supplement its direct military interventions (Glazebrook, 2013), while much of its border policing has also been outsourced (see Chapter 3). Domestically, since the 1990s, 'civil society' has been increasingly incorporated within processes of capitalist state governance under successive governments, from Labour's social capital interventions to the Conservatives' 'Big Society' under David Cameron and the populism of Theresa May, while many services previously provided by the state have been outsourced or privatised (see Chapter 4). Some of the most significant changes have concerned local state bodies, typically organised at a county, city or borough level, and referred to as 'councils' or 'local authorities' in the British context. Many civil society organisations have been co-opted into state-directed processes of governance, representing an intensification of imperialist hegemony and associated regimes, limiting possibilities in thought and action. Alternatives have been increasingly marginalised, facilitated by a discourse that has played on the fear of terrorism to construct a category of 'non-violent extremism' that has included as 'warning signs' disagreement with British foreign policy and criticism of the mainstream media (Kundnani, 2015). Within all these dimensions of the British state, borders and racism play an important role.

Migration: structuring human mobility through borders

Bloch and McKay (2016: 5) note the 'uneven opportunities to migrate, with border controls aimed at excluding some groups while the global elite can move freely; the growth of forced migration as a consequence of North/South relations and the need of capitalism for low-paid and often precarious workers'. In recent decades, a hardening of borders has been accompanied by increased 'cooperation as neighbouring states work together against shared threats to their sovereign control over their territories' (Jones, 2016: 68–9). The class basis for migration has become increasingly naked, with 'Citizenship by Investment' programmes offering residency rights and a fast track to citizenship for wealthy capitalists, while for the majority, rights to residence have become increasingly dependent on demand for one's labour (Hanieh, 2018).

Just as imperialism develops as a direct consequence of the internal contradictions of capitalism, racism and immigration controls are driven by the imperialist division of labour (Cross, 2013). The migration of labour and export of capital are part of the same process: countries' relation to capital shapes conditions for migration by their citizens, and where labour-intensive processes are required close to the point of consumption, it is difficult to export production and so labour is often imported to imperialist countries instead. Social care, catering and hospitality, construction, and some parts of food processing and agriculture are all typical of this tendency (RSA, 2018). Immigration controls regulate mobility according to the needs of capital and create differential terms for inclusion. Racism reflects these differentiated conditions and encourages their acceptance as 'natural'.

Maintaining imperialist divisions of labour

Foster et al (2011) point to the dependence of imperialist super-exploitation on the immobility of labour, highlighting the role of borders in containment and differentiation, as well as exclusion. For example, refugees continue to be concentrated in oppressed countries, with 86 per cent taking refuge in neighbouring countries that are mostly low- or middle-income states (Crawley et al, 2018: 15), and this concentration is even more pronounced in relation to countries' wealth (Sassen, 2014: 61).

This is part of a longer history. Feldman (2012) points to the similarities in intent behind contemporary restrictions on migration from poorer to richer countries and previous policies of 'containment' against the Soviet Union, which aimed at undermining the potential for socialist countries to inspire revolution in Europe and elsewhere. He quotes the American diplomat George Kennan, credited with designing the Cold War containment strategy, who wrote in 1948:

> We [the US] have 50% of the world's wealth but only 6.3% of its population. In this situation, our real job in the coming period … is to maintain this position of disparity. To do so, we have to dispense with all sentimentality … we should cease thinking about human rights, the raising of living standards and democratisation. (Cited in Feldman, 2012: 78)

This parallel between the containment of socialism and the containment of the poor is not coincidental. The relative privileges of large sections of the population of imperialist countries depend on both maintaining the incorporation of oppressed countries within capitalism and preventing their populations from escaping exploitative conditions through migration. To put this another way, autonomy of mobility for some workers is enabled through restrictions on geographical mobility for other workers, which enforce productive mobility within the capitalist labour process. Feldman (2012: 115) points to the way this is expressed through the association between freedom of movement within the EU and controls on entry from outside, through which 'the apparatus functions to maintain a large-scale apartheid between the North and South precisely because the prosperity of the former cannot be universalized to include the latter, regardless of the hope invested in development projects'. This relationship between free movement and restrictions is explored further in Chapter 3.

Migration and immigration controls

The percentage of the world's population who are resident outside their country of origin has not changed substantially in recent decades, although a growing global population has led to an increase in absolute numbers (Crawley et al, 2018: 14). While movement between places has always been a feature of human societies, imperialism results in structural tendencies for migration from oppressed to imperialist countries on terms that leave little agency for migrants. Some of the main drivers include: conditions of poverty and inequality that lead families to sponsor some of their members to move for work and send back remittances; authoritarian state practices in many oppressed countries, driven by the need to enforce exploitative conditions; wars, often resulting from imperialist countries' direct and indirect pursuit of profits against their rivals, or as the intervention of last resort against governments that refuse to cooperate with imperialist exploitation; and environmental destruction resulting from the unplanned and relentless expansion of capitalist production. Many conflicts that appear to be based around ethnic or tribal divides, or local competition for resources, are fundamentally rooted in imperialism (Kundnani, 2007). 'Development' under imperialism does not reduce out-migration; indeed, within sub-Saharan Africa, wealthier countries tend to have higher rates of out-migration than poorer ones (Bakewell, 2011: 132–3). This reflects the resources needed to cross borders, as well as differences between oppressed countries' role in global production. As Cross (2013) shows in detail regarding West African migration to the EU, movements of people have been shaped, in part, by the systematic dispossession of households from their means of production and subsistence, alongside the development of sites of transit and recruitment that create opportunities for the sale of labour power.

Remittances provide an important source of foreign currency for oppressed countries to buy imports, benefiting multinational companies, and support the reproduction of labour power in oppressed countries despite a lack of waged labour or state welfare. For example, in 2012, Bangladeshi migrants sent US$14 billion in remittances, accounting for 11 per cent of Bangladesh's GDP. Smith (2016: 44) reports that 'in 2013 each of Britain's 210,000 Bangladeshi migrant workers remitted an average of $4,058, three times the annual wages of his (most Bangladeshi migrant workers are male) wife, sister, or daughter working in a garment factory back home'. The World Bank (2018) estimates that remittances to low- and middle-income countries totalled US$466 billion in 2017, and the real figure is likely to be higher because many informal transfers are unrecorded. One in seven of the world's population, more than a billion people, are involved in remittances as senders or recipients (Hanieh, 2018). The reliance of family and friends on remittances encourages migrants to tolerate poor working conditions. A survey of low-paid migrant workers in London found that 71 per cent sent money home, remitting 20–30 per cent of their income on average, mostly as contributions to daily subsistence. Those with the highest levels of remittances were also those working the longest hours (Datta et al, 2007b: 51–9). Migration and remittances have not declined as expected following the economic crisis, explained by Schierup and Castles (2011: 17) through people's willingness 'to endure considerable hardships to support their families back home'. In our survey of 402 migrants in North-East England, 40 per cent reported sending remittances. Among those who said that they lacked sufficient money for necessities for themselves, 31 per cent said that they remitted money. Thus, remittances do not combat inequalities within imperialism, but rather sustain them in multiple ways.

Migrants' experiences are becoming increasingly polarised in terms of 'access to labour markets but also modes of entry into nation states' (Bloch and McKay, 2016: 16). Yet, compared to an earlier period following the Second World War, today 'not only less skilled but also skilled migrants are now subject to temporary-migration schemes' (Piper, 2011: 70–1). This conditional mobility of labour combines with highly mobile capital to result in a situation in which 'workers everywhere no longer have a quasi-monopoly of jobs but must now compete with an apparently "inexhaustible pool of potential labour" in the global economy, creating for capital a supply of labour of comparable efficiency but at different prices' (Lewis et al, 2015: 581). For example, Hardy (2008: 18–19) cites reports by Polish trade unions of multinational companies relocating to Poland for the low wages and treating workers in an 'undignified way', and where they could not relocate to Poland, 'poaching' workers to move and work elsewhere. In the EU, 13.5 per cent of highly skilled migrants are African, with concentrations by country and sector – for example, estimates suggest that more than half the doctors and a quarter of the nurses trained in Ghana emigrate (Bakewell, 2011: 136–7). This 'brain drain' represents another form of national exploitation.

'Replacement migration' chains have developed based on countries' relative positions within imperialism, involving, for example, the migration of British nurses to the US or Canada, being replaced by South African nurses, who are, in turn, replaced by Zimbabwean nurses, all seeking better conditions, or similarly Polish nurses migrating to Sweden and being replaced by Moldovan nurses, in patterns that are sector-specific and gendered (Piper, 2011: 64). Farris (2015: 6–7) points to the connection between the precariousness of migrant women's work and their concentration in the so-called 'reproductive sector', with 42 per cent of migrant women across the EU15 countries working in 'the care–domestic sector in private households, the care sector in hospitals, residential care and home care and cleaning activities', not including undocumented migrants performing private domestic work in households in the 'shadow economy'. In many major destination countries, an increase in female participation in the labour market has created demand for low-paid care-related services, contributing to concentrations of migrant women in this work (Piper,

2011: 65–6; see also Farris, 2015). Gendered migration has thus enabled an increase in non-migrant women's availability for waged labour.

International inequalities in wages, conditions, state support and the overall standard of living lead some people to accept wages and conditions that are poor by the standards of their country of residence but that compare favourably to those in their country of origin (Anderson, 2010b; Wills et al, 2010: 7). This reflects circuits for the reproduction of labour power that extend across borders, for example, through circular migration and transnational family structures, which partially extend the lower costs for reproducing labour power in oppressed countries to migrants from these countries within imperialist countries (Hanieh, 2018). This contributes to qualitative differences in workers' relationship to capital, combining with differential rights connected to immigration status. Hardy (2008: 14) summarises the relationship between labour, welfare and immigration in state policy: 'The state faces the dilemma, on the one hand of maximising the supply and flexibility of its national labour force, while on the other minimising the cost of reproducing and maintaining those workers'. Borders help states manage these competing demands. As Anderson (2010b: 301) argues:

> Immigration controls function both as a tap regulating the flow of labour, but also … as a mould shaping certain forms of labour. Through the creation of categories of entrant, the imposition of employment relations and the construction of institutionalised uncertainty, immigration controls work to form types of labour with particular relations to employers and to labour markets.

Mezzadra and Neilson (2013: 101–2) argue that immigration controls 'mould' not only those who cross international borders, but also wider class structures. Categories produced through borders have material, legal and ideological dimensions, combining to harness the creative capacity of living human beings to generate surplus value for the capitalist class. This idea will be explored further in the chapters that follow.

As Anthias (1980: 55) points out, with reference to women workers, it is important to separate out the advantages to capital of employing particular forms of labour, both economic and non-economic, and the reasons that this labour is employed. All migration has implications for labour, not only that which takes place under formal economic migration categories. Complementing this, Anderson (2010a: 109–11) points out the complexity of the factors that lead to segmented labour markets, including employers' stereotypes about 'types' of migrants and the requirements of jobs, from formal skills to 'soft skills', as well as preparedness to work in certain conditions. Social networks can also play an important role in structuring migrants' position within the workforce, helping migrants find work but sometimes sustaining disadvantaged positions and carrying obligations that can deepen migrants' oppression (Bloch and McKay, 2016: 12).

Migration allows for fluctuations in demand for labour and provides skilled labour without the normal costs of training. Hardy (2008) argues that migrant workers are used to reduce wage bills through employment on lower wages and with poorer conditions, as well as through flexible contracts that enable employers to only pay for the precise amount of labour time they need in each week or year. This is supported by Pemberton et al (2014: 13), who survey literature pointing to the temporary and insecure nature of much employment for migrants in Britain, linked to the prevalence of agency employment (see also Sporton, 2013). This is part of converging trends globally towards temporary and seasonal labour migration under a discourse of 'managed migration' (Piper, 2011).

The role of racism

Often, academic literature focuses either on migration *or* race. For example, Datta et al (2007a: 404) note the predominant framing in much of the British industrial relations literature of workers according to ethnicity regardless of migration background. Yet, as Smith (2016: 46) points out, racialisation is shaped not only by identities or differential conditions within Britain, but also international competition and consumerism:

> The increasingly global character of the social relations of production and the increasing interdependence between workers in different countries and continents objectively strengthens the international working class and hastens its emergence as a class 'for itself' as well as 'in itself', struggling to establish its supremacy, yet, to counter this, capitalists increasingly lean on and utilize imperialist divisions to practice divide and rule, to force workers in imperialist countries into increasingly direct competition with workers in low-wage countries, while using the cheap imports produced by super-exploited Southern labor to encourage selfishness and consumerism and to undermine solidarity.

Migration forms a particularly intense component within this wider system of divisions, leading to the racialisation of British immigration controls (Sivanandan, 1991).

Racism has a long history, pre-dating capitalism, but in its current form, it is shaped by the divisions produced through imperialism. National oppression forms the basis of racism towards migrants from oppressed countries (Williams et al, 1979), their descendants and anybody else associated with these countries through skin colour, religion, accent, dress or other markers. This explains the targeting of people who may be diverse in many ways but have in common an association with an oppressed country. Hierarchical racialised categories shift over time, for example, Karakayali and Rigo (2010: 127–31) trace the dominant 'figures of migration' in Europe since the Second World War, moving through the 'guest worker' to the 'refugee' to the 'illegal migrant'. Connections can be traced from this to the changing needs and conditions of European capitalism as the labour needs of the post-war boom gave way to the political utility of providing asylum to Cold War 'dissidents' in order to demonstrate the supposed moral superiority of capitalist democracies (Schuster, 2003), and then to the deepening capitalist crisis and consequent drive to create super-exploitable workers without rights through 'illegalisation' (Oliveri, 2012).

Today, racialised systems of governance reconcile systematic violence and the deprivation of liberty with liberal values and obscure borders' political role:

> One of the most shocking features of this new racism is its capacity to develop reasonable discourses, apparently based on matters of fact, race-neutral principles and politically correct postures, through which discriminations become de facto and de jure acceptable for a large share of the population, still believing in democratic and egalitarian values.... Besides the crucial criminalizing frame, there are many other discursive strategies that essentialize, racialize and orientalize migrants while depicting them as a threat and as a resource in relation to the main interests of the receiving societies – security, well-being and identity. The representation of migrants as victims completes the picture: it contributes, at the same time, to patronize and de-politicize them and to offer a positive self-presentation of Western societies as 'doing good things for migrants' such as rescuing them from oppressive regimes, miserable living conditions and backward cultures. (Oliveri, 2012: 800–1)

Furthermore, Mishra (2018: 6) describes the connections between racialisation and imperialist foreign policy: 'launching military campaigns, often without bothering to secure the consent of a frightened people, and while supporting despotic leaders they talk endlessly of their superior "values" – a rhetoric that has now blended into a white-supremacist hatred … of immigrants, refugees and Muslims'. Racialised minorities are thereby placed in an oppressed position susceptible to super-exploitation. This helps shape class in contemporary Britain.

Class: structuring exploitation within Britain

The increasing mobility of capital, enabled through transformations in communication and shipping and driven by the over-accumulation of capital in imperialist countries, has led to the transfer of many industrial jobs to oppressed countries (Magdoff and Magdoff, 2004). Across the EU, 4.2 million industrial jobs were lost between 2008 and 2012, accounting for 12 per cent of manufacturing employment (Pradella and Cillo, 2015). The consequent shift within Britain from industrial to service sector jobs has corresponded with changes in the nature of work for large parts of the working class:

> Increasingly, and especially prevalent in the service sector, is employment based on temporary, short-term, part time, informal job arrangements as well as various forms of self-employment and subcontracting.… Such work arrangements affect 75% of the global workforce … with 50% of the jobs created in the Organization for Economic Co-operation and Development (OECD) since the mid-1990s being of this type. (Harvey et al, 2017: 20)

There are exceptions to this general trend. For example, Bromma (2013: 12) highlights the special considerations concerning the arms industry: 'For security reasons, the shipyard needs to be located inside the "homeland" and staffed by people supportive of its aims. These warships definitely aren't going to be outsourced to China'. This helps to explain the continuing vitality and security of employment in arms manufacturing, which directly employed 363,000 people in Britain and the North of Ireland in 2016, around 12 per cent of the total manufacturing workforce, with a turnover of £72 billion (ADS, 2017).

Compared to previous periods of capitalist crisis, the post-2007 crisis in Britain was marked not by a dramatic rise in unemployment, but rather by an accelerating shift to various forms of insecure and low-waged work. This combined long-standing forms – such as seasonal labour in agriculture, involving an estimated 64,000–77,000 people, 14–17 per cent of the agricultural workforce (RSA, 2018) – with new forms enabled by digital technologies, often referred to as the 'gig economy', employing 1.1 million people (Shafique, 2018), such as the courier and transport platforms operated by Deliveroo and Uber. Half of the new jobs created following the recession were formally 'self-employed', and from 2008 to 2016, average wages for self-employment fell 22 per cent to £207 per week, less than half the average for their employed equivalents.[6] Many forms of labour in the gig economy represent piecework, in which workers are paid for completed work rather than via a wage, afforded fewer protections and held responsible for maintaining both work materials and their own labour power (De Stefano, 2016). In other cases, work is 'put out', with payment for completed work made to an individual who then employs a team on wages, prevalent in sectors such as agriculture, construction and care. Braverman (1998 [1974]: 43) suggests that this was a 'transitional form, a phase during which the capitalist had not yet assumed the essential function of management in industrial capitalism, control over the labour process'. The return of these and other labour practices from earlier periods of capitalism's history (Harvey et al, 2017) is indicative of the crisis and breakdown of capitalism, as well as a shift in the balance of forces against the working class through the breakdown of collectivity and the growth of insecurity. This is part of an international shift in the balance of class forces against labour and in favour of capital. These shifting conditions are producing a 'making, unmaking, and remaking of class', whose form cannot yet be clearly seen (Carbonella and Kasmir, 2018: 4).

Shafique (2018: 46) summarises evidence showing the current direction for the working class in Britain, with material insecurity becoming more widespread and increasing in intensity at the extremes:

> The growth of low-paid employment and the rise of non-standard work have become key features of the UK labour market and its 'recovery' from the 2007–2012 recession. The number of self-employed workers grew from 3.23 million in the final quarter of 2000 to 4.81 million by August–October 2017 [which represents] 15% of the UK workforce.... There were 865,000 agency workers in 2016, an increase of 30% since 2011.... Employment in low pay (70–85% of average earnings), and very low pay sectors (below 70% of average earnings) ... has grown steadily since 2000 and dramatically

since 2012. By contrast, employment in all other sectors in 2016 was only modestly higher than 2000.

The British government's extension of the period during which workers lack protection and reductions in the costs of ending contracts have made temporary employment more prevalent in real terms, even where positions are technically classified as 'permanent' (Standing, 2011: 58). A total of 55 per cent of people in poverty are in a working family and 21 per cent of employee jobs pay less than the living wage (Shafique, 2018: 16–17). In a major study of poverty, Gordon et al (2013) found that across Britain and the North of Ireland:

- over 30 million people suffer financial insecurity;
- nearly 18 million cannot afford adequate housing;
- nearly 12 million are 'too poor to engage in common social activities considered necessary by the majority of the population';
- around 4 million lack adequate food and more than one in four adults consciously limit their own eating so that others in their family can have more; and
- one in three cannot afford to adequately heat their homes and 29 per cent have to turn the heating down or off or only heat part of their homes.

The number of people with a standard of living below socially accepted minimum standards doubled between 1983 and 2013. By 2017, 14 million people, one fifth of the population, were living in poverty and 1.5 million were destitute, unable to 'buy the bare essentials that we all need to eat, stay warm and dry, and keep clean' (Fitzpatrick et al, 2018: 50). This is partly about the changing nature of work, with an average reduction in real wages of £24 per week from 2008 to 2018,[7] and also the weakening of a range of other sources of security, from the community to the state. In 2018, a report by the UN Special Rapporteur on Extreme Poverty and Human Rights concluded that 'poverty is a political choice' and that government policies have created 'great misery' 'unnecessarily'.[8] This has taken place alongside a growing dominance of waged labour over the entirety of human experience and potential, or the 'time of life'.

Work colonising the total time of life

Mezzadra and Neilson (2013: 21) draw together recent developments in class relations using the concept of the 'multiplication of labour', which represents:

> a conceptual tool for investigating the composition of living labour in a situation characterized by a high degree of heterogeneity. In part it refers to the intensification of labour processes and the tendency for work to colonize the time of life. It also attempts to grasp the subjective implications of the diversification and heterogenization of workforces that are the other side of the growing relevance of social cooperation in contemporary capitalism. The concept of multiplication of labour is therefore meant to accompany as well as supplement the more familiar concept of the division of labour, be it technical, social, or international.

Illustrating one form of the colonisation of the time of life, a welfare rights worker reported that in their experience, "it's a requirement from employers now ... that the staff members need to be fully flexible for not much commitment on the employer's behalf, 'I'll give you an eight-hour [per week] contract but you have to be available 24-7' [24 hours per day, seven days per week]" (interview P8). Similarly, Sporton's (2013) research with migrants in Doncaster highlights the potential for insecurity to enable employers to command all of workers' time, with no space for other priorities:

> Several interviewees talked about the *control* that agencies held over them, in particular, if they were unable or unwilling to work they would not be contacted again. Similarly, if they were not available for any reason, for example, a visit to their child's school or the doctor, they would not be contacted again. (Sporton, 2013: 451; emphasis in original)

As Standing (2011: 58) notes for 'temping', in such work relations, 'the time someone must put aside for labour exceeds the time' spent actually working. This shifts the costs of the reproduction of labour power onto workers by divesting capitalists of responsibility outside periods of key demand.

Again, these 'new' developments echo conditions from a much earlier period of capitalism's history. Braverman (1998 [1974]: 46) describes attempts at total control over workers' lives 'before the rise of industrial unionism' as 'the capitalists were groping toward a theory and practice of management'. He gives the example of the ironworks of Ambrose Crowley, which, with associated enterprises, employed more than 1,000 workers in the second quarter of the 18th century and housed them together with a wide range of facilities as part of a 'method of total economic, spiritual, moral, and physical domination, buttressed by the legal and police constraints of a servile administration of justice in a segregated industrial area' (Braverman, 1998 [1974]: 46). This might be compared to the practices of some agencies employing migrant workers today, who control many aspects of workers' movement to Britain, provide housing tied to their employment and extract numerous other charges, discussed further in Chapter 4.

In other cases, an abdication of responsibility by employers and the state leads to hidden and informal additions to the labour expected from workers, which can also involve them in processes of self-governance in the interests of capital. In some cases, this involves expectations to engage in activities such as studying company literature and answering emails outside waged hours, or the kind of survival strategies that Datta et al (2007a) found among Bulgarian workers in London, including careful budgeting and shopping around for bargains. This represents additional unpaid labour subsidising employers. Contemporary employment in Britain thus combines practices from earlier stages of capitalism, producing distinctive and differential forms of subjection. This reflects conditions of systemic decay (Yaffe, 2006) and the need to extend the field of profit-making to alleviate the capitalist crisis.

How borders structure the working class in Britain

Bromma (2013: 2) questions the essential unity of the working class on the basis that the term:

> doesn't really identify a single community of material interests under modern capitalism ... there's no way to finesse the fact that sizeable chunks of the working class have benefitted from – and therefore embraced – capitalism's program of privilege, national oppression, patriarchy, exploitation, and genocide. That's a reality too weighty to ignore.

James (2012 [1983]) makes similar observations regarding differences within the working class that are rooted in different positions within the productive process and also give rise to oppressive relations between working-class people. Charnock and Starosta (2016: 9; emphasis in original) argue that the division of the working class is a fundamental characteristic of capitalism, which has taken new forms within the international division of labour, whose "'essential" general content ... consists in the *international fragmentation of the productive subjectivity of the working class'*. Grady and Simms (2018) argue that the financialisation of society has driven further divisions among workers.

Phizacklea and Miles (1980: 6) use the concept of 'class fractions' to describe 'objective position[s] within a class boundary which [are], in turn, determined by both economic and politico-ideological relations', and whose composition and relationships must be empirically established. This offers a way of understanding the class divisions produced through imperialism. Borders play a prominent role in class fractioning, and given their disarticulation from geographical boundaries, discussed previously, the fragmentation that they produce occurs within and across national boundaries. This can be applied to several significant cleavages within the working class in Britain, comprising: polarisation within long-established racialised-minority sections of the working class; differentiation among recent migrants, contributing to further polarisation; and forms of relative privilege enabled by imperialist super-profits, giving rise to a 'labour aristocracy'. The remainder of this chapter considers each in turn. The term 'opportunism' (Lenin, 2005 [1915]) is used to express political perspectives that reflect the narrow, short-term interests of particular class fractions rather than the long-term interests of the entire working class. These divisions are unstable, and while processes of fractioning are always underway, distinct fractions often become visible only in moments of intense struggle, when underlying processes burst to the surface in mass collective action. Consequently, this book generally discusses processes of class fractioning, rather than defined fractions.

Racialised divisions in contemporary Britain

Racialised divisions have played an important role in class fractioning in Britain. In recent decades, the increasing complexity of ethnic categorisations has gone together with continued systematic discrimination and inequality (Wilkinson and Craig, 2011), highlighted in May 2018 by the UN Special Rapporteur on Racism.[9] More than 50 per cent of people who defined themselves in the 2011 Census as Indian, Pakistani, Bangladeshi, Black Caribbean or Black African were born in Britain. In general, racialised minorities in Britain are more likely to be subject to state repression,[10] and less likely to benefit from state welfare, discussed further in Chapter 4 (see also Vickers, 2012). There are persistent racialised inequalities in access to work and concentrations of racialised-minority workers in low-paid and insecure sectors, such as social care, hospitality, food processing and agriculture.

Since the 1980s, racialised-minority sections of the working class in Britain have become polarised. While most remain concentrated among poorer sections of the working class, a numerically significant middle class has emerged. Sadiq Khan epitomises this development – a bus driver's son who became a solicitor and then a career politician and the Mayor of London in 2015. Figure 2.1 presents some indicators of the differences between some of the largest racialised-minority groups and the general population by work role and pay.

These racialised-minority groups are thus both more concentrated in 'unskilled' roles and more polarised between the proportions classified as directors, managers or professionals or as unskilled, with smaller proportions in the middle category compared to the general population.

Since the 1980s, the British state has promoted forms of multiculturalism that have encouraged 'ethnic communities' to compete for resources, displacing earlier forms of black politics based on anti-racist solidarity, which often made common cause with liberation movements in oppressed countries (Williams et al, 1979; Sivanandan, 1991). In effect, a degree of cultural acceptance and the promise of economic mobility for some have been exchanged for loyalty to British imperialism. As part of the same process, resources have been granted for community projects and salaries for community leaders on the condition that anti-racist, political demands

Figure 2.1: Imperialism, migration and class in the 21st century

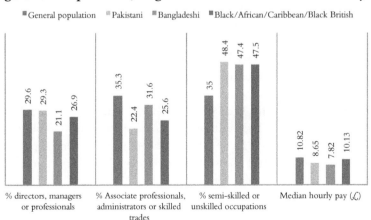

Source: Labour Force Survey, April 2014–March 2015.

were abandoned in favour of 'ethnic' interests, which have been defined increasingly narrowly (Gilroy, 1998). This has created a middle-class layer within racialised-minority communities, alongside the continued super-exploitation of the majority. During the 1997–2010 Labour government, state multiculturalism shifted into a focus on 'community cohesion'. This represented some forms of cultural difference as a threat in order to legitimate the state's wars in the 'Middle East' and isolate and terrorise any signs of opposition within Britain by demonising Muslims as hostile to 'British values' (Kundnani, 2007).

The enduring insecurity of racialised-minority sections of the working class was vividly illustrated by the attacks on the 'Windrush Generation', which made headline news in 2018. The Windrush Generation refers to people who moved from the Caribbean to Britain in the decades after the Second World War as Commonwealth citizens, symbolically represented by the docking of the MV Empire Windrush on 22 June 1948. They were granted British citizenship as part of the Immigration Act 1971, alongside restrictions on further migration. In 2016, reports began to appear about people within this group being refused access to state services because they had no documents to prove their citizenship, for example, Albert Thompson, who arrived from Jamaica as a teenager 44 years before and found himself denied cancer treatment by the National Health Service (NHS).[11] Others were deported.[12] Home Secretary Amber Rudd responded to the ensuing public outcry by saying that this was all a mistake and subsequently resigned, and Prime Minister Theresa May promised compensation. Yet, these apologies are undermined by the existence of a Home Office pamphlet, first issued in 2010, *Coming home to Jamaica*, which offers guidance to those deported after decades living in Britain. This demonstrates the extent to which lines of entitlement are shifting in the current British context, and how borders are expanding their operation to ensnare growing numbers of people. As Schierup and Castles (2011: 24) argue, established members of racialised-minority groups have weaker claims to social citizenship than white citizens, and in the context of the capitalist crisis, they are moving closer to the situation of temporary migrants and refugees.

The British state has been very effective at dividing and neutralising resistance to racism. The creation of a substantial racialised-minority middle class laid the basis for new forms of opportunism. One expression of this is the turn towards individualistic responses to racism, sometimes under the banner of 'intersectionality'. While Crenshaw (2018), who is credited with coining the term, advocates intersectionality as an approach to structural injustices, it tells us little in itself about their causes. In practice, contemporary intersectionality often focuses on personal identity and challenging individual acts of discrimination, something that Hill Collins (2009: ix) describes as part of an unfortunate 'turning inward' in social analysis. This diverts energy from the kind of coordinated, collective movements that are needed to confront the British state.

New migration to Britain

Low-skilled, strongly gendered and often temporary migration to the EU from outside has grown rapidly in recent decades, alongside highly skilled migration from outside and various forms of movement within the EU, with increasing polarisation. Schierup and Castles (2011: 23) identify tendencies across Europe towards the inclusion of migrants in formal rights, alongside ongoing 'real economic and social exclusion', enforcing acceptance of low-paid, insecure work. Migration continued despite the economic crisis, and continued mobility for 'highly skilled' workers has been a major concern within Brexit discussions.[13] In total, around 8.3 million residents of Britain or the North of Ireland were born abroad, of which around 1.9 million come from the EU (Alberti, 2017).

In 2008, the Labour government introduced a Points-Based System for migrants from outside the EU, representing a new stage in the fine-tuning of immigration to the needs of British capital. This system allocates points according to attributes, including qualifications, skills, English-language competence, age and income, with a top tier in which 'high-skilled' migrants, generally from more middle-class backgrounds and speaking excellent English, are granted greater rights, followed by workers with more limited rights, often tied to specific employers. The bottom tier, for 'low-skilled migrants', was indefinitely suspended as soon as the system was launched given the availability of labour from other parts of the EU. Differences in migrants' class position within Britain are influenced by the position of their countries of origin within imperialism. As Datta et al (2007a: 412) note:

> those coming to Britain from high-income countries have been crucial in helping meet a still growing demand for high-skilled workers, with around a third (36 per cent) of those coming from Japan and a little under a quarter (23.1 per cent) of migrants from Germany who are now living in London finding employment in managerial positions.

A policy advisor from a large regional membership organisation for businesses reported that the ability to quickly meet skill needs in response to changing customer demands was a significant motivation for companies to recruit internationally (interview P4). They indicated the existence of migration chains in some sectors, with graduates qualified in digital and information technology (IT) industries leaving North-East England for London, increasing the need to bring in workers from elsewhere or outsource to workers resident in another country. At the other end of the workforce in terms of status and pay, key sectors of the British economy are reliant on low-skilled migrant labour. Since the 1990s, for example, the low prices and 'just-in-time' methods of British supermarkets have depended on a flexible, low-paid and disposable workforce mainly composed of migrants, who can be out of work at times and suddenly called upon to work 70-hour weeks at others according to consumer demand, and who are kept in their super-exploited position by dependency on gangmasters for food, work and board, together with threats and intimidation (Kundnani, 2007: 59–60). Many of those sectors where migrants are concentrated were also hardest hit by the economic crisis, leading to a further intensification of precarity for these workers (Pradella and Cillo, 2015: 50–1).

In 2004, eight formerly socialist countries in Eastern Europe joined the EU, followed by Bulgaria and Romania in 2007. They entered the EU in a position subordinate to the interests of the big European imperialist powers; this offered British capital access to a substantial new source of labour and their subordinate status was reflected in the treatment of migrants from these countries. Poland was the largest single source of EU migrant labour during this period. Prior to joining the EU, Poland had experienced the fastest growth and fastest privatisation of all the former socialist countries in Eastern Europe, the highest unemployment rate of any EU member state, and lower per capita GDP than many other Eastern European countries. It shared other typical features of the formerly socialist countries, wherein:

> Job security has been replaced by insecurity, through casual contracts.... [The] unemployed rely on low-value state benefits and on informal legal and illegal income-generating activities.... The uncertain legal status of temporary contracts, reflecting their relatively recent appearance in CEE [Central and Eastern Europe] labour markets, has seen employers resort to the use of self-employment contracts, enabling avoidance of health and safety responsibilities, regular pay increases and payment of social contributions, and to shed staff more easily.... In some workplaces employers have been quick to

> dismiss workers who try to join or organize unions. (Hardy,
> 2008: 6)

This offered a ready supply of unorganised labour under pressure to migrate.

Migrant workers from Eastern Europe have faced systematic discrimination within Britain, based on markers such as accent, names and language (Ashe and Nazroo, 2016; Vickers et al, 2016), and have been disproportionately concentrated in poorer sections of the working class. In 2014/15, 83.7 per cent of Polish adults in Britain were classified as economically active, compared to 59.4 per cent of the general population. Furthermore, 31.4 per cent of Polish migrants in work were employed in 'elementary occupations', more than three times the percentage for the general population, and Polish workers' median hourly pay was £7.94, compared to £10.81 for the general population. The reliance on EU migrant labour in some sectors reached around 40 per cent for 'Packers, bottlers, canners and fillers' and 'Food, drink and tobacco process operatives' (Morris, 2017: 24–5). Dustmann and Frattini (2014) show that EU migrants who arrived during 2001–11 made a net contribution of £20 billion to Britain's public finances, representing a massive transfer of wealth to Britain. This is part of a wider pattern in which 'those coming ... from the Global South, and East and Central Europe have emerged as a major new source of labour for London's expanding low-wage economy' (Datta et al, 2007a: 412). Although demographics and sectoral compositions differ across Britain, the evidence of differential inclusion is consistent. Labour segmentation has coincided with social exclusion, including divisions between migrants from different countries, undermining the potential for class-based solidarity against exploitative working practices (Datta et al, 2007a: 422–3). Since 2008, growing numbers of people have moved to Britain from Southern Europe, fleeing the even more intense impacts of economic crisis and austerity in those countries (Alberti, 2017).

Meardi et al (2012: 8) argue that the benefits of EU10 migrants for employers have resulted as much from their mobility as from their readiness to accept low wages:

> It would be simplistic to see intra-EU mobility as just a strategy, by governments and employers, to lower labour costs and weaken trade unions.... In fact, wages seem to have been affected only marginally in the EU15.... [R]eal wages had already been stagnant in Western Europe for a while, and unions declining, so there was no urgent need for EU

employers to import foreign labour to stop wage or union growth.... [M]ore than low costs, the specific attractive feature of the new labour supply relies exactly on their 'mobility', which offers a corrective to the long-blamed 'sclerosis' of European labour markets.

Sporton (2013: 445) connects the deregulation of labour markets since the 1990s and the shift to 'managed migration' since 2002 as part of a neoliberal drive to create a workforce that is 'flexible' from the perspective of employers but 'precarious' from the perspective of workers themselves. As part of this shift, they point to the explosion of agency employment, from 775,000 to 1.37 million between 1997 and 2007. In a survey of over 1,000 employers, all of those who employed a disproportionately large number of EU migrants had recruited them via an agency (CIPD, 2013: 16). This has led to invisibility for many migrant workers at the bottom of supply chains because their employment via agencies means that they are recorded in the category of 'administration, business and management' – the largest sector of employment for Eastern European workers by far according to the Border and Immigration Agency in 2008 (Hardy, 2008: 10).

The tailoring of immigration controls to the needs of British capital has been further reinforced by restrictions on migration on grounds other than employment or investment, for example, to study, for family reunification or asylum, discussed further in Chapter 3. This reflects waged labour as the dominant form of conditionality for migration to imperialist countries.

The labour aristocracy and the crisis of labourism

Standing (2011) describes a crisis of 'labourism', which he defines as a prevailing approach to workers' organisation associated with 'Fordist' employment conditions in the second half of the 20th century. Standing (2011) uses Fordism to refer to labour relations in which workers could expect to maintain full-time employment with the same employer for a large portion of their lives, with various forms of labour-related security backed by powerful trade unions. Yet, these conditions were only ever enjoyed by a minority and 'presupposed vast amounts of unpaid domestic labour by women and hyper-exploited labour in the colonies' (Mitropoulos, 2006: 91).

Standing connects the crisis of labourism to the growth of 'precarity', which Casas-Cortés (2014: 207) conceptualises within 'four main tracks':

'(1) labor after the rollback of welfare state provisions; (2) the new paradigm of intermittent and immaterial labor; (3) the unceasing mobility of labor; (4) the feminization of labor and life'. All of these are relevant to this book: track (1) is addressed in Chapter 4, arguing that recent changes to the British state represent not simply a 'rollback', but a shift towards greater control through conditionality; track (2) relates to the tendency for work to colonise the total time of life, although the apparent shift to immaterial labour needs to be contextualised by the discussion earlier in this chapter about outsourcing much of capitalism's material labour to oppressed countries; track (3) is discussed in some senses in Chapter 3 and is of central concern for Chapter 5; and in defining track (4), the feminisation of labour and life, Casas-Cortés cites Maló:

> [The feminization of labor] is the process through which traits that usually characterized women's work and lives such as flexibility, vulnerability, total availability, high degrees of adaptation, talent for improvisation, and the ability to assume simultaneous roles and tasks (as housewives, wives, mothers, grandmothers, daughters, nurses, teachers, midwives) are nowadays spreading through a growing spectrum of types of employment, for both men and women. (Maló, 2001: 75, quoted in and translated by Casas-Cortés, 2014: 219-20)

In other words, 'women's work' has always been precarious, and the growth of precarity can be understood as an extension of those conditions to other sections of the working class. This can be understood as a shrinking of those privileged class fractions produced by imperialism, which poses a threat to their continued loyalty to capitalism, prompting alarm and a sense of crisis among sections of the ruling classes, their state representatives and their allies in the trade unions.

Within Britain, trade unions have often failed to represent the interests of the whole working class, and have instead tended to consolidate the position of a labour aristocracy whose privileges rely on the maintenance of imperialism and are consequently complicit with racism (Clough, 2014; Carbonella and Kasmir, 2018: 14). This gives the labour aristocracy an interest in the fragmentation and subjugation of the working-class majority. This provides a material basis for chauvinism and racism among the working class, beyond the purely ideological dimensions discussed by Virdee (2014), and suggests that such divisions are intrinsic to imperialism.

Britain's labour aristocracy has taken various forms, concentrated in sectors directly connected to colonialism in the late 19th century, skilled industrial workers in the mid 20th century, higher-paid public-sector workers in the second half of the 20th century and workers in the financial sector today. Today, trade unions in Britain largely fail to organise among, let alone represent, the most oppressed sections of the working class. Membership has fallen, in absolute terms and as a proportion of the workforce, and has become more middle class (BIS, 2017). In 2016, union membership among people earning over £1,000 a week was proportionally higher than among those earning less than £250 a week (BIS, 2017: 29). Higher-paid trade unionists outnumbered those in lower-paid roles by 4:1 in 2016, increasing from 2014, when it was 3:1. This was at a time when there were 5.1 million low-paid workers (D'Arcy, 2017). The concentration of highly paid workers within Britain's unions is not accounted for by gains won through struggle. Indeed, the 'trade union premium'[14] fell between 1995 and 2016, from 15.3 per cent to 7.6 per cent for the private sector, and from 30.4 per cent to 14.5 per cent for the public sector (BIS, 2017: 41).

Following a series of mergers, Britain's trade union movement has become dominated by massive monopolies, with the biggest three unions – Unite, Unison and GMB – together accounting for over half of Trade Union Congress (TUC) membership. Mergers have combined unions whose members are employed at very different levels of seniority, meaning that low-paid workers may be forced to be in the same branch as their managers. These mega-unions have a significant stake in the system, with major investments in properties and shares, and leaders paid six-figure salaries. In 2009, the big three unions received a total income of £386.5 million and paid out only £3 million in strike pay (Clough, 2010). These characteristics of union membership and structures help to explain the historical tendency for British trade unions to be reluctant to support migrant workers, or to be outright hostile (Richmond, 2002). In 2016, trade union membership was 16.2 per cent among workers born outside Britain, compared to 25 per cent among workers born in Britain (BIS, 2017: 5). The absence of migrants among trade union officials is even more pronounced, and there has been a lack of attention to specific attacks on migrants, particularly since the onset of the crisis (Pradella and Cillo, 2015: 52).

Yet, despite these tendencies to divide the working class, disunity and antagonism are not a foregone conclusion. The labour aristocracy is not a mechanical consequence of relative privilege, but also political, and therein lies the possibility for opportunism to be challenged and alliances to be formed. The engineering construction worker strikes of 2009–10 provide an example of both the pressures towards opportunism and the possibility for more internationalist positions to win through.

These strikes began on 28 January 2009, when workers at Lindsey Oil Refinery in North Lincolnshire were told that IREM, an Italian company that was due to take over a third of the contract on behalf of the French multinational Total, was refusing to employ British labour. Another subcontractor, Shaw's, had issued 90-day redundancy notices in mid-November, meaning that workers already facing redundancy in mid-February would not be allowed to apply for the IREM jobs. They were also told that the Italian and Portuguese workers that IREM was planning to employ would be housed on floating barges for the duration of the job, and would be bussed back to the barges for lunch, which was interpreted as an attempt to keep them separate from British workers and trade unions. The entire workforce across all subcontractors voted for strike action, and the following day, over 1,000 workers from the Lindsey, Conoco and Easington sites picketed Lindsey. The strike called for international equality and unionisation, driven by grass-roots unofficial action, as Gall (2009: 418) describes:

> when the assembled workers voted to walk out, the entire stewards' committee (on advice from Unite EUOs [Employed Union Officers]) resigned in order to distance the union from 'unlawful action'. An unofficial strike committee was then elected which formulated the strikers' demands following approval at a mass meeting on the strike's third day. These were: no victimisation for taking solidarity action; all ECI [Engineering Construction Industry] workers in Britain to be covered by the NAECI[15] agreement; union controlled registering of unemployed and locally skilled union members, with nominating rights as work becomes available; government and employer investment in proper training/apprenticeships for a new generation of ECI workers; all migrant labour to be unionised; union assistance for immigrant workers – including interpreters – and access to union advice to promote active integrated union members; and building links with construction unions on the continent.

Following this, the unofficial strike spread to over 20 sites across Britain.

Neither local strike leaderships nor their unions ever officially endorsed the slogan 'British jobs for British workers', which some workers used on placards in the early days of the strike, quoting then-Prime Minister Gordon Brown. Attempts by the Far-Right British National Party (BNP) to intervene in the strikes and recruit to their 'Solidarity' union front were firmly rebuffed, and BNP members were reportedly chased out of the car park outside a mass meeting at the Lindsey plant.[16] Yet, 'British Jobs for British Workers' was used to characterise the strikes in much of the capitalist media, ignoring the context in which it had been raised in the first days of the strike:

> Following the government's spending billions of pounds of public money in bailing out banks and indemnifying them against their losses, the strikers sought to make the point that they too demanded government protection.... The first strike at Lindsey concerned IREM's practice of exclusively using Italian and Portuguese workers specifically brought into Britain for this work, and excluding local labour, whether British or non-British. So this was not a strike against the use of overseas workers per se, and the strikers did not call for the expulsion, repatriation or sacking of 'foreign' workers.... After the strike committee asserted itself, the slogans on the placards changed to 'Fair access for local labour' where 'local' meant already domiciled worker, and was not a cipher for 'British' or white 'British' workers. The two unions then repeatedly made statements like, 'Our fight is with the employers who want to tear up our [NAECI] agreement and undermine our hard-won conditions at Staythorpe and wherever else. Not with the workers they seek to exploit'. (Gall, 2009: 422)

The strike was settled with an agreement that included an end to the segregation of foreign workers.

Following these successful strikes, in June the same year, 51 workers employed by Shaw's at Lindsey were made redundant without consultation or the industry norm of transferring to another of the site's contractors, and with only a week's pay in lieu of notice. Simultaneously, another subcontractor at the site took on 60 new workers to perform similar work. According to a GMB union press release, a senior manager at the site blamed the refusal of a transfer option on 'an unruly workforce who had taken part in unofficial disputes and who won't work weekends' (GMB, 2009). Workers responded by calling for unofficial solidarity actions across the industry. Three days later, contractors, with the backing of Total, announced the sacking of a further 647 workers for participating in unofficial strikes. Total initially agreed to talks with unions and the Advisory, Conciliation and Arbitration Service (ACAS)[17] but failed to turn up. The 647 workers were given the option to reapply for their jobs, seemingly an attempt to weed out leading trade unionists. Workers responded by publicly burning their dismissal notices. Solidarity strikes spread to more than 20 sites, including Polish workers at Drax in North Yorkshire, with 900 contract workers at the Sellafield plant in Cumbria stopping work for three days. Faced with such unity, Total made a statement expressing hope that its subcontractors at Lindsey would soon reach an agreement allowing work to resume. As 2,000 workers rallied outside Lindsey, the Unite and GMB unions announced their official endorsement of the strikes, with GMB pledging a £100,000 hardship fund. The strike ended with an agreement between Unite, GMB and the managing contractor Jacobs, including the full reinstatement of all sacked workers for at least four weeks, following which national terms would be followed for any further redundancies.

These strikes demonstrated that despite material divides within the working class, as well as attempts by the capitalist media and politicians to encourage chauvinism, a more internationalist approach can win out. Faced with determined and independent action by workers, the unions had little choice but to give official support, if only to end the dispute. The strike committee at Lindsey played a crucial role in maintaining a degree of independence from the union leadership to drive the action forward. However, it is important not to overstate these victories: even after the 2009 strikes, employers continued to employ migrant workers below industry rates (Gall, 2009: 426–7). Similarly, the danger of a chauvinist direction to trade unionism in the industry did not disappear and required constant political struggle. Other examples suggest continuing failures by Britain's major trade unions to integrate migrants, leading to splits in recent years from Unite and Unison to form new workers' organisations, including the IWGB (Independent Workers' Union of Great Britain) and United Voices of the World (Alberti and Peró, 2018).[18]

Conclusion

This chapter has analysed contemporary British capitalism, focusing on its international position, the role of the state, its relation to migration and some of the most significant conditions shaping exploitation. This sets the context for: Chapters 3 and 4, which examine the changing nature of the state in response to the capitalist crisis; Chapter 5, which considers the implications of this for wage labour; and Chapter 6, which relates this to discursive struggles.

Notes

1 See *The Guardian*, www.theguardian.com/politics/2008/sep/11/gordonbrown. economy
2 See, for example, *Financial Times*, www.ft.com/content/11f38928-ca6f-11e5-be0b-b7ece4e953a0, and *Business Insider*, http://uk.businessinsider.com/the-next-recession-could-be-worse-than-the-great-depression-2018-3/
3 See: http://databank.worldbank.org
4 For more recent applications, see Yaffe (2006) and Petras and Veltmeyer (2013).
5 'Britain and the North of Ireland' is used throughout the book instead of the more conventional 'United Kingdom' because the latter normalises British occupation.
6 See: http://blogs.lse.ac.uk/businessreview/2016/09/12/self-employment-is-precarious-work/
7 See: www.tuc.org.uk/blogs/17-year-wage-squeeze-worst-two-hundred-years
8 See: www.ohchr.org/EN/NewsEvents/Pages/DisplayNews.aspx?NewsID=23881&LangID=E
9 See: www.ohchr.org/EN/NewsEvents/Pages/DisplayNews.aspx?NewsID=23073&LangID=E
10 See: www.ethnicity-facts-figures.service.gov.uk/crime-justice-and-the-law/policing/stop-and-search/latest
11 See *The Independent*, www.independent.co.uk/news/uk/home-news/albert-thompson-windrush-cancer-treatment-date-radiotherapy-a8320836.html
12 See *The Guardian*, www.theguardian.com/uk-news/2018/jun/05/991-people-deported-to-caribbean-in-year-before-windrush-row
13 See the *Financial Times*, www.ft.com/content/eb27252d-94d8-328f-a0e3-76b890601484
14 The wage difference associated with trade union membership.
15 National Joint Council for the Engineering Construction Industry.
16 See *The Socialist*, https://www.socialistparty.org.uk/articles/6851/04-02-2009/lindsey-refinery-workers-show-their-strength
17 See: www.acas.org.uk/
18 See: https://iwgb.org.uk/; www.uvwunion.org.uk/

3

Deconstructing Migrant Crises in Europe

Introduction: immigration policy and the crisis of imperialism

Bassel and Emejulu (2017: 3) suggest that England is 'experiencing a backlash against multiculturalism ... fuelled by an existential crisis of national identity'. The origin of this crisis of national identity can be found in the crisis of imperialism. British capitalism is simultaneously highly dependent on capturing surplus value produced in other parts of the world (see Chapter 2) and incapable of defending its international interests alone. This produces contradictory tendencies towards national protectionism and collaboration with other imperialist states. The capitalist crisis is both fuelling rivalries between the imperialist powers, making cooperation more difficult, and reducing the material concessions that can be afforded to sections of the working class within Britain, increasing the importance of racism, nationalism and other ideological means of securing loyalty to the ruling classes. This echoes the rise of national protectionism, racism and xenophobia in many imperialist countries in an earlier period of crisis at the end of the 19th century (Mishra, 2018: 3).

The capitalist crisis has made the international struggle for sources of profit increasingly desperate, and this has contributed to an aggressive militarised foreign policy by imperialist states. Military interventions have combined with support for non-state proxy forces and repressive states, as well as concentrations of poverty and environmental degradation in many oppressed countries to put pressure on people to move internationally as a matter of survival. In 2015, 12.4 million people were newly displaced, although not all crossed an international border, and the proportion of the world's population who are migrants has remained consistent for decades (Crawley et al, 2018: 14). Restrictions on migrants' rights, reinforced by racism, serve both to insulate imperialist countries against the worse consequences of imperialist crisis and to create special conditions of legal and social insecurity that enable a reduction of wages and conditions. Defining a state of crisis through migration has involved:

- material elements (such as checkpoints, immigration prisons and guards), restrictions on migrants' access to resources and militarised attacks on migrants and those assisting them;
- the legal identification of human beings through migrant categories;
- cultural representations of migrants that are classed, racialised and gendered; and
- ideological definitions of the crisis as caused by people moving rather than the borders that define and impede that movement.

The combined effect has been to facilitate an ongoing reorganisation of the British state, and many other states, to increase the extent and intensity of control over the working class.

This chapter traces the proliferation of British border controls internally, through the cultivation of a 'hostile environment', and externally, through Europe's so-called 'migrant crisis'. The last part of the chapter considers the potential for social movements and campaigns to both reinforce and contest these bordering practices.

Internalising Britain's borders: the 'hostile environment'

Increased differentiation of rights through immigration status is a Europe-wide trend (Carmel and Cerami, 2011). Within Britain, shifting depictions of 'asylum seekers', 'migrant workers', 'highly skilled migrants' and other categories have been played off against one another, as well as against a posited 'British worker', who is implicitly white and male (discussed further in Chapter 6). Increased differentiation of rights has contributed to the class fractioning discussed at the end of Chapter 2 and further in Chapter 5. Border controls have extended into more and more aspects of everyday life, combined with the state-sponsored cultivation of a populist hostility to migrants, forming a complex 'border regime' whose core components are outlined by Corporate Watch (2018).

The discussion here focuses on a policy agenda that has come to be known as the 'hostile environment', a phrase first coined by then-Home

Secretary Theresa May in 2012,[1] although its origins go back much further. Its core elements have evolved over the course of the Labour government of 1997–2010, the Conservative–Liberal Democrat Coalition of 2010–15 and the Conservative government since 2015. Between 1997 and 2010, the Labour government passed six immigration laws, each more restrictive than the last. As discussed in Chapter 2, a ready supply of low-waged labour from other European Union (EU) countries combined with the Points-Based System to fine-tune immigration to the labour needs of capital, complemented by attacks on the right to asylum (Vickers, 2015). From 2010, the Conservative–Liberal Democrat Coalition and the Conservative government that followed implemented a cap on net migration and passed new Immigration Acts in 2014 and 2016, further extending controls.

The consistency of this trajectory across different governments reflects deep roots in the needs of British capitalism in crisis. It connects to longer histories of British state racism in which national citizenship has 'mark[ed] out ... populations ... contained within the state as an "interiorized other"', 'producing paralysed, dejected and "deportable" populations of non-citizens within the internal borders of the nation' (Tyler, 2013: 48). During the 2017 Conservative Party conference, the term 'hostile environment' was replaced by Immigration Minister Brandon Lewis with 'compliant environment'.[2] This rebranding may have been an attempt to make the approach seem more reasonable, but it also emphasised its disciplinary character. The hostile/compliant environment has made immigration status *the* defining characteristic for those subject to immigration controls, overriding both shared humanity and any other characteristic or identity. It can be further defined as embodying several core elements: the idea of the nation under threat; the presentation of migrants as a burden; conditional acceptance of some migrants in the 'national interest'; systematic surveillance and repression; and the extension of responsibility for border controls to the whole of society. Each of these elements is explored in the following.

The nation under threat

Around the turn of the century, British foreign policy underwent a significant shift, normalising a constant state of war. The idea that Britain was under threat from international terrorism was central to the government's justification for state interventions, including the invasions of Afghanistan in 2001 and Iraq in 2003, alongside the expansion of its repressive apparatus domestically (Kundnani, 2015). Race and nation also went through significant changes during this period, from a form of multiculturalism in the Labour government's early years to an aggressive assimilationism that offered a degree of acceptance for racialised-minority sections of the working class in exchange for loyalty to 'British values' and complicity with the continued exclusion of newcomers (Vickers, 2012). The 'assimilationist turn' (Phillimore, 2012) reached new levels in December 2016 with the publication of the Casey Review into 'integration and opportunity' (Casey, 2016), commissioned a year before by then-Prime Minister David Cameron.

The review was led and authored by Dame Louise Casey, who also oversaw the 'Troubled Families' programme that followed the urban uprisings in 2011 (Crossley, 2018). That programme shifted the blame from police racism, poverty and cuts to the supposed moral failings of working-class families. Similarly, the Casey Review on integration blamed Muslims, particularly those of Pakistani and Bangladeshi descent, for the inequalities they face. It defined integration as 'the extent to which people from all backgrounds can get on – with each other, and in enjoying and respecting the benefits that the United Kingdom has to offer' (Casey, 2016: 20). 'Anti-Western' attitudes and a lack of nationalist identification with Britain were raised by the review as points of concern – in other words, 'integration' seems to have been interpreted as the extent to which all people, and particularly racialised minorities, can be relied on to express gratitude to their rulers and stand with them against workers of other countries. Casey explicitly rejected the oft-cited 'two-way street' metaphor for integration, and instead described it as 'a bloody big motorway and you have a slip-road of people coming in from the outside … people in the middle in the motorway need to accommodate and be gentle and kind to people coming in from the outside lane but we're all … heading in the same direction'.[3]

The Casey Review explained racialised inequalities and a range of other issues – particularly the oppression of women and child abuse – as the result of cultural difference. It expressed concern at the number of British Pakistani people marrying new migrants from Pakistan, and suggested that this reduced levels of spoken English and fostered regressive social attitudes. The review's recommendations followed its nationalist, assimilationist perspective: more teaching of 'British values' in schools; a requirement for migrants to take an 'integration oath'; more focus on the English language; and 'women's emancipation in communities where they are being held back by regressive cultural practices' (MHCLG, 2016). In short, the role of racism and other structural factors in producing disadvantage were ignored and, instead, ethnic difference was pathologised (Ashe, 2018).

The government responded to the Casey Review with an Integrated Communities Strategy Green Paper. This exemplified a further intensification of the assimilationist turn. As Phillimore and Sigona (2018) say:

> Similarly to the Casey Review, in the Green paper, isolation, deprivation, lack of participation [among racialised minorities] are invariably constructed as having little to do with the conditions of their lives in Britain and factors such as structural discrimination and wealth inequality. Instead, the causes of the integration deficit and the onus of integrating are placed on 'them', migrants and ethnic minorities.

Portraying the nation as under threat encourages national loyalty in exchange for protection. It constructs racialised minorities as an internal threat to the nation, especially where they express solidarity with those perceived as external threats, and the perpetrators of their own oppression through cultural difference.

Migrants as a burden

Migrants have often been portrayed as a financial burden on British citizens. This characterisation pre-dated the economic crisis and public sector cuts that followed, but intensified alongside them. Large sections of the press and many politicians have blamed migrants for the falling wages, precarious work and deteriorating public services facing large sections of the working class.[4] Whereas migrant workers and refugees were often played off against each other in the past – each in turn held up as the 'model migrant' and then demonised (Kundnani, 2007: 4–5) – over the last decade, the main British parties have united in attacking those assigned to both categories. This escalating hostility has been facilitated in part by the coverage given to the UK Independence Party (UKIP) by the capitalist media, despite a small formal membership and very limited electoral success.

Illustrating this intensifying narrative, in the lead-up to the 2015 general election, the major political parties entered what amounted to a bidding war over who could promise more severe restrictions on access to welfare for EU migrants. Labour leader Ed Miliband said that immigration was at the top of his party's agenda, and that he would press for EU reforms to increase restrictions on migrants from new member states. The following month, Labour's Shadow Secretary for Work and Pensions, Rachel Reeves, used an article in the *Daily Mail* to announce that a Labour government would extend restrictions on out-of-work benefits for EU migrants to two years, and that access to in-work tax credits would also be restricted.[5] Evidence showing the net contribution that migrants make to public finances has been repeatedly dismissed by politicians. For example, in an interview on BBC Radio 5 Live in November 2014, Work and Pensions Secretary Iain Duncan Smith described Dustmann and Fratini's (2014) calculations as 'silly', claiming that 'they [migrants] literally change the schooling because so many people arrive not speaking English. You have then got problems you know with local services, transport, all that kind of stuff'.[6] This narrative fed directly into the campaigns around the 2016 referendum on Britain's membership of the EU, where it reached a crescendo.

Since the election of Jeremy Corbyn as leader of the Labour Party in 2015, the party has changed its headline rhetoric on migration but has continued to accept fundamental claims that migrants place a burden on British workers. For example, in July 2017, Corbyn claimed in an interview on the BBC One *Andrew Marr* show that 'wholesale importation of underpaid workers from Central Europe' had been used to 'destroy conditions' for British workers, and he committed Labour to ending freedom of movement within the EU and ensuring that migrants would only be allowed to 'come here on the basis of the jobs available and their skill sets to go with it'.[7] A speech by Labour's Shadow Home Secretary, Diane Abbott, in February 2018 at King's College London's Policy Institute exemplifies the contradictions of Labour's position. She spoke against the idea that migrants are responsible for low wages, pointing instead to a combination of 'globalisation', weak trade unions and 'predatory employers', but in the same speech said that the 'exploitation of migrant labour by unscrupulous employers ... serves to undercut wages for all', a claim without evidence.[8] She promised an end to the 'hostile environment' for migrants and rightly blamed the crisis in schools, housing and the National Health Service (NHS) on austerity rather than immigration. Yet, she went on to say that 'We do accept that a rising population creates challenges in education, health care and housing', and proposed the reinstatement of a Migration Impact Fund as a solution, rather than the allocation of resources to meet the needs of the local population, wherever they are from. This represents an attempt to placate opposition to the insidious racism of the government's hostile environment, while simultaneously maintaining the idea that migrants are a threat to 'British workers' that requires special measures.

The idea that migrants put a burden on services appears to explain some people's everyday experiences: areas where migrants are concentrated are often characterised by inadequate housing, overcrowded schools and poor health provision, but this is because they are more exploited by

British capital and receive a lower 'social wage' in the form of benefits and services, not because they are a drain on resources. What appears as a causal relationship between the presence of migrants and inadequate services is, in fact, a sign of migrants' super-exploitation (Paine, 1977). This helps explain why politicians' arguments have resonated with some sections of the working class in the absence of strong political movements fostering a more critical interpretation of their experiences.

Conditional acceptance

In common with many other EU member states during this period, the Labour government of 1997–2010 adopted a principle of 'circular migration', representing repeated cycles of migration and temporary settlement according to labour demand. Feldman (2012: 150–79) suggests that circular migration unites the concerns of neoliberals eager to ensure a continued supply of migrant labour, and 'neo-nationalists' determined to prevent longer-term settlement. It positions migrants as 'entrepreneurs' rather than workers, reducing them to a skill set to be sold on the market and enhanced through circulation; their subjection as workers is thus intensified even as their working-class identity is undermined. Polish workers were publicly valued during this period for their 'work ethic', and contrasted with the image of the 'bogus asylum seeker', who was simultaneously legally prohibited from working and portrayed as lazy and uninterested in contributing (Kmak, 2015).

The Labour government of this period also introduced a minimum wage, but its implementation represented a stark contrast to its immigration enforcement, as Anderson (2010b: 307) describes:

> projected costs for the enforcement of the National Minimum Wage (NMW) in 2009/10 [were] £8.8m, with the budget for the UK border force (not including Customs detection activity funding) for the same period at £248.6m.… The budget for in-country immigration control (work permits, Points-Based System, removals, asylum processes) was £884.3m. The NMW had 93 compliance officers in 2009 and the Gangmasters Licensing Authority had 25 inspectors.… The proposed number of UK Border Agency Staff for Local Immigration teams, the bodies tasked with bringing immigration controls to a local level, is 7,500.

This reflected the priorities of the British state and its Labour government, with a lack of restraint on the violence of wage exploitation accompanied by the direct violence of border controls. The shift towards increased repression, combined with the localisation of immigration controls, established a trajectory that would be continued by the governments that followed.

The Conservative–Liberal Democrat Coalition government pursued its net migration target by running campaigns targeting various migrant categories, including students attending so-called 'bogus colleges'[9] and those entering 'sham marriages'.[10] Home Office propaganda included photographs on its official Twitter feed on Valentine's Day showing marriage ceremonies being broken up by immigration officers[11] and advertising vans with a picture of handcuffs and the slogan 'In the UK Illegally? Go Home or Face Arrest' driven round some of the most diverse boroughs of London (Jones et al, 2017). In 2018, it emerged that the target for net migration had given rise to national and local deportation targets. After initially denying the existence of such targets, amid the Windrush scandal discussed in Chapter 2, Home Secretary Amber Rudd announced that targets did exist but promised that they would be scrapped.[12] This echoed deportation targets set by the Labour government in 2000 (Corporate Watch, 2018: 22).

New restrictions have made migrants' position more precarious and imposed further conditions on their presence in Britain. This includes restrictions on EU migrants' access to benefits, discussed further in Chapter 4, making their presence in Britain increasingly conditional on employment. In July 2015, new restrictions were announced for students on Tier Four visas, including a ban on students at publicly funded colleges getting a part-time job alongside their studies, a ban on their 'dependants' taking 'low or unskilled' jobs, a reduction in the maximum visa length for students in further education from three to two years, and new barriers preventing students continuing their studies beyond their initial visa, or transitioning to a work visa. New restrictions on Tier Two visas came into effect in 2016, limiting those earning less than £35,000 to six years in Britain, after which they must leave the country or face deportation, with no opportunity to apply for Indefinite Leave to Remain. This represents a guest worker programme in all but name, benefiting capitalists through a 'churn' of individuals that makes integration and solidarity more difficult.

The Labour Party's ongoing commitment to conditional acceptance was made clear in the February 2018 speech by Shadow Home Secretary Diane Abbott, mentioned in the previous section. Abbott proposed more selective filtering:

of who we accept and reject. We can adopt policies to attract some people such as nurses or engineers, we can adopt policies to apprehend others such as criminals, people traffickers, terrorists…. there are many sectors of the economy where we need people from overseas, whether it's agriculture, or astrophysics, teaching, IT [information technology], or sandwich making.

She proposed that such selections would be enforced under a future Labour government by 1,000 extra border guards. The continuing need for migrant labour was also expressed in the Conservative Party's 2017 election campaign, when the proposed continuation of the cap on net migration was criticised by some senior party members as detrimental to the economy.[13]

The combined effect of these changes was expressed by a local authority welfare rights advisor we interviewed: "the whole rhetoric around it has changed significantly … we're creating quite an inhospitable climate for people and it's, 'Yes be here, but work and don't expect any support, regardless of your circumstances'" (interview P8). Conditional acceptance expresses an attempt to reconcile the continued need for migrant labour with the need to maintain its super-exploited position. It operates together with a punitive and conditional approach to state welfare for the wider working class, which also affects migrants in special ways, discussed in Chapter 4.

Expanding the repressive apparatus

Between 1997 and 2010, immigration detention capacity expanded to more than 3,000 places. The most common category of detainees in 2010 was people who had sought asylum (Silverman, 2011); later, these same facilities were also directed at migrants from Eastern Europe, and by 2017, capacity had increased to more than 4,000. Investigative journalists and campaigners have repeatedly exposed abuse and overt racism within detention, for example, in 2015, a Channel 4 documentary filmed guards describing detainees as 'animals' and 'beasties', with one guard telling another 'Headbutt the bitch. I'd beat her up'. The Black Women's Rape Action Project and Women Against Rape (2015) documented other abuses. The charity INQUEST recorded 48 deaths of immigration detainees between 2000 and April 2018.[14]

In February 2018, 120 women in Yarls Wood Immigration Removal Centre went on indefinite hunger strike, the latest in a long history of resistance within detention (Webber, 2012). The strikers launched a set of demands that included: an end to indefinite detention; amnesty for everybody living in Britain for over ten years; an end to the employment of detainees for £1 an hour; and 'an end to charter flights and the snatching of people from their beds in the night and herding them like animals'.[15] Home Office figures show that in the five years up to 2018, it was forced to pay £21.2 million as compensation for the unlawful detention of migrants.[16] In 2018, a report was published following an inspection of Harmondsworth Immigration Removal Centre (HM Chief Inspector of Prisons, 2018), revealing that: over half of detainees felt unsafe; support for detainees identified as at risk of self-harm was inconsistent; use of force was excessive; segregation was used punitively; and some detainees were held for long periods, even where they had histories of being tortured. A previous inspection in 2015 had made 23 recommendations, of which only one had been implemented by 2017. Outside detention, asylum seekers are forced to sign regularly at immigration reporting centres or police stations, increasing a sense of criminalisation.

Bales and Mayblin (2018) document the extent of waged labour by detainees, which has operated since 2003. Many detainees cited the need to send remittances and pay for goods and services inside detention as reasons that they felt they needed to take the work, even at £1 an hour, and there was evidence that work was sometimes withheld as a disciplinary measure. Detainees performed 923,154 hours of such labour in 2015, much of it menial tasks contributing to the running of the centre, reducing costs for the private companies that run most detention centres. Many detainees would be legally prohibited from working if they were not detained; they thus represent captive labour subject to special conditions for exploitation, the implications of which will be further discussed in Chapter 5.

Refusal rates for asylum applications have remained high throughout this period, even during periods when fewer people have applied (see Figure 3.1). In 2013, a Home Office spokesperson admitted that officials dealing with asylum cases were given targets to secure refusals of at least 60 per cent of cases,[17] with bonuses for meeting a 70 per cent rejection target.[18]

As can be seen from Figure 3.2, various forms of 'voluntary' returns have increased, often with a cash incentive for the migrant. These are not formally classed as deportations, but often take place under conditions where the state has made people's lives so difficult that they are left with little alternative.[19]

Blinder (2017) expresses caution about drawing conclusions from these data about trends over time due to changing data-collection practices. Nevertheless, these figures indicate the mass scale of enforced mobility.

Deportations on the grounds of imprisonable offences are also significant: 6,171 people were deported in this way in 2016, sometimes due to survival-related offences such as theft of food or performing waged work

Figure 3.1: Asylum applications and refusal rates, 1999–2017

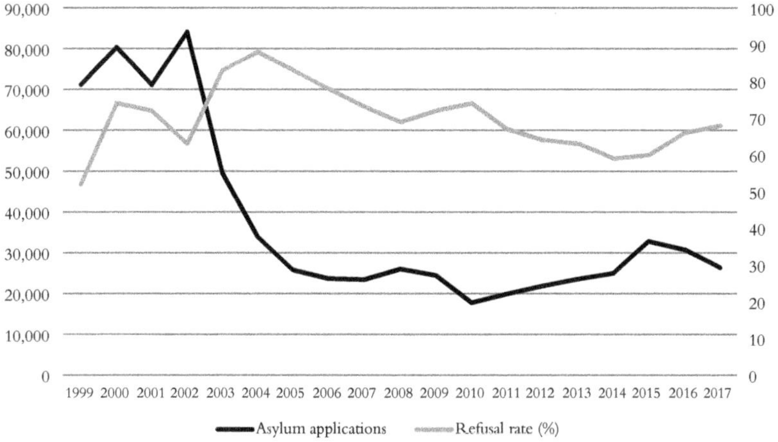

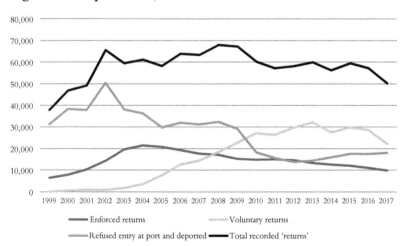

Notes: Applications include those at the port of entry and after arrival in the UK. Refusal rates represent final decisions, including applications made in a previous year.

Source: www.gov.uk/government/statistics

Figure 3.2: Deportations, 1999–2017

Source: www.gov.uk/government/statistics

while prohibited from doing so. Their ascribed criminality adds a further dimension to definitions of 'good' and 'bad' migrants (Griffiths, 2017). State repression has also intensified within communities. In 2013, businesses in London's Chinatown staged a shutdown in protest at repeated speculative immigration raids,[20] and this was repeated in 2018.[21] In another example, a December 2016 operation targeted hundreds of nail bars, leading to 97 arrests on immigration grounds. Bloch and McKay (2016: 18) show how such workplace raids have 'resulted in a retreat among undocumented migrants into less visible and more informal sectors of the economy', deepening conditions for exploitation. While the government has formally supported action against forced labour, including passing the Modern Slavery Act 2015, it has thus simultaneously created conditions for forced labour to flourish (Balch, 2015).

Following widespread resistance against deportations, the state has increasingly resorted to 'charter flights', whereby an entire plane is booked for deportation. By separating deportees from other types of travellers, and often involving companies that do not rely on commercial travellers, opportunities for resistance have been limited. Security 'escort' services on charter flights have been outsourced to a private company, Tascor, who took over the contract from G4S after the killing of detainee Jimmy Mubenga.[22] The Independent Monitoring Board's (2018) report on charter flights criticises the excessive use of force by 'escorts' and routine degrading treatment, such as denying detainees privacy to use the toilet, preventing them from using the toilet before leaving the detention centre and keeping them penned for hours on a coach. It also criticises the practice of allowing escorts to act as gatekeepers denying detainees access to legal advice.

Immigration enforcement in Britain has extended its net far beyond recent migrants. For example, Arthur Muir, who moved to Britain 17 years before, aged 13, and had a wife and two children in Britain, was deported to Jamaica in 2017 because his wife did not earn the £18,600 salary required for a spouse visa. He was told by a Home Office official that keeping his family together was not sufficient reason to halt his deportation because he 'would be able to remain in contact with them via modern methods of communication i.e. telephone, internet or by written correspondence'.[23] After being detained, he was found to be at risk of suicide. The same week, 52-year-old Irene Clennell was deported to Singapore, away from her children, grandchild and husband of 27 years, for whom she was the main carer. She had been living in Britain since 1988. After a legal battle, she was finally able to return to Britain.[24]

This repressive apparatus acts as a final measure of exclusion and plays a role in structuring differential inclusion through the fear it creates.

Furthermore, many police forces have admitted handing over victims of crime to immigration enforcement, weakening migrants' access to any protection from the state.[25] However, Corporate Watch (2018) point out that reductions in state budgets have also affected some elements of the repressive apparatus, increasing pressure to outsource some elements of the hostile environment to non-state bodies.

Co-opting non-state actors into border control

Forced dispersal of asylum seekers from 1999 drove the incorporation of voluntary sector organisations within migration management, setting a precedent that was later extended as part of the hostile environment. In many asylum dispersal areas, little preparatory work was done, forcing voluntary sector organisations, churches and refugee community organisations (RCOs) to respond quickly (Hewitt, 2002: 7). This contributed to a narrow focus on service provision and partnerships with the local state (Briskman and Cemlyn, 2005). Even among RCOs, critical voices were often sidelined as organisations were drawn into state-directed funding regimes, and many volunteers were also incorporated within hegemonic state practices (Vickers, 2012, 2016).

In 2013, the Home Office created the Interventions and Sanctions Directorate (ISD), with the explicit aim of building partnerships to push undocumented migrants out of Britain:

> The unit has overall responsibility for removing incentives for people to stay illegally and encourage those who are in the country unlawfully to regularise their stay or leave the UK.... The unit works closely with government departments and a range of other partners across the public and private sectors to identify those migrants accessing such services and benefits to which they are not entitled. (ICIBI, 2016)

In 2014, the government passed an Immigration Act that extended border controls into many areas of everyday life (Wemyss, 2015), including health care, private-rented housing, employment, banking and driving private vehicles. This built on pre-existing arrangements for data sharing to enable immigration enforcement, for example, a relationship between the Home Office and the Driver and Vehicle Licensing Agency (DVLA), established in 2005 and extended in 2008 (ICIBI, 2016), and restrictions on benefits and health care discussed in Chapter 4.

A new 'Immigration Taskforce' was created in 2015, chaired by then-Prime Minister David Cameron. A further Immigration Bill followed, passed in 2016 with no opposition from the Labour Party under its new leader, Jeremy Corbyn. During the second reading of the Bill, then-Home Secretary Theresa May outlined some of the outcomes of the 2014 Act: 11,000 driving licences revoked; 8,000 marriages investigated by the Home Office (out of which, 98.5 per cent were found *not* to be 'sham'); and charges for migrants to use the NHS that totalled £100 million. The 2016 Act created a new criminal offence for working without permission, potentially leading to a 12-month prison sentence, the confiscation of earnings as the proceeds of crime and an unlimited fine. Immigration officers were given new powers to enter and search premises, seize earnings and property, and shut down businesses, with a focus on small businesses that disproportionately affected racialised-minority owners. Prison sentences of up to five years were introduced for landlords renting to a migrant without a 'right to rent', which was made dependent on immigration status. The 2016 Act also created a criminal offence for driving without the appropriate immigration status and required banks to carry out quarterly checks on the immigration status of their clients and to hand data to the Home Office where account holders were found to lack the correct papers (Liberty, 2018: 21–2). This further marginalised undocumented migrants and increased their vulnerability to exploitation. Implications for health care and housing are discussed further in Chapter 4.

The hostile environment has also extended to education. In October 2016, it emerged that the Department for Education (DfE) was sharing data with the Home Office to target families for immigration enforcement. This affected up to 1,500 children and young people each month, together with their families (Liberty, 2018: 9). Activists responded with a campaign encouraging parents and teachers to withhold information about country of origin and nationality from the National Schools Census and launched a series of legal challenges.[26] Data were either actively refused or simply not completed for 25 per cent of pupils, and in April 2018, the DfE announced that it would no longer require schools to gather this information.[27] Universities have also become sites of immigration enforcement, with high fees for visas and courses, and academics forced to report on the attendance of international students to ensure that they comply with visa conditions. In 2018, it emerged that many asylum seekers were being prevented from studying, using powers under the Immigration Act 2016, even where they had been offered full scholarships to cover their fees.[28]

Businesses, local authorities, charities and Members of Parliament (MPs) have also been involved in the hostile environment. For example, Bales (2017) discusses the 'arrest by appointment' of 35 workers in July

2016 after their employer, Byron Burgers, told them to attend meetings deliberately timed to coincide with immigration raids. Protests opposing this collaboration followed outside several Byron outlets across Britain. As with many other elements of the hostile environment, this represented an intensification and systemisation of longer-term trends, with precedents including alleged collaboration between the University of London School of African and Oriental Studies (SOAS) and the Home Office to deport cleaners fighting for a living wage in 2009.[29] In another example, Corporate Watch (2018) document collaboration between at least 12 London borough councils, the Greater London Authority, homelessness charities and the Home Office to deport homeless migrants, with similar practices reported in Bristol, Brighton and other cities with large numbers of rough sleepers. A High Court ruling in December 2017 found the deportation of EU citizens on grounds of street homelessness to be unlawful, but campaigners allege that their involvement continued (interview A6). During 2012–18, MPs reported more than 700 people for suspected 'immigration abuse', presumably mostly constituents approaching them for help.[30]

The hostile environment has ostensibly been aimed at undocumented or 'irregular' migrants. In practice, it has targeted migrants from oppressed countries in particular, as well as those in a working-class position within Britain, because these migrants have less access to visas offering preferential terms and are more likely to rely on private-rented accommodation. As Liberty (2018: 5) points out: 'Far from intentionally trying to evade the rules, people often become undocumented because they're unable to scrape together ever-increasing application fees, challenge poor Home Office decision-making, or pay a solicitor to help them keep up with rapidly changing immigration rules'. The hostile environment has also encouraged a climate of suspicion towards anybody fitting the imagined profile of a 'migrant', whether through skin colour, accent, religion or dress, consequently targeting wider sections of racialised-minority workers. As Phillimore and Sigona (2018) put it: 'If you are not white and British you must now prove that you have a right to be here. The same rules do not seem to apply to the white British who emigrated to Britain having been born in the former colonies'. Supporting this, a refugee drop-in worker we interviewed said that she was encountering so many refugees who were having problems setting up a bank account, even though they were legally entitled to do so, that she was advising them not to even try and to go to a credit union instead (interview P5). The Home Office itself reportedly warned the government about these wider ramifications on several occasions during 2014–18, but these warnings were seemingly ignored.[31]

Beyond its direct effects in heightening everyday surveillance and repression, the hostile environment has incorporated additional layers of workers within the state's border regime, and its accompanying suspicion of racialised others. This is part of a wider international trend, summarised by Hanieh (2018). It is consistent with other developments in state welfare, discussed in Chapter 4, and is an important context for the growth of anti-migrant populism. Resistance to the hostile environment is discussed later in this chapter and in Chapter 4.

Externalising Britain's borders: 'Europe's migrant crisis'

Europe's so-called 'migrant crisis' or 'refugee crisis' is connected to contradictory impulses, both arising from the imperialist crisis, towards destabilisation as a means of expropriation and control as a means of exploitation. These two tendencies come together in struggles around the border. Feldman (2012: 83; emphasis in original) describes how a focus on individual rights has obscured the class character of immigration controls and their role in managing the surplus populations that are a structural feature of capitalism:

> To justify the apparatus in humanitarian terms, EU officials speak fluently in the language of human rights…. Emphasising the isolated individual allows the structural inequality behind the matter to remain obscure. This move succeeds only if EU officials treat migration as an *objective* threat or problem that arrives on their shores independent of any systemic political and economic relations between the EU and the wider world…. Border control … becomes a major security practice because an increase in redundant labor from the South, it is feared, would jeopardize the EU's internal social-cum-national order.

The crisis is thus ultimately rooted in the need to maintain imperialist divisions of land and labour, discussed in Chapter 2 (see also Jones, 2016: 28; Hanieh, 2018). As previous control mechanisms have been placed under pressure, the state has adapted, extending its control both within its territory, as discussed in the previous section, and far beyond it.

This section discusses: the emergence of the 'migrant crisis' as a public issue; the role of the EU, Britain and other member states in producing the crisis; the relationship between freedom of movement and restrictions;

and the outsourcing of border control away from the imperialist centres. These tendencies are then examined further through a case study of British bordering in Northern France.

Defining the crisis

The idea of a migration crisis entered the public mainstream in the summer of 2015. During that year, authorities detected more than 1 million unauthorised border crossings into the EU, mostly via the Mediterranean and the Balkans. This figure includes an unknown amount of double-counting as some migrants' journeys involve multiple crossings of the EU frontier. Crawley et al (2018: 34–8) emphasise that this was not a single 'flow', and included people from many different countries moving for a variety of reasons, although, in most cases, with little choice over whether and where to move, and, in many cases, moving repeatedly over a period of years. There were significantly more recorded border crossings in 2015 than 2014, but this still only amounted to around 0.2 per cent of the EU's population. To put this in perspective with other population movements, in the same year, total migration into the EU totalled approximately 2.7 million and total migration out of the EU totalled approximately 1.2 million.[32] Large numbers of people moving between countries is thus accepted as normal, but particular types of migration are treated as a problem. Although unauthorised migration occurs in significant numbers for some less developed countries, for example, India, Russia and South Africa, it 'tends to garner greater international attention as a challenge facing developed countries' (Friman, 2011: 89–90) – this reflects the challenge that it poses to the imperialist divisions of labour discussed in Chapter 2.

The public representation of the crisis in 2015 was marked by high-profile incidents, including the deaths of more than 1,200 migrants in two shipwrecks in April and a widely distributed photograph of three-year-old Aylan Kurdi, lying dead, face down, on a beach near the Turkish resort of Bodrum in September. This followed the British government's cancellation of funding for search and rescue operations in the Mediterranean, justified by the claim that rescuing people from drowning was creating, in the words of Foreign Office minister Lady Anelay, 'an unintended "pull factor"' attracting migrants to Europe.[33] Refuting this claim, Steinhilper and Gruijters (2018) analysed available statistics covering 2000–16 and found that reduced search and rescue operations were not associated with reduced migration, but were associated with increased loss of life (see also Crawley et al, 2018). The deaths in 2015 were part of a longer history, involving a combination of destabilisation within North Africa and West Asia, and EU border restrictions that have forced people to take increasingly dangerous routes. Carrier sanctions fine airlines for transporting people without a visa, forcing more people to travel by land or sea (Collinson, 1996). UNITED for Intercultural Action compiled a list of 34,361 confirmed individuals 'who have died in their attempt of entering the "Fortress" or because of Europe's immigration policies' from 1993–2018.[34] This only includes recorded deaths, and the actual total may be considerably higher.

Recorded deaths compiled by the Migrant Files journalist collaboration[35] and the IOM (International Organization for Migration) Missing Migrants project[36] give a minimum figure of 3,995 deaths in 2011, higher than the 3,785 deaths recorded in 2015. These figures call into question the idea that the public recognition of a crisis in 2015 was simply the result of the number of deaths. Crawley et al (2018: 26–7) argue that the sense of crisis in 2015 was heightened by the high proportion of migrants arriving via Greece (85 per cent), which lacked the infrastructure for 'managed disembarkation' and processing that existed in Italy – suggesting that the sense of crisis was connected to a loss of control by the border regime. De Genova (2017: 5) points to 'the sheer incorrigibility of migrant and refugee subjectivities and their mobility projects', referring to people's determination to move. This placed previous strategies of control under pressure and consequently produced splits in the ruling classes about how to respond, making it a public issue. Migrants' resistance may have helped force border deaths onto the public agenda, but the crisis was presented by capitalist institutions in ways that facilitated limited accommodation of migrants' presence within the EU, particularly where it could help address labour shortages, alongside increased repression.

Crawley et al (2018) suggest that the 'crisis' was driven by the EU's policies and its failure to mount an adequate humanitarian response. As new restrictions were imposed, people continued to find new routes, including several thousand who crossed into Norway via Northern Russia during 2015.[37] In many cases, the new routes that people resorted to carried higher risks, for example, Crawley et al (2018: 117–18) found smugglers in the Mediterranean crossing at night or in bad weather to reduce the chance of detection. The mortality rate, or number of deaths per 1,000 people attempting the crossing, increased from 4/1000 in 2015, to 14/1000 in 2016, to 18/1000 in 2017, to 24/1000 in the first half of 2018 (Carling and Hagen-Zanker, 2018). There are parallels here with the US–Mexico border, where more than 6,000 bodies have been recovered since the 1990s, estimated to be only one third of the total who have died. Most of these people died due to the hostile terrain, which they were forced into as part of a 1994 National Border Patrol Strategy, which states: 'The prediction is that with traditional entry and smuggling routes disrupted, illegal traffic will be deterred, or forced over more hostile terrain, less suited for crossing and more suited to enforcement' (cited in Jones, 2016: 45–6). The deadly consequences of migrants being forced into 'hostile terrain, less suited for crossing' should come as no surprise.

Immigration controls produce not only death, but also profits within an extensive migration industry, which includes legal and illegal elements. Friman (2011) shows how the illegal migration industry is shaped by state interventions that deny infrastructure for legal border crossings, creating conditions for a wide range of interlinked for-profit providers delivering services to fill the gap through a stratified market depending on how much people can afford to pay, affecting, for example, modes of transport and the associated risks. The existence of such a market in the Mediterranean has been used by the British state since 2015 to justify further repressive interventions, justified by the claim that people-smugglers encourage undocumented migration. This represents a 'mutually constitutive' relationship between the market and the state (Friman, 2011: 94; see also Crawley et al, 2018). Britain and other imperialist states are further implicated in creating the crisis through foreign interventions that put pressure on people to move (Bauman, 2016), driven by the defence of international assets and investment opportunities.

EU imperialism and forced migration

The strategic geopolitical position of West Asia and North Africa, together with their oil deposits, has made them significant targets for British domination for hundreds of years. British interventions have played a major role in forcing millions of people to become refugees, including military operations in Afghanistan (2001), Iraq (2003), Libya (2012) and less openly Syria. Ten years after the 2001 invasion of Afghanistan and with 140,000 troops still in occupation, it was the source of a quarter of the world's refugees, the highest of any country, followed next by Iraq (Sassen, 2014: 56). As a refugee called Abraham put it while speaking at an event at the Tate Modern in May 2018, British asylum policy is like somebody setting fire to a house and then telling the residents they must stay inside. The broad context for these interventions is the need to challenge rival imperialists and eliminate any forces that might promote a course of development independent of imperialist priorities. The most recent of these interventions, in Iraq, Libya and Syria, are discussed in the following.

Britain has a long history of interference in Iraq. The British state imposed its borders and subjected the country to a brutal occupation following the First World War, including the use of chemical weapons against civilian Kurdish villages, under Britain's first Labour government (Tripp, 2007). Subsequently, British interests were defended by a monarchy installed by the British state, which continued until the 1958 Revolution. This revolution was overturned by a military coup in 1963, led by Saddam Hussein with the active collusion of Britain and the US (Aburish, 1997). Britain's Royal Air Force (RAF) was created in 1918, and bombed Iraq in seven out of the ten decades that followed (Rayne, 2016). Britain was the principal partner to the US in the 2003 invasion, against a backdrop of Iraqi government deals with China and Russia and a decision by Iraq to trade its oil in euros instead of US dollars. Following the invasion, contracts were handed to British and US companies, including Anglo–Dutch Shell and British Petroleum, and the oil currency was switched back to dollars (Momani, 2008). The occupation forces encouraged sectarian divisions, exposed in incidents such as the arrest in September 2005 by Iraqi police of two British soldiers disguised as Arabs and driving a car packed with explosives[38] amid a spate of bombings of mosques that were attributed to rival sectarian militias. This is consistent with Britain's long experience in sowing divisions as part of counter–insurgency strategy, spelled out in Kitson (1973). Out of this context of destabilisation, occupation and sectarianism grew Islamic State and other organisations that would go on to play a major role in the conflict in Syria and other parts of the region (Cockburn, 2015).

Britain played a leading role in the North Atlantic Treaty Organisation's (NATO's) 2012 military campaign in Libya, which killed thousands of people through aerial bombardment alongside support for armed insurgents, and left much of the country in ruins, fought over by rival factions (Kuperman, 2013). Prior to this, Libya had both been a major destination for migrants, with a higher level of economic development than much of Africa (Glazebrook, 2013), and also become a major partner for EU border controls following a deal with the British government in 2004. The 2012 intervention followed popular uprisings in Tunisia and Egypt, and represented a reassertion of influence in the region by imperialist powers. It contributed to a context in which migrants continued to arrive through well–established networks to be met with widespread racism, indefinite detention, forced labour and violence. Crawley et al (2018: 67) conducted extensive interviews with migrants from other parts of Africa who were trying to cross from Libya to Italy. They found that many people had not originally planned to go to Europe, but had moved to Libya without realising the severity of the situation there, and were looking to Europe to escape.

Regarding the conflict in Syria, it is difficult to be sure exactly when Britain's involvement began. The British government held a parliamentary vote to begin bombing Syria in 2013, in which it was defeated, but it succeeded in another vote in 2015 and again in 2018. Bandeira (2017: 264) suggests that British Special Forces were already operating in 'rebel' areas, including Homs, as early as 2011. Britain's close allies in the Gulf states and Turkey have been deeply implicated in support for armed groups fighting the government since the early days of the war, and in May 2013, the British and French governments proposed lifting an arms embargo to make it easier to arm insurgents. In June 2015, the case against Bherlin Gildo, accused of attending a terrorist training camp between 2012 and 2013, collapsed in a British court when it became clear that the organisation he was working with had received weapons and other assistance from British intelligence services.[39] By 2016, the presence of British Special Forces in Syria, working with anti-government armed groups, was openly acknowledged. The British government have been clear from the earliest days of the conflict that their objective is regime change (eg Prime Minister's Office, 2011).[40] This could result in a more compliant government, would weaken the regional influence of Russia and could open the way to more direct threats towards Iran. The conflict has brought catastrophe for Syria's population, including the displacement of more than 6.3 million people internally displaced and over 5 million forced to seek asylum in other countries, together accounting for more than half the country's population.[41] High-profile European aid programmes have played a political role in justifying continued intervention, taking various forms. For example, London's 'Supporting Syria and the Region Conference' in 2016 had as its primary objective 'turning the Syrian refugee crisis into a development opportunity' in order to 'expand investment, promote exports and public–private partnerships', and resulted primarily in non-concessional loans conditional on structural adjustment policies that would open the region to greater imperialist exploitation (Hanieh, 2018).

Most people displaced by these imperialist interventions have remained within the region, but in many countries, their rights have been severely restricted. For example, in Lebanon, a country of 4.3 million where 1.5 million Syrians were living by 2016, increased restrictions in 2015 led around a million to become undocumented, restricted in their movements by checkpoints, denied state support, prohibited from taking paid work and with large fees to even apply for regularisation, making people liable to extreme forms of exploitation (Janmyr, 2016).[42] Refugees have faced similar restrictions in many other countries. In December 2014, the World Food Programme suspended food aid for 1.7 million Syrian refugees in the region due to a lack of funding (Crawley et al, 2018: 21–4). This has increased pressure for people to move further, in some cases, to the EU.

The connection between EU imperialism and pressure to migrate also takes forms that are less militaristic, though no less violent. Feldman (2012: 80) gives the example of Senegal, where:

> the fishing industry suffered a devastating blow as a result of seventeen agreements with the EU. These agreements gave the EU the right to fish in Senegalese waters while setting tight quotas on Senegalese exports back to its markets.… The resulting economic difficulties contributed to an increase in attempted illegal entries into the EU.

Depictions of migrants reflect on their countries of origin, simultaneously justifying international interventions and controls against migrants:

> The fact that rule breakers … are portrayed as coming disproportionately from particular regions (Africa, Mexico, South Asia) becomes not so much a consequence of economic disparities as an explanation for them.… In the absence of any accounting for their desperation, their anxiety and their disregard for the rules, these traits come across as regional personality attributes – a kind of irrational and wilful persistence – rather than the expression of desperation in the face of poverty or oppression. (Andrejevic, 2011: 67)

Britain and other EU member states are thus not responding to migrant flows that are already given facts. They are implicated in actively – though not necessarily intentionally – shaping migration flows at their point of origin and throughout their movement.

Free movement and Fortress Europe

The principle of free movement within the EU and restrictions on entry from outside might appear contradictory, but Karakayali and Rigo (2010: 123) point to 'continuity between the externalization of border control regimes and the internal migration policies of the European Union … [producing] the European legal and political space as a space specifically dedicated to governing mobility, both inside and across the EU's official borders'. Consistent with this, Crawley et al (2018: 136–7) point to an underlying principle of containment within EU migration policy. The governance of mobility is necessary to create an imperialist bloc that has sufficient economic and military might to compete with imperialist rivals for foreign sources of profit, while maintaining the imperialist division of labour on which these profits depend. However, European states face a contradiction because there is not a single European ruling class, but multiple national ruling classes, each jealously guarding their interests against rivals within the EU and outside. For example, while member states decided in principle in 2016 to pay Turkey to help with EU border enforcement, discussed later in this chapter, they have struggled to agree on who will actually pay.[43]

'Fortress Europe' is a relatively recent phenomenon. As Jones (2016: 26) reports: 'Prior to 1974 ... France allowed migrants to come and go freely. Spain allowed North Africans to enter freely until 1991'. Removal of border controls within the EU, established under the Schengen Agreement signed in 1985 and implemented in 1995, drove the reinforcement of external borders, 'lest undesirable commodities and people from outside circulate unchecked through the entire Schengen area' (Feldman, 2012: 61).[44] This was underlined in 2016 when Greece was threatened with expulsion from the Schengen area if it did not increase restrictions on migration from outside the EU.[45] Immigration policy was initially included under the third of the EU's legal pillars in the 1992 Treaty of the European Union, which meant that individual member states and the European Commission (EC) (the administrative arm of the EU) could initiate legislation but it required a unanimous vote by the European Council to be passed. The 1997 Treaty of Amsterdam moved immigration and asylum to the first pillar, meaning that only the EC could propose legislation and this only required a majority vote by the European Council to pass and be transposed into member states' national legislation. The Treaty of Amsterdam was followed by the 2002 Seville Council, which increased cooperation in border control and laid the foundations for Frontex,[46] an 'effort of total surveillance of the external border' that draws together bodies including the European Police (EUROPOL), the European Union Satellite Centre (EUSC), the European Defence Agency (EDA), the European Maritime Safety Agency (EMSA), the European Space Agency (ESA) and the European Centre for Disease Control (ECDC) (Feldman, 2012: 84).

In 2003, the EURODAC (European Asylum Dactyloscopy Database) system was launched to compile digitalised fingerprints of asylum-seekers and unauthorised entrants to EU territory. Later the same year, the European Council adopted the concept of the 'virtual maritime border'.

This allowed for border policing interventions by member states against vessels whose nationality was uncertain, 'irrespective of the geographic distance ... [from] the coastlines of member states' (Karakayali and Rigo, 2010: 124). The 2004 Hague Programme designated the Schengen countries 'an area of justice, freedom and security', implying 'a morally elevated space composed of decent individuals in need of protection from the threats of transnational criminal and terrorist networks' (Feldman, 2012: 63). This was transposed to the EC through the creation of a Directorate-General for Justice, Freedom and Security, which became responsible for harmonising migration policy among all member states and was accompanied by a variety of other initiatives (Feldman, 2012: 60–72). In July 2016, EU officials completed proposals for a new EU asylum system that would further reduce rights and make it easier to deport people to countries previously deemed unsafe.

The Mediterranean border space has become increasingly militarised. Britain played the leading role in drafting plans for a military intervention targeting migrants' boats, approved by the European Council in June 2015 as 'Operation Sofia'. This involved 24 countries with a force of five ships and 1,300 personnel. A document outlining the operation makes clear that it lacked a clearly defined 'end state' and envisaged progression to land-based operations in Libya (EUMC, 2015). A report on the operation's first six months (EEAS, 2016) is quite open about its political role, stating that 'the main message to the International Community is that the EU is capable of launching a military operation in record time, displaying a strong resolve and remarkable unity of intent', and reports positively on a trip to Washington and New York to promote its success. This represented a show of force against the EU's rivals in the context of the destabilisation of West Asia and North Africa and recent military successes of the Syrian state backed by Russia. In February 2016, NATO deployed its own forces to the Aegean Sea, including British warships, with the stated aim of intercepting ships taking migrants from Turkey to Greece. Intense struggles also developed during this period in the Balkans, where determined resistance by migrants forced gaps in the border regime but was met by increasing repression (Kasparek and Speer, 2015).

The net effect of these measures was to produce groups of people subject to special controls. Differentiation between categories played a central role in maintaining a liberal humanitarian appearance alongside mass state repression. For example, German Chancellor Angela Merkel made clear when accepting Syrian refugees that refugees from Balkan states would be deported because their countries were designated 'safe'. On 9 September 2015, EC President Jean-Claude Juncker used his annual State of the Union address to say that the EU would do more to welcome refugees but also engage in 'stronger joint efforts to secure our external borders', 'separate better those who are in clear need of international protection … and those who are leaving their country for other reasons which do not fall under the right of asylum', and turn migration into 'a well-managed resource' (Juncker, 2015: 9–10). Supporting this approach, the EC pushed forward its Smart Borders package, aiming to create a single biometric database for all foreign travellers within the Schengen area, easing the mobility of some while constraining others (European Commission, 2018).

European border violence has been given a 'common-sense' cover through the frame of criminality. By denying people a safe, legal route to cross borders, hundreds of thousands have been criminalised every year. Growing numbers of people across Europe have also faced prosecution for aiding migrants, such as 'Ahmed H' in Hungary[47] and Cédric Herrou in France.[48] In 2018, 15 activists went on trial in a British court, charged under anti-terror laws for non-violently obstructing a deportation charter flight.[49] Organisations and individual volunteers rescuing migrants at sea have been arrested by Greek authorities on charges of trafficking, while organisations including Médecins Sans Frontières (MSF) and Sea-Eye report being violently attacked by Libyan coastguards.[50] The threat of further attacks was used by European authorities to deter MSF from continuing its rescue operations.[51] In the summer of 2017, the EC backed an Italian proposal to require anybody rescuing migrants at sea to operate under the authority of the Italian and Libyan coastguards – the same forces that non-governmental organisations (NGOs) alleged were allowing people to drown or were returning them to Libya.[52] This situation came to a head in 2018 when the Italian state prevented the NGO ship Aquarius from disembarking 630 people that it had rescued. The Aquarius eventually docked in Spain, but further obstructions of NGO ships followed.[53] MSF estimates that this resulted in more than 600 people dead or missing in the following four weeks alone.[54]

Outsourcing border policing

The violence required by Fortress Europe has been directly contracted out to other states on behalf of imperialist countries, most systematically since 2004, when a meeting of the European Council endorsed a proposal by the British Labour government to systematically involve 'third countries' in the management of migration into the EU. Mezzadra and Neilson (2013: 172) suggest that this represented a 'dream of remaking migration systems in the light of the economic and labor market needs of EU

Member States'. Geography has combined with economic, political and military status to assign the role of border guards to countries on the EU periphery and beyond, including: Southern European countries like Italy and Greece, suffering under economic crisis and austerity and required by the EURODAC Regulation to register and fingerprint all those entering their territory without authorisation (Lovett et al, 2017); formerly socialist Balkan states such as Macedonia and Bulgaria, incorporated as junior partners to European imperialism[55]; aspiring member states trying to prove their worth, like Serbia and Turkey (Collett, 2016; European Parliament, 2016); and African countries of origin and transit for migrants, like Libya, Eritrea and Sudan (Crawley and Skleparis, 2018).

The Dublin Regulation, last updated in 2013, enables states to deport refugees back to the first EU country in which they were registered. Germany has made particularly extensive use of this, increasing its annual requests for a Dublin 'transfer' from 11,469 in 2012 to 64,267 in 2017. A total of 7,102 people were removed from Germany in this way in 2017 (ASYL, 2017). Proposals to resettle some refugees from Italy and Greece to other parts of the EU have been contested by many member states and have been implemented at a slow pace (Crawley et al, 2018: 136). Agreements have also been signed with many countries outside Europe to facilitate the deportation of their citizens. Crawley et al (2018: 127) show that, in practice, such deportations are not necessarily the end point for migration, but can contribute to circular mobility, where people move, in some cases settle, are forcibly returned and then move again.

The European Neighbourhood Policy (ENP) was launched in 2011 with the aim of encouraging countries bordering the EU to the south and east[56] to adopt EU practices for migration management 'in exchange for more favourable terms on other issues under negotiation' (Feldman, 2012: 88). The Moroccan state's policing of its border with the Spanish enclave of Melilla brings the violence of this outsourcing into sharp relief. The Spanish state began to build barriers to keep migrants out of Melilla in 1993, and in 2013, the EU signed an agreement for Morocco to help police the border. The Spanish fence is sometimes described as 'humanitarian' because it lacks barbed wire or razor wire, whereas the Moroccan fence, built in 2015 with EU funds, 'consists of rolls of concertina wire wrapped with barbed wire, with sentry posts every hundred metres' (Jones, 2016: 15). In 2015, Moroccan authorities destroyed migrant camps, burned shelters and belongings, and forcibly transported migrants to detention centres in the south of the country (Jones, 2016: 13–15).

The EU border regime continues to expand. Development assistance to African countries has been tied to their compliance in policing migration as part of the Rabat process beginning in 2004 and the Khartoum process launched in 2014 (Crawley et al, 2018: 139). In September 2015, a summit of EU interior ministers agreed to build a series of 'reception centres' in African countries and elsewhere outside the EU in order to detain refugees and prevent them reaching Europe. As part of the same agreement, an 'EU–Africa Trust Fund' was established to 'encourage' African states to accept deportees.[57] This echoed proposals originally made by the British Labour government in 2003 to create 'transit processing centres' outside the EU to detain migrants who arrive at Europe's borders, and potentially also those en route (Karakayali and Rigo, 2010: 125). At an EU summit in Malta in January 2017, British Prime Minister Theresa May announced further plans to remove refugees attempting to enter Europe, and to resettle them in Latin America and Asia.[58] *The Independent* cites assurances by a government source that refugees' participation would be voluntary, but given the desperate conditions facing many refugees stranded at the EU's borders, there would seem to be enormous pressure to accept resettlement.

In March 2016, the EU signed an agreement with Turkey to help police migration in exchange for billions of pounds of EU funding and the liberalisation of visa controls on Turkish nationals. The deal enabled the mass expulsion of asylum seekers from Greece to Turkey. Crawley et al (2018: 103–4) describe the extremely precarious situation for refugees in Turkey. Turkey is designated a 'safe country' by the EU, but it is not a full signatory to the 1951 Refugee Convention, meaning that once refugees have been removed to Turkey, they can be more easily deported elsewhere. Within hours of the deal being signed, Turkey deported a group of 30 refugees to Afghanistan. In response, five major aid agencies, including the United Nations High Commission for Refugees (UNHCR), suspended their operations in many of Greece's refugee centres, arguing that they had been turned into holding centres for deporting refugees to Turkey.[59] There have also been reports of Turkish coastguards attacking boats and burning life vests.[60]

The EU alliance with Turkey was presented as a positive example to inform further agreements with countries in North Africa and elsewhere (European Commission, 2016). In August 2016, an agreement was signed for EU navies to train Libyan coastguards. By November 2016, Libyan coastguards reported that they had intercepted and returned to Libya more than 11,000 people. Agreements were also signed with Tunisia and Morocco. In July 2017, the EC launched a new action plan on migration, which included €46 million of additional funding for Libyan authorities, the creation of a new Maritime Rescue and Coordination Centre in Libya, EU involvement in policing Libya's southern border, collaboration with the governments of Niger and Mali to intercept migrants suspected of travelling to Libya, and further 'readmission agreements' whereby governments would facilitate the deportation of their citizens (European Commission, 2017). These developments have parallels in other parts of the world, for example, since 2010, the US state has provided nearly US$100 million to the Mexican state to assist in policing its southern border, together with other forms of cooperation (Seelke and Finklea, 2017). The containment strategies outlined earlier will be further explored through a discussion of border struggles in Northern France, where the British border has operated since 2003.

Calais: British bordering in France

Makeshift camps have existed along France's northern coast since the late 1990s, populated by people trying to reach Britain, many of whom are trying to rejoin family. The camps are often referred to by authorities and their residents as 'jungles', informal settlements ranging from tens to thousands of people, which King (2016: 105) describes as 'ultimately, the safest and most efficient way that people can meet their needs in resource-limited situations'. The Le Touquet treaty was signed by the British Labour government in 2003, extending British border enforcement into France. It was followed by a continuous campaign of state violence that claimed more than 200 lives by 2018,[61] injuring many more and leaving thousands stranded in squalid conditions. The camps' inhabitants have been subject to repeated repression by French authorities in collaboration with the British state, accompanied by violent attacks by racist gangs.[62] By late 2015, the population of the camps had grown to an estimated 6,000 people. Growing desperation led to people jumping on and off trucks, hiding beneath the axles of vehicles, entering the sea, or crossing on foot through the Channel Tunnel. More recently, people have begun to resort to boats to cross the English Channel.[63]

Dhesi et al (2015) investigated environmental health conditions in the camps, finding: inadequate food storage facilities, contributing to widespread vomiting and diarrhoea; unsafe drinking water; only one usable toilet per 75 residents (compared to the UNHCR recommended minimum of one per 20 people); insufficient health care; overcrowded conditions fostering scabies; leaking shelters leading to soaking bedding with few opportunities for drying; and smoke inhalation from cooking and heating fires creating breathing difficulties. They also highlight the risk of fire created by 'Structures in close proximity, constructed of flammable materials, heated and lit with naked flames, and with no means of fighting fire or raising the alarm' (Dhesi et al, 2015: 2). Within months of this report, fires spread, causing injuries and destroying many people's belongings, documents and more than 100 shelters. The response to the fire relied on self-organisation among the camps' residents, who raised the alarm and got people to safety.[64]

A short episode in 2015 illustrates the wider pattern of state violence and resistance around Calais. On 2 August, hundreds of migrants marched for three hours from the main jungle to the Eurotunnel entrance leading to England in order to demand that the border be opened. They were driven back by riot police using tear gas, but demonstrations continued in the weeks that followed, sometimes daily. On 20 August, Britain's then-Home Secretary, Theresa May, and French Minister of the Interior Bernard Cazeneuve visited Calais and were met by protests. Riot police prevented migrants from entering Calais, and migrants responded by occupying the motorway for over an hour, giving others the opportunity to enter trucks heading for Britain. On 3 September, migrants staged a picket of the Jules Ferry aid centre, and issued a statement that said:

> People are blockading the government distribution centre because they no longer want to live in worse conditions than those they left behind.… People have a right to dignity and many people are badly injured and left with no medical provisions to die in the jungle. La Vie Active [a charity] who run the Salam centre profit from justifying people's prolonged stay in the jungle. Today the demonstration will continue at the gates of the centre and everyone informed why and asked not to go inside.[65]

The next day, 200 migrants marched into the centre of Calais. For the first time, the Mayor of Calais, Natacha Bouchart, came out to speak to them but, according to activists, offered only excuses. More protests followed. On 10 September, 150 Syrians held a candlelit vigil outside the town hall, calling for a legal and safe route into Britain to claim asylum. They were attacked by police, including seven vans of CRS (riot police), who dispersed the protest and forced people back to the jungle. On 21 September, riot police and council workers evicted migrants from three camps outside the main jungle, bulldozing tents, seizing belongings (including passports) and putting them through a rubbish compactor.

The main camp near Calais was subject to a major demolition by French authorities in October 2016, following which the British government established a limited scheme for unaccompanied minors to join family members in Britain. However, after only a few hundred had been accepted, this scheme was put on hold and then scrapped just months after it was launched, leaving an estimated 1,000 children stranded in France who had a legal right to enter Britain based on family reunification.[66] From 2015 to 2017, French police launched 34 operations targeting homeless migrants in Paris, and in 2017, the French government announced a 'zero tolerance' policy on makeshift shelters.[67] MSF reported police harassing migrants who could not get into Paris's single overcrowded official shelter, preventing them from sitting down as they queued for a place, waking them in the middle of the night and using tear gas.[68] Several hundred people continued to camp near Calais, where the French human rights ombudsman reported dire conditions. Calais Migrant Solidarity reported regular evictions of squats without court orders, in breach of the law, and migrants' sleeping bags and tents being removed or slashed by the police.[69]

In January 2018, a UK–France summit at Sandhurst Military Academy agreed a new treaty. This included an additional £45 million from the British government to bolster the already formidable security apparatus in Northern France, bringing the total to £160 million since 2016. It was accompanied by promises to speed up asylum applications for refugees with family in Britain and unaccompanied minors, but, as discussed earlier, similar previous initiatives have fallen far short of what was promised. The treaty also established a Joint Information and Coordination Centre for the 'management and prevention of threats to public order', 'crisis management in the event of acute migratory pressure' and 'support of action to counter the operations of smuggling rings, human traffickers and criminal networks' (Prime Minister's Office, 2018). As discussed earlier in this chapter, there has been a growing tendency to criminalise migrant solidarity actions, suggesting a risk that they may be included in the definition of 'criminal networks'. Just days before the summit, French President Emmanuel Macron visited Calais and announced that the French state was taking over food distribution, shutting down charities' operations. In the context of previous state interventions around the border, this gives greater control to the state and makes it easier to drive people away from the border through hunger. The treaty also included agreements to cooperate in deportations, as well as plans for 'joint actions in illegal immigration source countries' (Prime Minister's Office, 2018: 3). The latter is a programme for further imperialist intervention beyond European territory and was explicitly connected to military cooperation in summit discussions, with references to British support for French military operations in the Sahel region of Africa.

Shaping migration narratives through struggle

The state does not operate alone, but in interaction with civil society. This relationship is unequal, and civil society is thoroughly penetrated by the state, materially in the form of funding and the exchange of personnel, and ideologically in the form of shared practices and discourses. Nevertheless, spaces exist within civil society where capitalist interests can be challenged.

The narrative of a 'migrant crisis' has been challenged by grass-roots activism. For example, Oliveri (2012) describes the wave of protests that started in Rosarno, Italy, in 2010. They were characterised by the militant assertion of rights by irregular migrants, the rejection of 'paternalistic approaches of trade unions, NGOs and political parties that saw them as unable of acting autonomously', political demands including 'the right to stay for everyone', and solidarity from sections of Italian society beyond the usual 'militant milieu' (Oliveri, 2012: 798–9). Yet, civil society practices and campaigns can also reinforce and legitimise framings of migration that support imperialist interests. This can be seen as a consequence of the material divisions within the working class discussed in Chapter 2, which give rise to opportunist trends that direct opposition to imperialism's most obvious and violent consequences into 'respectable' channels that leave imperialism's core structures undisturbed. This is further explored in the following through a discussion of recent activism in Britain.

Advocating for the contributing migrant and the needy refugee

The binary separation between 'migrants' and 'refugees' has been contested by academics (eg Bloch and McKay, 2016; Kyriakides, 2017) and activists, both on the empirical grounds that migration patterns and individuals' reasons for moving are rarely so simple, and on the political and ethical grounds that such distinctions have often been used to justify repression and the denial of resources by portraying some categories as less 'deserving' than others. Yet, this binary has also been actively promoted by some campaigners. In 2015, as migrant struggles against border controls intensified in many parts of Europe, the distinction between 'refugee' and 'migrant' took on renewed political significance, with prominent social actors from *Al Jazeera* to the celebrity Bono calling for 'refugee' to be used in place of 'migrant' to describe those crossing Europe's borders on the basis that this would emphasise the seriousness of their needs.[70]

The presentation of refugees as particularly 'deserving' has been an important source of protection but has also been used to justify attacks on other groups of migrants (Jones, 2016: 22-3). Reflecting and reinforcing this narrative, the humanitarian convoys that were organised from towns and cities across Britain to migrant camps in Calais towards the end of 2015, often quite informally, enabled British citizens to assume a position of benevolence towards migrants who were assumed to be passive and helpless. Numerous reports emerged on social media, where many of these convoys were organised, of donations that were inappropriate to the needs of recipients, being driven by the desires of those giving amid an abundance of surplus consumer goods.

In another example of activism that operated within hegemonic categories and gave them new legitimacy, a high-profile campaign was built around an amendment to the Immigration Act 2016 tabled by Lord Alf Dubs, calling for unaccompanied child refugees to be granted asylum. Dubs was himself rescued from Nazi-occupied Czechoslovakia as part of the 'Kindertransport', which brought Jewish children to Britain in the months before the Second World War. The campaign's focus on children played directly to a narrative of refugees deserving help because of their passivity and victimhood, intensified through an 'essentialized view of "the child," grounded in racialized, Eurocentric, and advanced capitalist norms' (Rosen and Crafter, 2018). It echoed the practices of exclusion that are also part of the same history as the Kindertransport, in which the majority of Jewish adults who applied for asylum in Britain were refused and left to die (Kundnani, 2007: 67–8). Such distinctions reconcile the pretence of humanitarian values with the practice of state violence, and deny migrants' agency.

At other times, a special case has been made for migrants based on their 'contribution' to British society, often defined in the narrow terms of waged labour. For example, in August 2015, two calls for action were made by EU migrants, which embodied different conceptions of migrants' relationship to Britain. First, the *Polish Express* newspaper published a call by Polish workers for a one-day strike in defence of migrants' rights. However, this lacked an organisational infrastructure and did not deliver significant collective action.[71] Other migrants responded with a call for a mass blood donation. Conditionality was implicit in both calls, in different ways. The first attempted to make migrants' labour conditional on the granting of civil and political rights. The latter made no explicit demand, but implicitly called for social acceptance based on migrants' willingness to sacrifice for British people, to the extent of giving their own blood. The first is a form of negotiation, with migrants claiming agency, the latter involves migrants giving themselves over to the benevolence of a posited British society.

The fight against deportations and detention in Britain

In the early 2000s, growing numbers of asylum seekers who had been waiting years for answers to their claims gave rise to a wave of resistance, often in alliance with other sections of society, building on long-standing traditions (Vickers, 2012; Webber, 2012). After 2007, when a 'legacy exercise' resolved many of these long-standing cases, and with the increased use of charter flights for mass deportation, the movement in communities went into decline (Vickers, 2014), but resistance continued inside immigration detention centres, organised by groups like Movement for Justice,[72] Right to Remain[73] and Detained Voices.[74] The following account (interview A3) by an individual who was detained and subsequently became an activist demonstrates the potential for such processes of oppression and resistance to help inform a critical analysis:

> 'when I came out from detention, I was really on the border of becoming depressed. I started having anxiety and stress while in there.... They suggested to put me on antidepressants, which I said "No. I know the problem, I know why I am feeling this way, so if you take away the triggers, it will stop".... I said, "Well, there is a demonstration I've heard that is taking place … at [a detention centre]", that was the first time I spoke about it to people whom I had not met, and when I got there, I just talked to the crowd and I've not looked back since.'

For this individual, these experiences gave new relevance to theories they had studied in Nigeria and Britain, including the ideas of Kwame Nkrumah, discussed in Chapter 2: "so many things that Nkrumah says … when I looked at them, I thought maybe they don't fit into the real world. But now I get where he was coming from, because he actually studied here in the UK, so he knew first-hand". They explained the widespread use of immigration detention as a mixture of incompetence and private profit-making:

> 'I saw a system where when people leave [detention], for example, if a lot of people get [released], then the following week, a lot of people get detained. So … it's like a production line. It's an industry at full capacity … it justifies keeping people in there for as long as possible.'

They connected this to imperialist interventions leading to the disenfranchisement of the mass of the population in oppressed countries:

'the neo-colonial relationship is only possible because there's this disenfranchisement of the people. And so that's why I think when you see countries that are the richest countries like the DRC [Democratic Republic of Congo], you see that it is perpetually in conflict because that's the only way you can [take the resources].'

They anticipated resistance developing through a movement connecting opposition to neo-colonialism and racism through the idea of justice:

'It's going to take that process where many young people will rise up and say "No, we've had enough of the IMF, we've had enough of the World Bank ... we don't know what you really bring to Africa".... I see them already saying that ... "We don't need your aid".... When I have a look at these demonstrations ... the majority of those there are very young.... Last time I chose a young British girl, her dad was from England and mum is from France, and I just asked her, "Why are you involved with this?... you don't have any tangible benefits to receive from this and you've never been in detention". She said, "I've been to Calais several times, I've got so many friends, I just think it's unjust".... So, she's fighting for the concept of justice for its sake ... when you see the mixture of people fighting for the sake of justice, justice is not something that you can paint in a different colour, so if that doesn't arrive, people are not going to stop.'

This highlights the potential for shared values and political commitment to form the basis of alliances between people who occupy a range of positions within the system (see also Vickers, 2014).

There has also been recurring resistance within communities, some of which is reported by Corporate Watch (2018). For example, in June 2014, the Home Office launched Operation Centurion, intended as a high-profile campaign of immigration raids on businesses and homes. Documents detailing the operation were leaked in advance to the Anti-Raids Network, including specific targets. This exposed the use of racial profiling – with targets including 'Vietnamese nail bars in the Manchester area', Nigerian security guards in Sussex, and phone stalls in the North of Ireland that Home Office 'intelligence' reports stated were targeted on the basis that they 'appear to have foreign nationals working on them – some of which don't speak fantastic English'.[75] Activists across Britain and the North of Ireland mobilised to warn nearly 200 of those being targeted, and to inform people of their rights. Reports suggest that the operation resulted in only 20 arrests, and the Home Office were unable to claim it as a victory or use it to generate positive publicity. Activists simultaneously undermined the narrative that the state was seeking, disrupted the physical operation and exposed its racist character.

Fighting everyday bordering

Following the 2014 and 2016 Immigration Acts, campaigns developed to challenge the internalisation of borders discussed earlier in this chapter. Some of these were organised predominantly online, such as Docs Not Cops,[76] Homes Not Borders[77] and Against Borders for Children,[78] and some were more localised, such as the Newcastle-based Migration and Asylum Justice Forum[79] and North East London Migrant Action.[80]

An activist (interview A5) who had experienced several campaigns against deportations and restrictions on access to housing and health care spoke about how their perspective had developed through their political experience, from sympathy for asylum seekers to class solidarity:

> 'When I first got involved ... I definitely was coming at it from a liberal position of, "Oh, these poor victims, this is an attack on human rights".... I've understood that actually an attack on migrant rights and asylum rights is an attack on everybody's rights.... And that's not saying that I'm only involved in these struggles because of some sort of self-interest, but I think it's the process of identifying the people who are directly affected by the immigration controls with the fight for the rights of the working class internationally.... Some examples of that are the Azure Cards [used to deliver welfare payments to some asylum seekers, and] ... at the same time ... there's been a lot of changes in the benefit system for British citizens [which has] become increasingly more restricted and controlled....
>
> Big companies will try and get away with paying migrant workers less ... because of insecure immigration status, people will accept more temporary insecure zero-hours contract labour, and that's increasingly becoming the norm.... I don't think we can divorce what's happening to asylum seekers, their living conditions and illegal working conditions or the fact that they're not allowed to work ... to what's happening to EU migrants, especially in the context of Brexit.... Or people ... who are in work but are now being forced to claim Universal

> Credit and, even if they're a part-time worker, expected to do job searching to top up their part-time hours just to get the housing benefit, I think that all those kinds of attacks on the working class are interrelated.'

This highlights, in concrete terms, the need to identify points of connection among a heterogeneous and differentially included working class.

A campaigner (interview A16) with experience of struggles over council services and housing suggested that racism played a major role in undermining these struggles:

> 'I think people are very easily led to believe what they're fed. People think the hospital waiting times are this long because there are too many immigrants and we don't have enough money because there are immigrants.... People are always looking to blame someone else, rather than actually blaming the government. There is enough money; it has nothing to do with more people being here. If you want to blame things in the NHS on more people, you could say it's the ageing population. I work in a hospital, and 90 per cent of the people I see are white and over the age of 70 ... but people don't see that. There is money for it, but it's where money goes. It doesn't go to the people who need it. Taxes are higher than they've ever been.... There seems to be so much more casual racism now than there used to be.'

This highlights the importance of ideological struggle as a prerequisite for effective organisation, even in defence of immediate needs. Another activist (interview A14) cautioned against making claims for one group, in this case, the 'Windrush Generation' discussed in Chapter 2, in ways that legitimate the oppression of other groups:

> '[This] continual going back to the idea that these people come here as citizens ... and that they are rightfully thus British.... On the one hand, you're right, but don't just solely say that because then you're undercutting and fucking over everyone else who didn't.... By creating another category of rightful citizens, you're also attendantly producing unrightful citizens of people who shouldn't be here.'

The political tendency that they are criticising can be understood as a form of opportunism, discussed in Chapter 2, highlighting the need to actively draw out the long-term interests of the whole working class within each particular struggle.

Conclusion

As discussed in Chapter 2, capitalism in its imperialist form relies on a division of the world along national lines as a way of organising a division of land and labour to enable continued accumulation despite capitalism's inherent tendency towards crisis. Borders are thus used 'instrumentally ... to affix a dominant spatiality, temporality, and political agency' (Rajaram and Grundy-Warr, 2007: x), fundamentally shaped by the law of value (see Chapter 1). What appears as a crisis caused by migration – the geographical mobility of people structured by nation states – is actually a crisis in systems of control that underpin this system of division. The capitalist crisis has driven an intensification of inter-imperialist rivalries, leading to aggressive foreign interventions by imperialist states and their proxies to defend international investments. The resulting wars and political upheavals have led to an increase in forced migration globally. Simultaneously, the capitalist crisis has driven a tightening of discipline over labour, which finds expression in a fine-tuning of immigration controls to the needs of employers. Thus, increasing numbers of people forced to move because of their need to survive come up against borders that allow entry only on the condition of labour demand or private wealth. This contradiction between two manifestations of the capitalist crisis finds expression in Europe's 'migration crisis'.

The imperialist response has been to reorganise systems of control in an attempt to neutralise resistance. This reorganisation has been justified through articulations of crisis (see also De Genova, 2017). The ruling classes do not need to invent a sense of crisis; it is widely and deeply felt because people are integral to the capitalist system and the system is in crisis. The ruling classes simply redirect this sense of crisis through a racialised lens, shifting attention from the operations of the state to the actions of the people it is oppressing. This takes another form, intertwined with representations of the migration crisis, in the multiple crises of state welfare, as discussed in Chapter 4.

Notes

[1] See *The Telegraph*, www.telegraph.co.uk/news/uknews/immigration/9291483/ Theresa-May-interview-Were-going-to-give-illegal-migrants-a-really-hostile-reception.html

2   See *The Guardian*, www.theguardian.com/politics/2017/oct/02/post-brexit-immigration-white-paper-delayed-until-late-autumn

3   See *The Independent*, www.independent.co.uk/news/uk/politics/immigration-integration-tsar-louise-casey-not-two-way-street-a7517936.html

4   See, for example, *Politics.co.uk*, www.politics.co.uk/comment-analysis/2012/06/22/ed-miliband-s-immigration-speech-in-full; and the *Daily Mail*, www.dailymail.co.uk/news/article-2542352/Exclusive-Ministers-new-crackdown-Housing-benefit-ban-jobless-migrants.html

5   See the *Daily Mail*, www.dailymail.co.uk/news/article-2839327/Labour-ban-jobless-EU-migrants-claiming-benefits-TWO-YEARS-plan-curb-welfare-tourism.html

6   See *The Guardian*, https://www.theguardian.com/politics/2014/nov/16/iain-duncan-smith-eu-immigration-schools-changing

7   See the *New Statesman*, www.newstatesman.com/politics/staggers/2017/07/jeremy-corbyn-wholesale-eu-immigration-has-destroyed-conditions-british

8   Portes (2018) surveys the available evidence. He concludes that immigration has little effect on wages, potentially having a small positive effect overall and, at worst, depressing wage growth for the lowest paid by an average of 1 penny per hour, while other factors, such as technological change, tax credits and minimum wage rates, have far more impact.

9   Referring to institutions that allow people to register to access 'Tier 4' student visas rather than for genuine study.

10 Referring to marriages to gain rights to residence in Britain rather than a 'genuine' relationship.

11 See: https://nandosigona.info/2013/02/14/happy-valentines-day-by-the-home-office/

12 See *The Guardian*, www.theguardian.com/politics/2018/apr/26/amber-rudd-makes-a-staggering-admission-over-immigration-targets

13 See the *Evening Standard*, www.standard.co.uk/comment/comment/evening-standard-comment-it-s-time-to-scrap-the-tory-migration-cap-a3541346.html

14 See: www.inquest.org.uk/deaths-of-immigration-detainees

15 See: https://detainedvoices.com/2018/02/25/the-strikers-demands/

16 See *The Guardian*, www.theguardian.com/uk-news/2018/jun/28/wrongful-detention-cost-21m-as-immigration-staff-chased-bonuses

17 See *The Observer*, www.theguardian.com/uk-news/2013/oct/26/asylum-cases-home-office-fix

18 See *The Guardian*, www.theguardian.com/uk-news/2014/jan/14/home-office-asylum-seekers-gift-vouchers

19 See *The Prisma*, http://theprisma.co.uk/2013/03/24/there-is-no-such-thing-as-voluntary-return-only-voluntary-deportation/

20 See *The Guardian*, www.theguardian.com/commentisfree/2013/oct/24/chinatown-london-immigration-fishing-raids-ukba

21 See *The Guardian*, www.theguardian.com/uk-news/2013/oct/22/chinatown-protest-immigration-border-agency-raids

22 See *The Guardian*, www.theguardian.com/commentisfree/2014/dec/22/g4s-convictions-deaths-employees-racial-overtones

23 See *The Guardian*, www.theguardian.com/uk-news/2017/mar/07/home-office-tells-jamaican-man-talk-to-family-online-after-removal

24 See *The Guardian*, www.theguardian.com/uk-news/2017/aug/25/irene-clennell-deported-british-woman-finally-granted-uk-visa

25 See *The Guardian*, www.theguardian.com/uk-news/2018/may/14/victims-crime-handed-over-police-immigration-enforcement

26 See: www.schoolsabc.net/

27 See *Schools Week*, https://schoolsweek.co.uk/dfe-ends-divisive-pupil-nationality-data-collection/

28 See *The Guardian*, www.theguardian.com/uk-news/2018/apr/08/young-asylum-seekers-education-ban

29 See: https://freesoascleaners.blogspot.com/; and *The Guardian*, www.theguardian.com/education/2009/jun/17/soas-occupation-ends

30 See *The Independent*, www.independent.co.uk/news/uk/home-news/hostile-environment-imigration-mps-home-office-abuse-report-david-lammy-a8413111.html

31 See: *The Independent*, www.independent.co.uk/news/uk/home-news/theresa-may-ignored-home-office-warnings-migrant-policies-hostile-environment-windrush-immigrant-a8312996.html

32 Source: http://ec.europa.eu/eurostat. Due to differences in countries' reporting, these figures include refugees for some countries but not for others.

33 See *The Guardian*, www.theguardian.com/politics/2014/oct/27/uk-mediterranean-migrant-rescue-plan

34 See: http://unitedagainstrefugeedeaths.eu/

35 See: www.themigrantsfiles.com/

36 See: https://missingmigrants.iom.int

37 See *The Independent*, www.independent.co.uk/news/world/europe/refugee-crisis-arctic-frontier-between-russia-and-norway-one-of-the-fastest-growing-routes-despite-a6731581.html

38 See *BBC News*, http://news.bbc.co.uk/1/hi/uk/4263648.stm

39 See *The Guardian*, www.theguardian.com/uk-news/2015/jun/01/trial-swedish-man-accused-terrorism-offences-collapse-bherlin-gildo

40 See also *The Independent*, www.independent.co.uk/news/uk/politics/isis-and-assad-must-be-both-be-defeated-by-hard-military-force-david-cameron-signals-uk-is-close-to-10493072.html

41 See: www.unhcr.org/uk/syria-emergency.html

42 See also: http://reporting.unhcr.org/node/2520

43 See *Spiegel Online*, www.spiegel.de/politik/ausland/eu-tuerkei-deal-deutschland-und-andere-mitgliedslaender-wollen-nicht-mehr-zahlen-a-1200973.html

44 The Schengen area includes Austria, Belgium, the Czech Republic, Denmark (excluding Greenland and the Faroe Islands), Estonia, Finland, France (excluding overseas departments and collectivities), Germany, Greece, Hungary, Iceland, Italy, Latvia, Liechtenstein, Lithuania, Luxembourg, Malta, Netherlands (excluding Aruba, Curaçao, Sint Maarten and the Caribbean Netherlands), Norway (excluding Svalbard), Poland, Portugal, Slovakia, Slovenia, Spain (with special provisions for Ceuta and Melilla), Sweden and Switzerland.

45 See *Reuters*, www.reuters.com/article/us-europe-migrants-ministers-idUSKCN0V315L

46 Since September 2016, the full name of Frontex is the European Border and Coast Guard Agency.

47 See *Al Jazeera*, www.aljazeera.com/news/2018/01/hungary-retrial-highlights-vilification-refugees-180112202923432.html

48 See the *New York Times*, www.nytimes.com/2017/08/08/world/europe/france-farmer-migrants-asylum.html

49 See *IRR News*, www.irr.org.uk/news/stansted-15-face-trial/

50 See *The Independent*, www.independent.co.uk/news/world/africa/libyan-coastguard-attack-shooting-refugee-rescue-boat-msf-medecins-sans-frontieres-armed-bullet-a7512066.html; and the *New York Times*, www.nytimes.com/2018/05/07/world/europe/greece-migrants-volunteers.html

51 See Médecins Sans Frontières, www.msf.org/en/article/hindrance-humanitarian-assistance-will-create-deadly-gap-mediterranean-sea
52 See *The Independent*, www.independent.co.uk/news/world/europe/refugee-crisis-ngo-rescue-ships-mediterranean-sea-italy-libya-eu-code-of-conduct-deaths-2300-latest-a7866226.html
53 See: https://alarmphone.org/en/2018/07/27/from-the-sea-to-the-city/
54 See Médecins Sans Frontières, www.msf.org/drowning-skyrockets-european-governments-block-humanitarian-assistance-central-mediterranean
55 See: http://bulgaria.bordermonitoring.eu/
56 The ENP includes Algeria, Armenia, Azerbaijan, Belarus, Egypt, Georgia, Israel, Jordan, Lebanon, Libya, Moldova, Morocco, Palestine, Syria, Tunisia and Ukraine.
57 See *The Guardian*, www.theguardian.com/world/2015/sep/14/refugee-crisis-eu-governments-set-to-back-new-internment-camps
58 See *The Independent*, www.independent.co.uk/news/uk/politics/eu-malta-summit-refugees-europe-redirect-settle-asia-latin-america-theresa-may-30-million-aid-plan-a7561296.html
59 See *Reuters*, www.reuters.com/article/us-europe-migrants-greece-idUSKCN0WP1KY
60 See *Watch the Med*, https://alarmphone.org/it/2016/03/13/weekly-reports-bad-weather-violence-and-ongoing-movements-in-the-aegean-5/
61 See *Medium*, https://medium.com/thedigitalwarehouse/calais-update-4-4-2018-130152da54b9; see also https://calaismigrantsolidarity.wordpress.com/deaths-at-the-calais-border/
62 Documented at: https://calaismigrantsolidarity.wordpress.com
63 See *The Telegraph*, www.telegraph.co.uk/news/2018/11/27/border-force-cutter-could-relocated-english-channel-tackle-growing/
64 See: https://calaismigrantsolidarity.wordpress.com/2015/11/22/another-big-fire-destroy-an-eritrean-camp-last-night/
65 See: https://calaismigrantsolidarity.wordpress.com/2015/09/03/peaceful-protest-outside-salam-food-distribution-center/
66 See *The Guardian*, www.theguardian.com/world/2017/feb/08/dubs-scheme-lone-child-refugees-uk-closed-down
67 See *The Guardian*, www.theguardian.com/world/2017/jul/07/french-police-evict-2000-refugees-and-migrants-sleeping-rough-in-paris
68 See Médecins Sans Frontières, www.msf.org/en/article/france-critical-situation-refugees-and-migrants-stuck-paris-streets-winter-approaches
69 See: https://calaismigrantsolidarity.wordpress.com/2018/01/17/encore-une-expulsion-illegale-aujourdhui/
70 See: www.aljazeera.com/blogs/editors-blog/2015/08/al-jazeera-mediterranean-migrants-150820082226309.html
71 See *The Guardian*, www.theguardian.com/uk-news/2015/aug/20/polish-workers-strike-blood-donation-nhs-uk
72 See: https://en-gb.facebook.com/movementforjustice/
73 See: www.righttoremain.org.uk/
74 See: https://detainedvoices.com/
75 See: https://mappingimmigrationcontroversy.com/2014/06/26/operation-centurion-the-communication-of-fear-and-resistance/
76 See: www.docsnotcops.co.uk/
77 See: https://homesnotborders.net/
78 See: www.schoolsabc.net/
79 See: https://en-gb.facebook.com/migrationandjustice/
80 See: https://nelmacampaigns.wordpress.com/

4

Deconstructing Welfare Crises

Introduction: state welfare and the crisis of imperialism

This chapter further develops an analysis of the British state, focusing on state welfare. It argues that increasing conditionality has combined with long-standing forms of differential inclusion to tighten labour discipline and create conditions for more intense exploitation. This builds on the introductory discussion in Chapter 2 and the examination of the state's role in regulating international migration in Chapter 3. The chapter begins by connecting the crises of state welfare in Britain to the capitalist crisis. Changes to the character of welfare are considered, with attention to the growth of outsourcing and the presentation of austerity as an economic necessity. This is followed by an examination of policy and practice relating to three welfare domains that have been presented as sites of crisis in recent years: the National Health Service (NHS) and social care; housing; and the benefits system. The last part of the chapter explores counter-narratives within social movements and campaigns for the insights that they provide about alternative understandings of the nature and causes of welfare crises and their relation to migration and borders.

British state welfare: roots of the crisis

Expansions and contractions of capitalist state welfare have operated largely on a national basis. Welfare provision in each country is shaped by its relationships to global capital, mediated by economic conditions, the strength and politics of working-class organisation, and the example of rival systems.

State welfare is socially useful but does not produce value in a capitalist sense; it therefore represents a deduction from surplus value produced elsewhere (Yaffe, 1972). In this sense, state welfare is a concession to the working class, whereby a portion of the wealth produced by workers and seized by the ruling classes as surplus value is 'given back' in the form of services or benefits, making workers less dependent on wages. This helps to explain the determination with which capitalist governments have sought to restrict welfare spending, intensifying in periods of capitalist crisis. Capitalist state welfare plays other roles as well. It subsidises employers by allowing them to pay poverty-level wages while state welfare makes up the difference to enable the reproduction of labour power. In Britain, this includes cash payments such as tax credits and housing benefits, as well as state-funded services such as health care and education. Capitalist state welfare also disciplines working-class behaviour, consumption patterns and free time through various forms of conditionality and means testing. Even at the high point of capitalist state welfare, 'entitlement to most benefits was dependent on regular participation in the labour market' (Standing, 2011: 70), and was thus tied to the sale of labour power. Contemporary examples of conditionality are discussed later in this chapter. Lastly, state welfare helps to sustain a reserve army of labour, which puts pressure on those currently in work through competition, enables a regular turnover in the workforce to facilitate worsening conditions and disrupt organisation, and provides for future increases in labour demand (Magdoff and Magdoff, 2004). The reserve army is discussed further in Chapter 5.

The 'post-war boom', outlined in Chapter 2, enabled significant concessions for large sections of the working class, including the NHS, extensive social care, a council house-building programme and a range of benefits to support the low paid, unemployed and those unable to work due to long-term illness, age or disability. This was partially funded through the exploitation of oppressed countries and migrant labour within Britain, discussed in Chapter 2 and later in this chapter. It also occurred under the pressure of the Soviet Union's example of providing economic security to its citizens (Petras, 2012). State provision for the working class in Britain was never complete and, for the most part, denied access to non-citizens and, in some cases, also large numbers of working-class citizens.

Capitalist state welfare has always operated differential inclusion, whereby different sections of the population experience qualitatively distinct treatment. As Stevenson (1978: 459) puts it when discussing the US, while elements of service and control are always present, the balance differs across the population, for example, 'the service aspect is dominant in New York City schools when teachers teach white middle-class students. The control aspect is dominant when they teach black and Latino working-class students'. This contributes to class fractioning (see Chapter 2). Under conditions of capitalist crisis, combined with a historic low for the strength of working-class organisation in Britain, the conditional character of welfare has become increasingly dominant across the working class, and lines of differentiation have become more acute. This has been expressed discursively through oppositional categories such as 'strivers' and 'skivers', promoted at times by politicians from all the major capitalist parties. Resources, and even political representation, have been made increasingly conditional on the sale of labour power. For example, in 2015, Labour's Shadow Work and Pensions Secretary, Rachel Reeves, said: 'We are not the party of people on benefits. We don't want to be seen, and we're not, the party to represent those who are out of work'.[1] This complemented the Conservative government's use of categories such as 'hard-working families', counterposed to 120,000 'troubled families', who were identified as needing urgent intervention following the 2011 riots. Evaluation of the subsequent Troubled Families Programme showed that it brought no discernible benefits for anyone (Bonell et al, 2016).

In the context of imperialism, racialised differences in state welfare have contributed to super-exploitation. A line of continuity can be drawn from the granting of suffrage to working-class men in the 19th century to the establishment of the NHS and other institutions in 1948 in a process incorporating a section of working-class people into a nationalist alliance with the British ruling classes. Early reforms to provide state welfare after 1900, including old-age pensions, school meals and public housing, benefited working-class people but were driven by ruling-class concern to appease an increasingly militant working class in order to ensure healthy workers for the army and factories, and to limit emigration (Williams, 1995: 151–5). The term 'welfare state' first entered common usage during the Second World War in order to contrast the British state's care for its citizens with its fascist rivals (Harling, 2001: 154). From the beginning, it was thus linked to ideas of national superiority. After the war, state welfare supported post-war rebuilding by maintaining mass consumption, drew women back into unpaid domestic work under the concept of the 'family wage' while wartime childcare provision was withdrawn, and afforded limited concessions to pacify the working class and undermine the attraction of socialism (Williams, 1995).

Differences associated with migration interact with racialised and gendered divisions. As state welfare reduces the burden of unwaged caring on women, differential access to welfare produces gendered differences in caring arrangements and unwaged labour. For example, Datta et al (2007a: 420–1) found that childcare strategies among migrants in London included leaving children with a friend or relative in their country of origin, particularly for people with limited social networks within Britain, or parents working alternate shifts so that they could provide childcare at all times within the household. Differential rights to family unification and connections between earning thresholds for certain immigration statuses and family size extend state control into the realm of reproduction (Lonergan, 2015).

Qualitative differences in state welfare according to racialisation and immigration status have also been reflected in the patterns of cuts since 2010. Collett (2011: 18–19) identifies some of the cuts that specifically targeted migrants in the first years of austerity:

- the cancellation of several community cohesion programmes, such as Connecting Communities, alongside a retargeting of funding to 'counter radicalisation', reducing resources and increasing social control;
- the cancellation of the £50 million Migration Impacts Fund, which funded many small community organisations;
- restrictions on eligibility and reductions in funding for English-language provision, including the removal of the £4.5 million Learner Support Fund used by low-income migrants to help with course fees, and the merger of the Ethnic Minority Achievement Grant into general education budgets; and
- cuts to funding for non-governmental organisations (NGOs), including a 62 per cent reduction in state funding for the Refugee Council in 2011 and the termination of the Refugee Integration and Employment Service.

Hall et al (2017) calculate that the already-announced benefit cuts and tax changes between 2010 and 2020 will mean an average reduction of annual income for the poorest third of households by 19 per cent for Asian women, 14 per cent for black women and 11 per cent for white women. They also assess the impact of service cuts in cash terms, representing a cut for the poorest 20 per cent of 11.6 per cent for black households, 11.2 per cent for Asian households and 8.9 per cent for white households.

To summarise, capitalist state welfare in Britain has only been possible under exceptional conditions that included imperialist super-exploitation, and even at its high point, fell short of meeting the needs of the entire working class and contributed to differential inclusion. Today, the character of state welfare is changing, with a shift in the balance between its resource/ service and control dimensions. This is connected to the incorporation of non-state actors, some of them profit-making, within state-directed capitalist governance.

Welfare outsourcing: unlocking profits, increasing control

Outsourcing public services has been driven by the need for British imperialism to find new opportunities for profitable investment by opening up services previously provided by the state and fostering the emergence of new multinational companies. Outsourcing is therefore a new form of capitalist plunder, the precedent for which was set by the wholesale privatisation of state utilities and industries over the previous 30 years (Alonso et al, 2013; TUC, 2015).

Public sector outsourcing was first introduced from the late 1980s and was significantly expanded by the 1997–2010 Labour government. Gosling (2011) and Wilks (2013) document the creation of powerful lobbying organisations, with close links to government and media, including:

- the Business Services Association (established in 1993), with 65 companies as members, employing a combined workforce of 2 million people and with an annual turnover of £80 billion, £50 billion of which was generated outside of Britain and the North of Ireland[2];
- Scottish Care (established in 2000), 'Representing the largest group of independent sector health & social care providers across Scotland'[3];
- PPP Forum (established in 2001), the 'private sector industry body for public private partnerships delivering UK infrastructure'[4];
- the Confederation of British Industry (CBI) Public Services Strategy Board (established in 2003)[5];
- the NHS Partners Network (established in 2005), representing 37 providers of outsourced services to the NHS[6]; and
- the English Community Care Association (established in 2007), later renamed Care England, representing independent care providers, whose website states that it 'is represented on key government and regulatory policy groups'.[7]

Supporting these lobbying activities, companies have sponsored research to promote outsourcing and, in some cases, set up their own 'research institutes', including the Serco Institute, the PricewaterhouseCoopers Public Sector Research Centre and the Centre for Public Service Partnerships at Birmingham University, which was created together with Balfour Beatty and directed by the former Head of Strategic Relations at Capita. This produced results: by 2014/15, a third of government expenditure went to external suppliers, totalling £242 billion, including around £100 billion for outsourced services, compared to the total wage bill for public sector employees of £194 billion (Sturgess, 2017).

At the pinnacle of Britain's outsourcing industry stands G4S. Based in Crawley, England, it is the world's third-largest private employer, with over 570,000 workers worldwide and operating in 90 countries. Its annual turnover was £7.8 billion in 2017. Next largest is Serco, based in Hampshire, England, employing 50,000 people and with a revenue of £2.9 billion in 2017. The activities of such companies have become vital to the interests of British imperialism because of its reliance on service exports, discussed in Chapter 2. This explains why British governments have consistently defended these companies and continued to grant them contracts despite numerous embarrassing failings. For example, after G4S botched security for the 2011 Olympics, leading costs to increase from £10 million to £125 million and requiring the police and army to be deployed to fill gaps, then-Home Secretary Theresa May ruled out a review of the company's government contracts, at the time totalling £1 billion, and encouraged police forces to continue with their outsourcing programme.[8]

Outsourcing welfare services is well advanced, with increasing concentration of ownership in companies like CareUK, which, in 2012, acquired Britain's largest medical General Practice (GP) out-of-hours provider, Harmoni, and by 2018 was providing services to 18 million patients each year.[9] CareUK is owned by London-based private equity firm Bridgepoint Capital and has diverted millions of pounds each year into profits and interest on the massive debts incurred when Bridgepoint purchased the company. This represents money not reinvested in services. Many of those employed in outsourced services have faced redundancy, lower wages and poorer working conditions (Mori, 2017), while service users receive less or nothing at all (Pensiero, 2017).

Another consequence of outsourcing is an in-sourcing of the endemic instability of capital within the operations of the state. Outsourcing allows companies to extract profits from public services but is distinguished from outright privatisation in that the state retains ownership and shoulders responsibility when things go wrong. For example, in January 2018, Carillion went into liquidation amid spiralling debts, with ramifications throughout its many public sector contracts. Carillion was Britain's second-largest construction company, also providing many services and employing 43,000 people worldwide. Carillion was part of a complex outsourcing chain, with 90 per cent of its work carried out by subcontractors. British government contracts accounted for 38 per cent of its income in 2016 and it was a major beneficiary of the Private Finance Initiatives (PFIs) that expanded rapidly under the 1997–2010 Labour government. Rayne (2018) describes the range of its activities, in which it managed:

200 NHS operating theatres, 11,800 NHS hospital beds, provided patients' meals, built motorways and bridges, designed and built 150 schools, provided catering at 875 schools, maintained and repaired prisons, managed several public libraries, was working on London's Crossrail and the HS2 high-speed rail project.... The government depended on Carillion to maintain its GCHQ [Government Communications Headquarters] building, which Carillion designed and built. It was the biggest manager of military bases for the Ministry of Defence and was building £1.1bn of new accommodation for British troops. Carillion had contracts worth a combined £685m to build the new Royal Liverpool University Hospital and the Midland Metropolitan Hospital in Birmingham.... Carillion maintained half of Britain's prisons.

On news of the company's collapse, 14 hospitals were forced to resort to emergency plans to cover services that it previously provided, while in Oxfordshire, the Fire Service was notified that it may have to deliver school meals (Rayne, 2018). Other examples include Barnet Council, left with £1.5 million in costs after Connaught, contracted to manage housing repairs, went bust, and forced to pay £10.3 million in compensation and costs when a contract with Catalyst for care homes went wrong, alongside other failings (Whitfield, 2012). Outsourcing is therefore particularly attractive to capitalists because there is no risk – the state acts as guarantor.

Outsourcing state welfare has contributed to the replacement of professional decision-making with contractual compliance. Charities have been incorporated into this process, beginning with the voluntary sector 'compacts' created by the Labour government in 1998, which reconceptualised charities as partners in governance, and renewed by the Coalition government in 2010. A shift from grants to 'payment-by-results' contracts has required charities to put forward large upfront investments. Bassel and Emejulu's (2017) research in England, Scotland and France found that funding cuts had made many voluntary sector organisations' previous ways of operating impossible, and, in many cases, had led to a breakdown of feelings of solidarity and the infusion of market ideas. Many charities have responded to cuts since 2010 by reorganising themselves into 'social enterprises'. These developments have been masked by the relabelling of the voluntary and community sector as part of a 'third sector' under the Labour government and then 'civil society' under the Conservative–Liberal Democrat Coalition. The first term encompasses social enterprises and the second can also include for-profit companies. Donovan et al's (2012: 8–9) research with the voluntary sector of

North-East England gives a vivid account of how this has been experienced on the front line of practice:

> Many practitioners spoke about feeling personally and professionally overwhelmed with the increased work they were being asked to do to cover for posts deleted, services cut and hours curtailed. The emotional toll was articulated in expressions of despair, bewilderment, low morale, ill-health and fears about their personal and/or their professional future and/or the future of their service and the future for their service users.

They found voluntary sector organisations responding to cuts through the increased use of volunteers, charging for services, diversifying funding streams, developing consortium bids and campaigning and lobbying. Respondents reported drawbacks of each of these responses: threatening quality and safeguarding (volunteerism); limiting access to those who cannot afford to pay (charging); distorting provision by introducing priorities other than need (charging and diversifying funding); and operating in ways that favour larger organisations who can afford specialists but may lack the local contacts and understanding of smaller locally embedded organisations (diversifying funding, consortium bids and campaigning). The combined effect has been a shift towards a two-tier voluntary sector of highly professionalised massive organisations and unfunded local self-help groups (Craig, 2011). Changes to state welfare and charitable provision have thereby moved in the same direction, reducing access based on need and increasing conditionality informed by capitalist reasoning.

Outsourcing welfare activities has gone together with the co-option of a wide range of individuals and organisations into processes of surveillance and control. Rowlands (2013) gives examples of some of the forms this has taken, evolving through successive governments, including:

- employers, private landlords and health-care providers monitoring the immigration status of their employees, tenants and service users, discussed in Chapter 3 and later in this chapter;
- requirements for universities to monitor and report to the Home Office on the attendance of international students on Tier 4 visas as part of the Points-Based System;
- Anti-Social Behaviour Orders, Criminal Behaviour Orders and Crime Prevention Injunctions, which rely heavily on members of the public reporting on each other's behaviour;

- 'crowdsourcing' schemes for the monitoring of closed-circuit television (CCTV) cameras;
- campaigns encouraging members of the public to report suspected benefit fraud, with the creation of a National Benefit Fraud Hotline that resulted in 253,708 reports during 2009–10, only 1.32 per cent of which led to further action (another scheme launched in 2009 called for people to report anyone they suspected of unlawfully subletting social housing, with the incentive of a £500 cash reward to the first 1,000 people whose tip-offs led to the repossession of a council house, and a similar reporting system exists for 'immigration crimes'[10]); and
- members of the public reporting 'suspicious activity' that might be indicative of terrorism, such as Metropolitan Police campaigns in 2008 and 2009 that encouraged people to report seemingly innocuous things like people taking photographs, items in neighbours' bins such as batteries or empty chemical bottles, or people paying too much attention to CCTV cameras (this has been followed by demands for a range of voluntary and statutory sector staff to undertake training in detecting 'extremism' as part of the 'Prevent' programme) (Kundnani, 2015).

Together, these schemes, and others like them, have drawn broad sections of society into state-directed systems of governance requiring habitual surveillance and judgement of other members of society. The state has thereby extended its systems of control even as it has withdrawn resources. These changes have been justified by an ideology of individualism and conditionality, promoted through austerity narratives.

Deficit narratives as justification for austerity

Kitson et al (2011: 292–3) describe the 'austerity consensus', in which 'Governments almost everywhere have embarked, or are embarking on, programmes of major cuts and reductions in public spending on a scale not seen for decades ... reducing the size of the state in favour of the private market'. Austerity has been described as the 'new common sense' in policy (Blyth, 2013), and has been adopted in practice by all of Britain's major electoral parties since 2010. Its effects have been extremely uneven, socially and geographically, with differences within and between countries (Beatty and Fothergill, 2013). Kitson et al (2011: 294) point to austerity's particularly severe impacts in regions that already 'suffered from structural problems, associated with deindustrialization and slow growth, and the economic downturn ... exacerbated and further exposed these problems'. The changes associated with austerity developed earlier in some countries, for example, through Structural Adjustment Programmes imposed on many African countries since the 1980s and following the restoration of capitalism in many Eastern and Central European countries in the 1990s; austerity's delayed arrival in Britain partly reflects Britain's privileged relationship to global capital.

The financial crisis of 2007–08 is directly connected to austerity in two senses: first, welfare spending offered a scapegoat to divert attention from massive state aid to the banking and financial sector, shifting the blame from wealthy bankers onto working-class benefit claimants; and, second, cuts to welfare provision increased workers' reliance on wages and therefore the pressure to comply with employers' demands, facilitating the more effective extraction of surplus value in order to mitigate the underlying crisis of profitability. Britain's net debt at the start of austerity was not abnormally high, at 57.2 per cent of national income in September 2010, below that of Germany, France, the US and Japan, and well below Britain's average debt between 1688–2010, at 112 per cent of national income (FRFI, 2011: 13). Kitson et al (2011: 292) identify the causes of rising debt for many countries as resulting from 'the banking crisis or the recession or both', with the cost of direct support to the banks totalling US$1.5 trillion. Yet, politicians effected an ideological 'reworking that has focused on the unwieldy and expensive welfare state and public sector, rather than high-risk strategies of banks, as the root cause of the crisis' (Clarke and Newman, 2012: 300). This was supported by a media narrative that explained the deficit as the result of welfare spending rather than bank bail-outs. Migrants have played several roles within this: as scapegoats blamed for putting pressure on public finances and resources, diverting attention from cuts; as workers excluded from access to state welfare in special ways due to immigration status and therefore both susceptible to super-exploitation and providing a testing ground for measures later extended to other sections of the working class; and as a relatively cheap workforce in key sectors of welfare provision, discussed later, keeping costs down.

Kitson et al (2011) suggest that the underlying argument behind austerity presents the public sector as a 'burden' on the 'wealth-creating' private sector, with the implication that the deficit should be reduced by cutting expenditure rather than by increasing taxes. Setting aside the socially useful character of state welfare in meeting needs, and considering value only in a capitalist sense, Marx offers a more fine-grained analysis of the relationship between different types of labour and the production of value in his discussion of productive and unproductive labour (Howell, 1975). Applying this analysis shows that huge sections of Britain's private sector produce no value but only influence how surplus value is distributed, for example, most marketing and advertising, many aspects of retail, and much of the financial sector. This activity is a huge burden on the wealth–producing sectors and, more importantly, a colossal waste of human potential, and yet it is ignored by narratives that describe the public sector as a burden.

Sassen (2014: 41–3) describes Europe's austerity programmes as cutting 'deep into the social economic fabric', and expelling sections of the population into 'alternative survival economies that … exist in a different economic space, one that falls outside formal measures and indicators'. This represents an abdication of responsibility by capitalists and the state for the reproduction of labour power outside the shrinking recognised economic space that Sassen describes, as well as an increased reliance on the kind of hidden reproductive work that has long been the burden of women within the home (James, 2012 [1983]). Austerity can therefore be understood as an intervention to shift the balance of forces against the working class, increasing the exploitation of waged and unwaged labour as the ruling classes attempt to escape the capitalist crisis.

From 2010 to 2016, cuts to local government funding amounted to 27 per cent in real terms for England and 11 per cent for Scotland (Hastings et al, 2015). This has affected many services, from children's and youth services, to respite services for informal carers, social care services, libraries, arts and culture, day centres for the elderly and disabled, subsidised public transport, parks, and waste collection. Many of these services were universal, and these cuts therefore removed some of the only sources of support for people excluded from many other services because of their immigration status. As local authorities were previously funded through a combination of central government subsidies and local taxes on businesses and households, and the cuts targeted the central government element, the overall effect has been to disadvantage poorer areas, where tax receipts are lower (Beatty and Fothergill, 2013). Councils have responded by increasing council tax and cutting services. As many councils in poorer areas were run by the Labour Party and central government over this period was run by a Conservative–Liberal Democrat Coalition and then the Conservative Party, each party could shift the blame onto the other.

Since the election of Jeremy Corbyn as leader of the Labour Party in 2015, he has rejected austerity at a rhetorical level, and has adopted the slogan that austerity is a political choice, not an economic necessity (LabourList, 2015b). However, in practice, the Labour Party under Corbyn has continued to implement austerity wherever it holds power within local authorities. Within months of becoming party leader, Corbyn issued a memorandum to Labour-run local authorities, co-signed by Shadow

Chancellor John McDonnell, instructing them not to set 'illegal budgets', meaning that they must pass on cuts from central government (LabourList, 2015a). This was made party policy at Labour's conference the following year, when 80 per cent of delegates voted to make it a disciplinary offence for Labour councillors to abstain, or vote against, budget cuts proposed by Labour-led councils.[11] In the 2017 general election, Labour ran on a manifesto that included £7 billion in cuts to welfare, in addition to those made by previous governments (Finch, 2017). This demonstrates that the drivers of austerity run deeper than party politics.

Structuring class through the crises of state welfare

The relationships between state welfare, borders and class have played out in different, but connected, ways in different welfare domains. The examples of the NHS and social care, housing, and the benefits system are discussed in the following. In each domain, borders differentiate people's treatment, reflecting imperialist divisions of labour and contributing to class fractioning that creates differential conditions of exploitation. Also within each domain, the appearance of crisis conditions reflects far-reaching reconfigurations of the state.

The crisis of the NHS and social care

The NHS was the second-biggest issue of public concern in 2018, close behind Brexit (Ipsos MORI, 2018). The crisis in health care and social care is often discussed in terms of inadequate funding. During 2010–14, despite growing demand, health spending increased by only 0.41 per cent per year and social care spending fell by 1.57 per cent per year, down from annual increases of 3.8 per cent for health care and 2.2 per cent for social care during 2001–10. In the poorest communities, social care spending fell by 14 per cent in real terms between 2010/11 and 2015/16 (Hastings et al, 2015). Underfunding led one third of NHS clinical commissioning groups to forecast an end-of-year deficit for 2018 (Murray et al, 2018; see also Meek, 2018). Watkins et al (2017) found that recent funding reductions were associated with a reversal of previously falling death rates, such that 45,000 more people died during 2010–14 than would have been expected based on previous trends. The roots of this crisis extend further back to a historical encroachment of profit-making into care.

The NHS was created in 1948, with principles that included care free at the point of delivery, based on clinical need rather than ability to pay, and available to everybody within Britain. There are considerable variations in how the NHS operates today, including different forms of devolution in England, Wales, Scotland and the North of Ireland. The 1997–2010 Labour government oversaw a process of restructuring, creating internal markets, whereby units of the NHS were made to treat one another as independent suppliers, and local trusts, which fragmented the NHS and weakened accountability (Pollock, 2005). PFIs financed hospital building, leading to debts to private investors that would result in repayment from public funds far beyond the actual costs of the building. Total PFI debt was £300 billion by 2016, equivalent to two-and-a-half times the NHS's annual budget, for construction projects that cost £55 billion, leaving £245 billion as a transfer from public funds to private profit.[12] Repayments have forced many hospitals into states of crisis, leading the Royal College of Physicians to warn that some acute care could be 'on the brink of collapse' (RCP, 2012). For example, Kings College Hospital in London was running a deficit of over £90 million by 2018. In the winter of 2016/17, the British Red Cross declared a 'humanitarian crisis' after it stepped in to supplement state provision in 20 Accident and Emergency departments.[13] The Health and Social Care Act 2012 removed the state's duty to provide universal health care in England. Sustainability and transformation plans (STPs), first announced in 2015, have been drawn up across the country with the aim of cutting expenditure, driving a process of rationing.[14] This has been justified by an ideology of individual responsibility and criteria such as weight and smoking. Differentiation in the experience of health care has also operated according to migrant categories and racialisation, discussed later in this chapter.

Since the 1980s, most social care in Britain has been privatised. Care companies have expanded and been subject to takeover and asset-stripping by private equity firms. This has contributed to repeated crises in the sector and deteriorating conditions for many workers and service users (Carey, 2008). For example, in 2011, the largest provider of care homes in Britain, Southern Cross, went bankrupt after being taken over by private equity firm Blackstone. These changes have been accompanied by a shift from structural and institutional approaches to a focus on individual behaviour and responsibility (Newman et al, 2008). Cuts to local authority funding since 2010 have reduced resources for social care, which has, in turn, increased demands on the NHS (Hudson, 2016). Profit imperatives for private companies have combined with funding cuts to squeeze services, worsening conditions for service users and staff, for example, through the common practice of limiting home visits to 15 minutes and not paying care workers for travel time between visits (Prentis, 2017). 'Cash-for-care' policies,[15] in common with other European Union (EU) countries such as France and Italy, have fuelled the growth of private, unregulated employment, adding to the general undervaluing of reproductive work under capitalism (Farris, 2015: 12–16).

Part of health care and social care contributes to maintaining the labour power of the working class and developing new generations of workers, but much of it is devoted to the well-being of those who have reached the end of their working life or are too unwell to be of use to employers. While there is therefore some benefit to the capitalist, this only applies to some types of care. All state-provided care represents a deduction from surplus value, although it has the appearance of being paid by individual contributions because it is first added to the wage and then removed through taxation (Yaffe, 1972). Migrant labour offers benefits here: making workers' residence in Britain conditional on the sale of labour power means that those who are too young, old or sick to find employment can be excluded from care, either through exclusionary access criteria or through expulsion from British territory.

At its creation, NHS services were formally available to anyone in Britain, regardless of nationality, but this quickly changed (Kundnani, 2007: 18). Charges for 'overseas visitors' accessing health care were introduced by a Labour government in 1977 and amended in 1988 and 2006, together with regulations introduced in 1982 and revised many times since (DH, 2004). Amendments to the regulations in 2004 departed from the principle of free access for those 'ordinarily resident' in Britain by introducing charges for secondary health care for undocumented migrants and refused asylum seekers, even if they had lodged an appeal. Although, in theory, some areas of care remained free for everyone, such as antenatal care, Yates et al (2007) report that, in practice, confusion among providers led to antenatal care being refused to some women because of their immigration status, unless they could pay several thousands of pounds upfront.

Restrictions have often been justified by claims of 'health tourism', whereby people are alleged to be visiting Britain simply to access free health care.[16] Yet, estimates commissioned by the government suggest that, at most, 0.3 per cent of the NHS budget is attributable to people travelling for health care, and this includes British emigrants returning to Britain to access a trusted doctor (Prederi, 2013). It also includes people in situations of desperation, such as that described by a worker from a Romanian organisation:

> 'this typical family … chose to come here because of the health…. [A man had] an accident at work [in Romania]. [He] was a healthy man, and two years ago, he's having this accident. He's not had recompense [compensation], nothing.

So, the guy has lost everything, and now to continue to be able to survive, he cannot pay for medication anymore [in Romania], so he has come in the last stage of desperation to have some more help.... So ... you stay in Romania and you carry on, or you die, or you survive and you take the risk.... He's had to sell everything, and he's come here.... [For] five months, he's been able to pay his own private rent and all that, but the money's finished.... He is so desperate, he didn't know what to do.' (Interview P9)

At this point, the family were evicted from their private-rented accommodation, including the man (who was in a wheelchair), his partner (who was providing him with 24-hour care) and their eight-year-old child. This occurred in a context where the destruction of socialism in Romania, and the re-entry of Romania into the capitalist system in a subordinate position, led to the stripping away of state services in the 1990s, including an exodus of health professionals recruited to work in imperialist countries (Stanciu and Jawad, 2013). To describe such a family's desperate movement to Britain as 'tourism' is obscene.

The Immigration Act 2014 changed the definition of 'ordinarily resident', as a condition for many migrants to access health care, to require indefinite leave to remain, and this was followed by a slew of regulatory amendments. The 2014 Act also introduced a flat-rate NHS surcharge for people from outside the European Economic Area without indefinite leave to remain, with those unable to pay automatically refused a visa (DHSC, 2018). In 2018, this surcharge was doubled. Starting in 2017, health-care providers were required by law to check patients' eligibility for care at the point of delivery, and to charge people ineligible for free NHS treatment upfront at a rate of 150 per cent of the actual cost (Cassidy, 2018). This initially included hospital departments, community-based health visitors, school nurses, community midwives, community mental health services, some abortion services and district nursing.[17] Following protests, some community services were exempted from these charges, including school nurses and health visitors.[18]

Exemptions were also made for certain treatments and for victims of trafficking, refugees and asylum seekers, but the track record of similar measures in the past suggests that the real extent of exclusion will extend beyond those formally targeted. For example, Jolla, who had initially come to Britain on a student visa and later claimed asylum and was refused, spoke at an event at the Tate Modern in May 2018 about how they had received a letter stating that their cancer treatments would be discontinued because of their changed immigration status. After challenging this, they were told that they would continue to receive their current treatments but that they should avoid falling ill with anything else because they would then be charged. Jolla described this experience as a loss of control, saying: "it's like being in an extra-tight box, where you have no control over your finances, no control over your life, but also now no control over your health". They also reported friends with precarious immigration status resorting to borrowing money from 'loan sharks'[19] to pay for chemotherapy. In 2018, the government raised the possibility of extending upfront charges to also apply to GPs and Accident and Emergency departments (Potter, 2018). Unpaid debts for health care can lead to the rejection of future immigration applications (Liberty, 2018: 17–18).

Data are shared by the Department of Health and Social Care with the Home Office, often without the knowledge or consent of patients or health-care practitioners. In 2016, information shared in this way was used for immigration enforcement against nearly 6,000 people (Liberty, 2018: 18). In January 2018, Parliament's Health Select Committee heard contributions from organisations representing or providing services to migrants, who reported that because of data sharing, many migrants were too scared to seek help with health problems and that this had already led to at least one death.[20]

Race has also played a significant role in differential experiences of health care. In mental health provision, there has been a history of racialised stereotypes associating black men with aggression and dangerous behaviour, which has seriously affected their experience of services (Newbigging et al, 2007: 113). Recent figures suggest that black people have relatively high rates of mental health problems but are less likely to receive treatment (Cabinet Office, 2018). In social care, assumptions that racialised minorities, and particularly South Asian people, prefer to 'look after their own' have justified a situation in which 'nearly one in five Pakistani women aged 30–pension age, and one in ten British Pakistani or Bangladeshi men aged 16–29, are also [unpaid] carers' (National Black Carers and Workers Network, 2008: 30). Research into the views of South Asian carers found that rather than a cultural preference, many people's decisions to care for family members were influenced by negative experiences of trying to access mainstream support (Mir and Tovey, 2003: 471). The lack of appropriate provision, particularly acute in some parts of the country, was highlighted by an experienced worker for a black and minority ethnic (BME) voluntary sector organisation in North-East England, who suggested that it 'cut across' immigration categories:

'if you look at mainstream provisions, so if you're looking at support for carers, and if you look at ... respite care for

maybe a BME older person that's been here for 40 years, or
... a refugee that's been here for five years, those issues are
not significantly different.'

They suggested that this situation had been worsened by cuts because of a
loss of experienced practitioners and specialist services. People identifying
as Indian, Pakistani, Bangladeshi or Chinese are the least likely to report
positive experiences of accessing GP services (Cabinet Office, 2018).
Hall et al (2017) describe the growing difficulties experienced by many
racialised-minority women trying to get an appointment, and identify
causes including cuts to interpreting services and increasing numbers of
GPs refusing to treat women who have no recourse to public funds because
of their immigration status.

While migrants and racialised minorities have been discriminated
against in receiving care, care provision has depended heavily on racialised-
minority and migrant labour. At its creation, the NHS required workers
who were actively recruited from areas such as the Caribbean, many
of them working for low wages, as porters or nurses (Williams, 1995).
This reliance has continued: 15,000 of the 20,000 nurses who joined the
medical register in 2003/04 had migrated and one third of doctors on the
register qualified abroad (Jameson, 2005; see also Kyriakides and Virdee,
2003). In recent years, the NHS has drawn labour from other parts of the
EU, but in anticipation of Brexit, many people are leaving and fewer are
arriving. Together with visa restrictions, this is worsening shortages of
nurses, with 40,000 unfilled vacancies,[21] and of doctors.[22] In 2018, the
government announced a new programme to recruit 5,500 nurses from
Jamaica to work in the NHS for three years before returning to Jamaica,
under the slogan 'earn, learn, return'.[23] Refugees are being retrained to
help fill doctor shortages, and, in some cases, must initially work on an
unpaid basis because their qualifications are not recognised.[24] There is a
substantial involvement of migrants in delivering social care, with one
study suggesting that a fifth of all care workers looking after older people
are migrants, with many employed by agencies. Widespread exploitation
has been documented, including excessive hours, rates of pay below the
minimum wage, deception about expected wage levels, little to no holiday
and cases of debt bondage (Wilkinson et al, 2009: 24–5). Together, recent
changes to health and social care have clawed back surplus value from the
working class, pushed provision for the working class down towards the
minimum required for the reproduction of labour power and enforced a
differentiation in who can remain in Britain if their health prevents them
from performing waged labour.

The housing crisis

Housing rose from the 18th most pressing public concern in 2010 to the third most pressing in 2018 (Ipsos MORI, 2018). Homelessness statistics provide a further indication of the crisis. From 2011 to 2016, core homelessness[25] increased year by year, for a total increase over the period of 33.4 per cent across Britain, to 159,900 people. If current trends continue, core homelessness will more than double by 2041 (Bramley, 2017). Street homelessness increased by 169 per cent from 2010 to 2018 and the number of families in temporary accommodation increased by 61 per cent (Clough et al, 2018: 2). Homeless Link (2017) surveyed organisations providing support to single homeless people and found that 39 per cent had experienced funding cuts over the last year and the number of bed spaces had fallen by 3 per cent overall and 9 per cent in London. National Audit Office figures show a 21 per cent reduction in housing services spending since 2010.

Much of the public discussion has focused on London, where a combination of soaring house prices and private rents, sell-offs of council housing, and cuts to housing benefit have put pressure on large numbers of working-class people to move to the outskirts of the capital or to other cities, described by some as 'social cleansing' (Lees and Ferreri, 2016; Watt and Minton, 2016). Difficulties accessing decent housing are also affecting growing numbers of better-off workers and young middle-class professionals, which Clough et al (2018) argue has been decisive in bringing the housing crisis into public discussion. There are also severe housing problems in other parts of the country, taking various forms. Access to housing is differentiated according to racialisation and migrant status, with extremes of deprivation clustering for particular groups, discussed further later in this chapter.

The predominant response to this crisis from Britain's main capitalist parties has been to promise house-building programmes. Yet, there is already considerable unused housing, with local authorities reporting over 205,000 homes in England empty for at least six months in 2017.[26] The problem is not simply a physical lack of housing, but that the system of private ownership prevents it being used by people who need it. Additionally, political parties' commitments to build 'affordable' housing for sale or rent means little when 'affordable' is generally defined as 80 per cent of local market rates and house prices increased by 255 per cent from 1997 to 2017.[27] The focus on house building also fails to address the insecurity of private tenancies and is aimed at the increasingly small number of middle-class people who can afford to buy a house. The main beneficiaries are landlords, a group who overlap significantly with the politicians implementing housing policy. Within the 40 English boroughs with the highest proportion of homes for private rent, one in seven councillors are landlords, and this rises to a third in some councils.[28] Many councils, such as Southwark, Lambeth and Greenwich, have been advised by estate agents like Savills, who have a massive stake in the expansion of private housing (Clough et al, 2018: 78–82). This embodies, at the local level, the confluence of interests between the state and landlords.

The principle that land can be privately owned by an individual, the enshrining of this principle in law and its defence by the repressive forces of the state combines under capitalism with the actual concentration of land ownership in the hands of a minority. This system enables both imperialist immigration controls, by establishing monopoly control over a geographical area, and the exploitation of the working class through waged labour, by preventing people from using land to produce for themselves. It also lies at the base of the housing crisis. As Clough et al (2018: 6) point out: 'Under capitalism, houses are built only if someone can make a profit out of them.... The developers, the land owners, the financiers and the construction companies all want a profit. It doesn't matter that millions of people need a decent home'. To build genuinely affordable housing for the working class at social rents that take into account local incomes would require state subsidies in London of £200,000 per housing unit – an impossibility under capitalism (Clough et al, 2018).

Marx (1991 [1894]) uses the theory of 'ground rent' to explain how the price of land is determined through an interaction between predicted earnings from its use and interest rates. The crisis of profitability for British capitalism, discussed in Chapter 2, has made land an attractive option for investors searching for something to do with their surplus capital. Investment in land entitles the landlord to a share of the total surplus value in exchange for allowing use of the land. In 2015, the average price of agricultural land in England was £21,000 a hectare, but with planning permission for housing, the price rose to £6 million a hectare (DCLG, 2015). This reflects the scarcity of housing on the market and the lack of other opportunities for profitable investment. Wealthy investors from around the world have bought up properties as an investment, often leaving them empty but pushing up prices. International investments in office space in Central London totalled £16.4 billion in 2017.[29] This has been actively encouraged by the state through a 'Citizenship by Investment' programme introduced by the Labour government in 2008 (Hanieh, 2018). Amid soaring land prices, local authorities have been collaborating with private developers like Lendlease to demolish council housing and take it over for profitable use, often with little or no consultation and in the face of determined resistance.[30]

Due to high private rents and a lack of social housing, increasing numbers of people lack housing security, even if they are in work. When Aditya Chakrabortty visited an emergency night shelter in London, one third of the 42 people staying there were currently employed, in some cases, by large multinationals.[31] There are also reports of homelessness among workers outside London, for example, McDonalds employees in Cambridge.[32] The widening incidence of working homelessness is corroborated by the Ombudsman for Local Government and Social Care, which reports increasing homelessness among people employed as nurses, taxi drivers, hospitality staff and council workers (LGSCO, 2017). *The Guardian* reports examples of the human consequences of housing insecurity:

- A couple with two young children who spent 26 weeks in a single room in a B&B [bed and breakfast]. Although they reported that the shower did not work and the room was infested with cockroaches, the council failed to ensure repairs were made.
- A mother whose baby had type 1 diabetes was placed in a dirty and unhygienic B&B room without access to cooking facilities. The baby contracted an infection and ended up in hospital. The hospital blamed the housing....
- A disabled single parent with four children was put up in B&B accommodation for nearly two and a half years after her benefits were capped. The council ignored letters from medical professionals outlining concerns that living in the property was affecting the family's health.[33]

Such conditions, which were previously considered temporary and exceptional, have become the norm for increasing numbers of people. The Community Law Partnership (CLP) in Birmingham report another case,[34] involving a family with three-year-old twins and a five-month-old baby, who were housed by Birmingham City Council in a hostel for several months before being evicted for allegedly breaking conditions that included restrictions on movement and freedom of association. They were given further temporary accommodation only after a legal battle. At one point, social services reportedly threatened to take the children into care – something CLP describe as the 'frighten them away card', which they have often seen used to deter people from insisting on the support that they are entitled to. A housing campaigner reported that this is common practice in London (interview A13). This reflects the increasingly punitive and exclusionary character of capitalist state welfare for the working class.

The history of housing in Britain helps explain the current crisis. Since the 1970s, there has been a steady reduction in state-subsidised council housing, driven by the so-called 'right to buy' for council house tenants, in which the state heavily subsidises the cost of the purchase (Malpass, 1990). This has led to large amounts of state-funded housing passing into private hands, and councils have been barred from using money from council house sales to build more housing. Over time, a lot of former council housing has become concentrated in landlords' hands. In London, more than one third of former council housing stock is now rented out privately. In some cases, councils have ended up renting back housing that they have sold to meet their legal requirements to house local residents, for example, Harrow Council spent £500,000 in this way in 2014 (Lansley and Mack, 2015).

Following the 2007/08 financial crisis and recession, fewer people exercised the right to buy. The government responded by launching a 'Right to Buy Reinvigoration', increasing the subsidies available. The number of council house sales increased again, to 13,427 in 2016/17. In 2013, the Conservative–Liberal Democrat Coalition imposed a cut to housing benefit for people renting from a council or housing association who were assessed as having a 'spare' bedroom, widely known as the 'bedroom tax'. As house building has historically favoured an oversupply of three- and four-bedroom homes in order to allow for growing families, this pushed many people out of social housing and into the private-rented sector. A Housing and Planning Act was passed in 2016, which included:

- an end to 'secure tenancies' for council houses, limiting new tenancies to two to five years;
- the extension of the right to buy to housing association tenants, subsidised by forcing councils to sell off housing designated as 'high value'; and
- planning permission for new developments on 'brownfield' sites that were defined as including council estates.

This paved the way for the further privatisation of land use.

Alongside reductions in council housing, private-rented housing has also become increasingly difficult to access for large sections of the working class. In 2008, the Labour government created new arrangements for housing benefit for private-rented accommodation, called the Local Housing Allowance (LHA), and limited it to the cheapest 50 per cent of private-rented housing in a local area for a given size of household. This was further restricted to the cheapest 30 per cent in 2011. In 2013, the Overall Benefit Cap set a maximum on the total that could be claimed from all benefits, particularly affecting larger families in London and other high-rent areas. The cap was lowered in 2016, increasing the numbers affected. LHA was frozen for four years from April 2016, a cut in real terms. Shelter (2017) estimates that by 2019/20, 83 per cent of England will be unaffordable for LHA claimants. Furthermore, Shelter (2016) found that 42 per cent of landlords surveyed said that they would not rent to anyone receiving LHA and a further 21 per cent 'preferred' not to rent to them. This narrows the options for poorer sections of the working class, constraining their residential mobility and forcing them into the worst private-rented housing. In 2016, 28 per cent of private-rented homes in England failed to meet the government's Decent Homes Standard (DCLG, 2017a). A 2017 White Paper, *Fixing our broken housing market* (DCLG, 2017b), proposed relaxing regulations on house quality and size – an attempt to cram more rent-payers into the same area of land. England already has the most cramped housing in Europe, with an average of 71.9 square metres per home (Weiner, 2017). The White Paper also included measures to encourage councils to sell land to private investors and set up public–private ventures to build more private housing, as well as to make it easier to obtain compulsory purchase orders to evict leaseholders from estates in order to open the way for redevelopment for sale.

There is a long history of racialised divisions in Britain's housing, with higher rates of overcrowding and homelessness for some racialised-minority groups, a lower likelihood for migrants to access social housing, and a higher likelihood that they will be concentrated in poor-quality private-rented accommodation (Cabinet Office, 2018). Pemberton et al (2014: 19) identify contributing factors, including restrictions on eligibility, the need for short-term housing and widespread poverty, leading to an inability to pay deposits and a priority to minimise short-term costs. The Localism Act 2011 allowed councils to more narrowly define who they had a duty to house, and many councils used this to impose a requirement for a 'local connection', first proposed by Labour MP Margaret Hodge in 2007.[35] This directly discriminates against migrants, other newcomers to the area and people whose period of local residence has been disrupted by living arrangements that restrict choice in location, such as those who have spent time in women's refuges or prisons. According to the CHAIN database, which combines information from multiple agencies, during 2016/17, over half the street homeless in London had a non-UK nationality and 30.3 per cent were from an EU country in Central or Eastern Europe (GLA, 2017). Racist harassment centred around the home has also contributed to the exclusion of racialised minorities from some areas because they feel unsafe (Chahal, 2007).

Asylum seekers have been subject to particularly acute forms of differentiation in housing. A separate housing system was created in 1999 in which asylum seekers are 'dispersed', with no choice over where they are sent. They have been subject to re-dispersal to a different property with only seven days' notice, a ban on anybody staying overnight and unannounced inspections for which landlords have often been reported to let themselves in without knocking. The main priority driving dispersal has been the need to find cheap, available housing (Hewitt, 2002: 7). All seven of the areas initially chosen for dispersal were in the top 20 most deprived areas in Britain (Phillimore and Goodson, 2006: 1717). Reports were common of tenants only rarely being moved because of problems, and housing contractors getting away with blatant abuse (Boswell, 2003: 324).

For many refused asylum seekers, even the limited housing and subsistence available while their cases are being processed is withdrawn, usually with 21 days' warning at most, or, in some cases, as little as seven days due to late notification (British Red Cross, 2010). Even for those with a technical right to support, the fear of detention and deportation has forced many underground and therefore out of touch with supporting services. By keeping people under constant threat of detention and deportation, these measures have deterred many refugees from participating in public political activity and have further isolated them from resources and potential allies. Dickensen and Grayson (2018) report growing numbers of refugee families who have had all support withdrawn and have fallen reliant on local authorities under section 17 of the Children Act, often housed indefinitely in totally inadequate circumstances, for example, B&Bs with steep stairs, no stair gates for small children and no any access to cooking facilities. In just one London borough, Haringey, the council reported supporting 71 households with no recourse to public funds, including 151 children.[36]

In 2012, new asylum housing contracts were issued, concentrating provision with two multinational companies, Serco and G4S, and the smaller Clearwater (Darling, 2016). These contracts were initially worth £150 million per year, and when they came up for renewal in 2018, their value was increased, totalling £4 billion over ten years (Grayson, 2017). This represents the creation of private housing monopolies through state aid. Appearing before the Home Affairs Committee in 2013, Serco's Chief Executive for the UK and Europe, Jeremy Stafford, made clear the longer-term implications of their involvement in asylum housing, providing a foothold in the housing market. Stafford explained that the company was 'very focused on building an accommodation business.... We felt that we could establish a very good platform that we felt was scalable.... Some of the services that we develop in the United Kingdom we then go and take to other geographies' (quoted in Grayson, 2013). Following the transfer to these new providers, there were widespread reports of worsening conditions. For example, in Yorkshire and the North-East, where G4S held the contract, there were reports of subcontracted landlords evicting tenants so that they could move in a larger number of people in order to reduce costs per head, leading to forced room-sharing, families being housed in filthy and even flooded properties, a lack of basic furnishings and cooking utensils, faulty electrics, and missing or broken crockery (Grayson, 2012). A parliamentary Home Affairs Committee inquiry into asylum housing in 2017 found 'vulnerable people in unsafe accommodation ... children living with infestations of mice, rats or bed bugs, lack of health care for pregnant women ... [and] inadequate support for victims of rape and torture' (Home Affairs Committee, 2017). In 2018 G4S lost its contract for asylum housing, but Serco secured a contract for another period.

Restrictions on housing have also extended to some other immigration categories. In 2009, the Borders, Citizenship and Immigration Act imposed new restrictions on local authority housing or homelessness assistance for 'Third Country Nationals' (Dwyer and Scullion, 2014: 5). In September 2012, Housing Minister Grant Shapps and Immigration Minister Damian Green announced a campaign against 'rogue landlords' providing poor-quality housing to migrants (MHCLG, 2012), referring to 'suburban shanty towns' that it was claimed 'blight entire neighbourhoods'. This carries racialised overtones of the shanty towns of oppressed countries intruding within the imperialist heartlands. In a series of showcase raids that were joined by the ministers and media, 19 tenants were detained on immigration grounds, contradicting the claim that this initiative was driven by concern for migrants' welfare. New guidance was issued to councils, including measures to arrest undocumented migrants, force them out of their homes and criminalise those who house them. There was no mention of providing decent housing as an alternative, despite the government's own statement admitting that the only options available to many migrants is 'to either live in these outbuildings or face living on the streets' (MHCLG, 2012). This trend towards restricting access and increasing repression, begun under the Labour government, laid the groundwork for restrictions on housing as part of the Immigration Act 2014.

The Immigration Act 2014 created a restricted 'right to rent', based on immigration status, applying to all private landlords in England. Over the first 18 months of the scheme, immigration enforcement teams gained access to 10,501 homes and issued 401 landlord referral notices for letting to migrants without the right to rent. The Immigration Act 2016 increased penalties for landlords. In a survey of 912 landlords, 55 per cent said that they would be less likely to rent to people from outside the EU because of this legislation, and 43 per cent said that they would be less likely to rent to someone without a UK passport (RLA, 2017). In another survey of 1,071 landlords, 44 per cent said that this legislation would make them less likely to rent to 'People who appear to be/I perceive to be immigrants' (Shelter, 2016). At the time of an inspection of the scheme in November 2017, 'there was no mechanism by which a migrant, or any other person, who believed that they had suffered discrimination from a landlord as a consequence of RtR [Right to Rent] could report it to the Home Office' (ICIBI, 2018).

The measures described here drive refugees and migrants towards the margins of the housing market, with many forced to accept the worst slum housing or homelessness. Some practitioners we interviewed expressed concern that restricted access to housing would push more people into 'tied accommodation', linked to exploitative employment (interview P8). A worker from a Romanian organisation described people in tied accommodation living ten or 15 people in a three-bedroom house, working for as little as £5 a day, forced to hand over most of the benefits they received to their employer-cum-landlord, and with little knowledge of how to escape (interview P9). While the individuals profiting from such arrangements are clearly culpable, the state also plays a role in creating the desperation that makes people susceptible to such exploitation. There are also wider effects. For example, Reeve et al (2016) found that because of immigration checks and other increased regulation, 48 per cent of landlords were more reluctant to let to benefit claimants, and 49 per cent were more reluctant to let to homeless people. The net effect is further restrictions on the availability and quality of housing for the working class, and for racialised minorities and migrants in particular.

In the supply of housing, there are concentrations of migrant labour in construction, where they have been disproportionately affected by injuries and deaths at work (Donaghy, 2009; Warburton, 2016) and by redundancies, at double the rate of UK nationals following the 2009 downturn (Meardi et al, 2012). This represents a manifestation of the general tendency of super-exploitation, in which migrants contribute more and receive less than the average, both in terms of the wage and their ongoing access to the social product of their collective labour.

Housing plays a central role in social reproduction and has multiple implications for mobility. It helps to structure geographical mobility by offering or denying shelter in particular places. This, in turn, influences employment opportunities and creates requirements for daily mobility to and from sites of employment. Housing influences the reproduction of labour power and is the workplace for domestic labour, whether paid or unpaid. Reduced access, quality and security of housing therefore reduce workers' control over their mobility.

The crisis of the benefits system

The crisis in the benefits system has been articulated, on the one hand, through growing numbers of people resorting to 'food banks' and other types of charitable support (Lansley and Mack, 2015) and, on the other, through politicians' suggestions that benefits provide a disincentive to work. For example, on 22 April 2015, then-Prime Minister David Cameron gave a speech attacking an apparent 'welfare trap laid by Labour, paid for by hardworking taxpayers ... that destroyed aspiration [and] created resentment', and proposed in its place 'the principle of something for something, not something for nothing ... where hard work is rewarded – where we make work pay'.[37] This is typical of a wider trend in government policy in which unemployment is understood not in structural terms, but as a question of individual motivation and 'employability'. As Standing (2011: 77) says, this paves the way for 'demonising the unemployed as lazy and scroungers'.

Beatty and Fothergill (2011) trace reforms to the benefits system under the Conservative–Liberal Democrat Coalition of 2010–15 back to the 'rights and responsibilities' approach begun with Labour's New Deal in 1998. During this period, access to many forms of non-means-tested support was reduced. In 2001, 'work-focused' interviews were introduced for Income Support claimants, establishing conditions for full receipt of the benefit. In 2008, the Work Capability Assessment (WCA) was created, together with a new benefit, Employment Support Allowance, replacing Incapacity Benefit and including expectations of 'work-related activity'. The WCA was outsourced to for-profit companies, first Atos, then Maximus. The WCA has faced fierce criticism from disability campaigners and others, who argue that it is punitive and fails to take people's needs into account. Over the first six years that the WCA was in operation, the rate of attempted suicides among out-of-work disability claimants doubled, from 21 per cent to 47 per cent.[38] In 2017, the UN Committee on the Rights of Persons with Disabilities criticised the British government's failure to uphold disabled people's rights.

Entitlement for lone parents claiming Income Support has also been restricted, with reductions in the youngest child's threshold age leading support to be terminated at an earlier date. A two-child limit was introduced in 2016 for some means-tested benefits, further weakening the principle that benefits should be allocated according to need (Machin,

2018). A digital 'Universal Jobmatch' system was introduced in 2012 to monitor people's job-seeking activities, with the requirement that anybody claiming unemployment benefits must be able to prove that they had spent 35 hours each week seeking work or undertaking other activities to 'prepare for work'. This fostered an industry of private suppliers teaching courses in things like basic information technology (IT) skills and completing a CV, often made compulsory whether or not someone already possessed these skills, under threat of losing their benefits. As part of the same 'workfare' approach (Deeming, 2015), people have been forced into unwaged work as a condition of receiving unemployment benefits, providing coerced labour at no cost to hundreds of major companies, local authorities and charities.[39]

Benefit 'sanctions' were introduced as part of the 1997 Labour government's 'New Deal', whereby a person's benefits could be suspended if they 'refused reasonable employment'. Their use increased significantly from 2007 and penalties were made more severe in 2012 (Tinson, 2015). There have been widespread reports of sanctions being applied for reasons such as missing a Job Centre appointment because it clashed with a job interview or because of illness or a close bereavement, or for arriving a few minutes late because of the length of the Job Centre queue.[40] Where benefits are refused, people have a right to appeal, but a freedom of information request in 2017 revealed that staff assessing the first stage of appeals were given a target of refusing 80 per cent.[41]

A new benefit, Universal Credit, began to be introduced from 2013, replacing six means-tested benefits, spanning in-work and out-of-work benefits and including around 3.2 million people in paid employment, many of them lone parents (Brewer et al, 2017). Universal Credit has extended conditionality to those in work by creating a Claimant Commitment, whereby those working less than 35 hours per week would be:

> forced into a 'work focused' interview programme, during which the DWP [Department for Work and Pensions] will dock their payments if they fail to attend regular appointments with Job Coaches. This is expected to hit working parents and shift workers hardest, as they are less able to rearrange their working patterns and caring commitments around the DWP's schedule. (Meehan, 2017)

People with other caring responsibilities or irregular work arrangements are also likely to be affected by difficulties attending appointments at set times. For those found not to be compliant, sanctions could amount to the loss of around £70 a week, lasting three months for the first infraction, six months for a second and three years for a third.[42] The National Audit Office (2018) estimates that Universal Credit will cost more than the benefits it replaces, and that its effectiveness in moving people into work will be impossible to assess. Together, these measures have extended capital's colonisation of the time of life, discussed in Chapter 2, reducing the time available for organising or other self-directed activity and providing a pool of state-subsidised labour for capital.

As with other elements of state welfare discussed here, migrants have experienced differential treatment, and this differentiation has become more pronounced. In recent decades, benefits and pensions have become increasingly linked to earnings, which has reduced access for migrants as they tend to spend less time directly employed in Britain (Sales, 2002: 460). Figures for the 1990s showed that only 62 per cent of elderly migrant households in Britain and the North of Ireland were in receipt of pensions, compared to 88.2 per cent of elderly non-migrant households. A far greater proportion of income for migrants is dependent on stigmatised means-tested benefits than universal benefits (Morrissens and Sainsbury, 2005: 650–3). Datta et al (2007a) found that among over 400 migrants, 91 per cent were paying tax and National Insurance contributions but only 17 per cent were claiming any form of benefits despite low wages. They explain this by a stratification of rights, involving 'a complex system of eligibility depending upon a person's immigration and residency status' (Datta et al, 2007a: 418). This has been further intensified through the concept of 'earned citizenship' based on various conditions, such as English-language proficiency, the absence of a criminal record and annual income levels (Dwyer and Scullion, 2014). The result is that 'Given that migrants' access to welfare and benefits is restricted, periods of unemployment not only exacerbate their financial and economic vulnerability but also push them into taking on any job, rendering them further vulnerable to an erosion of working standards during economic downturns' (Datta, 2011: 569). Pemberton et al (2014: 22) show that increasing numbers of EU8 migrants in Britain have relied on payments from family members in their country of origin, representing a further transfer from oppressed countries to British employers. Access to services has also been restricted. For example, English lessons are only accessible to many through a referral from the Job Centre, which will only be given if someone can prove that they have the right to work.

Restricting access to welfare was viewed by the 1997–2010 Labour government as a way to reduce asylum applications, justified by the unfounded idea that many people who claim asylum are attracted by Britain's welfare provision (Vickers, 2012). Access to mainstream benefits was removed and financial support for asylum seekers assessed as at risk of destitution was established under section 95 of the Immigration and Asylum Act 1999. This support was originally set at a rate equivalent to 70 per cent of mainstream welfare benefits, but this was not updated, so that by 2013, asylum seekers were receiving only 52 per cent of the rate for British citizens (British Red Cross and Boaz Trust, 2013). A court ruling in 2014 found that 'the Secretary of State had failed to factor into the assessment of the level of support necessary for essential living needs' the cost of household goods, including washing powder, cleaning materials, nappies and formula milk, as well as non-prescription medicine, and any costs for public transport, telephone calls or writing materials.[43] In 2015, the Home Office announced further reductions to the level of support for asylum seekers with children, representing a 26 per cent cut for an adult with two children, to £110.85 a week. Refugees who secure leave to remain gain rights to take paid work and access mainstream state support, but there is evidence of widespread poverty even then (Lewis et al, 2014; Vickers et al, 2016). Delays between asylum support stopping and mainstream benefits starting are common. A worker we interviewed from a refugee charity suggested that many refugees get into debt because of this transition period, often borrowing from lenders that charge high interest or carry other obligations, leading to ongoing precarity (interview P7). They reported some benefits, such as Child Benefit and Tax Credits, often taking a year to get set up.

Differential access to benefits has also applied to EU migrants and has been used as a significant disciplinary mechanism. As Alberti (2017; emphasis in original) describes, welfare restrictions have made EU migrants' presence in Britain conditional on '*retaining worker status*'. This is consistent with a wider trend across the EU in which welfare policies have been used to limit the mobility of some EU migrants, particularly since EU enlargement in 2004 (Lafleur and Mescoli, 2018). In Britain, initial controls on benefits for migrants from the new EU countries ended in 2011 for the A8 and 2014 for the A2 but were replaced with regulations restricting access for all EU migrants. These regulations denied access to benefits for the first three months in Britain, and limited subsequent unemployment support to a maximum duration of six months in most cases, with an absolute limit of nine months. In 2013, the European Commission initiated proceedings against the British government for its continued denial of benefits to EU citizens (Dwyer and Scullion, 2014: 3). These restrictions have been backed by the deportation of EU citizens found to be without the means to support themselves or to have committed crimes that may be survival related. The number of EU migrants detained on immigration grounds increased by five times from

2010 to 2017, and in the year up to June 2017, 5,301 EU nationals were deported and 2,726 were refused entry to Britain (Home Office, 2017). EU migrants have therefore faced severe pressure to accept whatever pay and conditions employers choose to offer, and to leave Britain if unemployed for more than a short period. This is ideal from the perspective of the capitalist because it removes the costs of reproducing the labour power of unemployed workers through welfare payments, as well as due to the fact that as these migrants' countries of origin are within Europe, they remain close at hand if needed again in the future (Datta et al, 2007b: 49).

A worker with a local authority welfare rights service told us that they were often called on to support migrants who were in crisis because of problems with the benefits system (interview P8). This included migrants from inside and outside the EU, and both newcomers and people who had been living in Britain for as long as 14 years but had still failed the 'right to reside' test needed to access benefits because they could not provide the necessary documentary proof. They described the impact of regulatory changes limiting EU migrants' access to benefits:

> 'I think it's putting the pressure on families that were scraping by before. They really had the rug pulled from under them. And there isn't any kind of safety net or protection or cushion for people and its people who are in quite unstable work anyway, either contract-based, or hourly, "Turn up, you might get a job today, you might not".... There's no cushion there for them.' (Interview P8)

This shows a differential impact of the changes to benefit rules, affecting already precarious workers, further reducing people's ability to turn down work because of poor pay or conditions, or any other reason. This welfare rights worker also suggested that the complexity of the law resulted in frequent wrong decisions by state officials, leading to benefit refusals that required a tribunal to correct. Cuts to legal aid – public funding for court proceedings – have reduced working-class access to legal challenges for almost all areas of social welfare, including benefits, employment, housing (except homelessness), immigration (except asylum) and family (except in cases of domestic violence). During 2012/13, 83,000 people received legal aid in benefit cases, and following legal aid cuts, this fell to just 440 during 2016/17, a 99.5 per cent decrease.[44]

Beyond the quantitative impact of benefit cuts, the growth of conditionality has weakened the position of labour. Shafique (2018) points out that only half of unemployed people currently receive jobless benefits, compared to 80 per cent in the early 1990s. He suggests that as well as increasing financial insecurity, this 'may also encourage risk averseness for those in insecure and low paid jobs: they may see their current work as more desirable than pushing for progression or alternative jobs if it risks unemployment and interaction with a tough benefits regime' (Shafique, 2018: 49). Similarly, Greer (2016: 170) argues that the welfare reforms described in this chapter translate 'into workplace discipline through the well-known mechanism of insecurity'. He also shows how a focus on moving people into work as quickly as possible has encouraged discrimination against those seen to be harder to place in employment, and created incentives for employers to take on workers through state-subsidised schemes instead of through regular employment on full pay (Greer, 2016: 169). This creates differential configurations of mobility/immobility, which involve structured movements as part of a system of control that undermines resistance to oppression and exploitation.

Developing counter-narratives of welfare crisis

The dramatic changes to state welfare described here have provoked responses, including mass student protests in 2010, urban uprisings and Occupy camps in 2011, local tenant-led campaigns against the bedroom tax in 2013, and numerous campaigns against council cuts, sanctions and other elements of austerity, particularly during 2010–15. The extent of the crisis means that there is no easy solution, and arguably no solution within capitalism. This creates a possibility for revolutionary change, which threatens not only the ruling classes, but also the labour aristocracy described in Chapter 2. The forms that resistance has taken, and their role in shaping counter-narratives of crisis, are explored in the following.

Electoral opposition to austerity

One response to austerity that seeks to contain resistance within capitalist hegemony is evident in the revived Labour Party under Jeremy Corbyn's leadership, its various allied anti-austerity campaigns, and interventions such as Ken Loach's film *The spirit of '45*. This film portrays the expansion of state welfare in Britain from 1945 and presents this as offering solutions for 2015. Campaign group The People's Assembly against Austerity organised showings of the film around the country.

Together, these forces have promoted the idea that austerity is driven purely by Conservative Party ideology and represents a mismanagement of capitalism. This is supported by the overtures made by Shadow Chancellor

John McDonnell to the financiers of the city of London, reassuring them that their interests would be safe under a future Labour government.[45] These narratives obscure both the colonial sources of funding that made earlier expansions of British state welfare possible, for example, through the plunder of Malaya (Clough, 2014: 91), and the reliance on low-paid migrant labour within the NHS. More fundamentally, they ignore the conditions of the post-war boom, which were exceptional within capitalism's history. They present capitalist state welfare in Britain as unambiguously positive for the working class, obscuring the oppressive dimensions that have always been present, which have also been racialised. While seemingly critical of the prevailing ruling-class narrative, these narratives thus operate comfortably within the limits of the hegemonic ideas that are consistent with the continuation of imperialism.

Those who have promoted opposition to austerity through the Labour Party have played a role in limiting other forms of resistance. Comparing the periods 2010–15, under the more obviously pro-austerity Ed Miliband, and 2015–18, under Jeremy Corbyn, there has been a notable reduction in grass-roots campaigns against austerity. More privileged sections of the working class who are politically opposed to austerity have flocked to the Labour Party (Bale, 2016), but have been largely inactive outside of this, while more oppressed sections have been left struggling to survive. Together, the Conservative and Labour Parties mark out the boundaries of capitalist hegemony. Alternatives have developed that locate austerity in an attack on the working class that goes beyond party politics. So far, they have been small, and have been subject to frequent attack, but they demonstrate that it is possible to struggle beyond capitalist hegemony, in theory and in practice. This section discusses examples emerging within struggles over housing and council services.

The fight for decent housing

In London, housing campaigns have focused around opposition to 'social cleansing', discussed earlier in this chapter. Among the most high profile has been the Focus E15 campaign,[46] which began in 2013 when a group of young mothers were threatened with eviction from their hostel due to council funding cuts and joined up with local communists (Watt, 2016). The campaign has built itself around weekly street stalls where anybody can speak about their problems and perspectives using an 'open mic', together with open organising meetings. In its first year, the campaign occupied two flats on the Carpenters Estate, which had been boarded up in a bid to sell off the land to private developers, and turned them into a base for organising. Within weeks, the council announced that they would open 40 properties on the estate to house local homeless people. Other examples include the Radical Housing Network[47] and Defend Council Housing.[48]

A London housing campaigner (interview A13) highlighted the inconsistent categories used by the local state to allocate housing, such that it seemed as if people could never be in the 'right' category:

> 'When you go to the housing office, they will always say that that person is not priority, so you'll get a single mother there and they will say, "Oh, it is working families that are priority", or you'll get a working family there, and they'll say, "It's single people". Or, one person I spoke to on the street stall last Saturday ... is a single person and she says that they refused to help them get housing because he hadn't tried to commit suicide and he wasn't abusing alcohol ... but at the same time, I've met homeless people who are suicidal and they'll have drinking problems and they say, "Until you get sober you're not getting housing". So, it's something that's used to divide people from each other but also to be able to pass the buck and say there is this person who is in more need but there isn't actually anyone who is in most need according to that.'

They emphasised the importance for people directly affected by housing problems to be "at the front of the campaign" (interview A13) and to gain a political education through making demands of politicians, organising collectively and participating in collective self-education. They suggested that the main influence undermining such education was "a lot of people on the Left ... that have a lot of experience with politicians and whatever, and then one comes along like Jeremy Corbyn, and I'm not against Jeremy Corbyn, but it's taken so many people away from the struggle" (interview A13).

This highlights both the importance of maintaining focus on extra-parliamentary activity and the potential for experienced left-wing organisations to undermine militancy, a point that will be returned to in Chapter 7.

Housing campaigns have also developed outside London. For example, in Newcastle-upon-Tyne, when the 'bedroom tax' was introduced in 2013, tenants who were affected organised in several local committees, together with other activists. They combined demonstrations and meetings with support for tenants submitting appeals.[49] The council first delayed, sitting on appeals for months without passing them to a tribunal, and eventually responded with a concession, in the form of a year's worth of rent relief for tenants who had appealed. This was issued as a Discretionary Housing Payment (DHP), despite the DHP scheme having different criteria to the appeal process and some tenants who received the payment having applied for DHP and been refused while others had never even applied for DHP. At the bottom of the letter notifying tenants of the DHP payment was a slip that they were invited to return to withdraw their appeal; the letter did not explicitly say that the payment was conditional on the appeal being withdrawn, but the implication was clear. Campaigners suggested that this was simultaneously a concession and an attempt to avoid the risk that a tribunal judgement might go against the council and set a precedent that would be binding on other tenants' cases (Bell, 2014).

A Newcastle-based campaigner (interview A10) who was personally affected by the bedroom tax located the causes of government policy in the close relationship between the state and corporations, with a consequent waste of people's potential: "the governments that are … in bed together with corporations…. They're not putting people to work thinking about things … they're not using people's brains … they're not spending that money on education or to even consider how they could make new work". They suggested that progress would depend on working-class organisation, although they were conscious of the barriers to this:

> 'there's more poor than there is rich people, so the country doesn't belong to the poor people, it belongs to the rich. And it's never, ever going to belong to the poor people if poor people can't get together and say more about it and change the government's minds…. I'm not responsible for the recession that came around…. It's still going on now, have they ever coughed up and said, "Oh well, we've been taking all this money for all these years off everybody but now we don't need to take that money because it's all been paid back tenfold". I just think the whole thing's totally unfair…. The sad thing is, though, working-class people, sometimes they haven't got the time because they've been working and they're too tired to go and say anything, join a political party or a movement.' (Interview A10)

This highlights the contradiction that the people with the most personal reason to organise often face significant barriers in doing so. Other campaigners spoke about the particular impact that insecure housing has on the ability to organise:

'You can't do anything unless you have an address…. [Lack of housing] economically damages them, it's a massive stress, massive life stress. But politically it also plays the role, I think, of fragmenting communities. Fragmenting any kind of solidarity between people who live next to each other. Breaking those old bonds in certain areas.' (Interview A12)

This underlines the importance of more secure sections of the working class organising together with those most severely affected, who have so many barriers that make it difficult to fight alone.

Fighting council cuts

In many cases, trade unions have helped to manage council cuts, prioritising the avoidance of compulsory redundancies but accepting voluntary redundancies and the transfer of staff to other services despite this representing a loss of services and jobs. Many campaigns have developed in defence of services, led by service users, with people coming together around residence in the same geographical area, and, in some cases, shared needs. For example, in Newcastle-upon-Tyne, Parents against Cuts was established in 2014 to oppose plans to cut 65 per cent of funding from Sure Start children's centres across the city. Frustrated at the inactivity of the local Unison union branch, who called one protest and said that the next would be several months later, parents organised themselves.[50] Some of these parents had significant experience of organising; others had never been to a protest before. They waged a campaign that organised primarily online but carried out physical actions, including 'messy play' protests in the city centre and outside council offices, and picketed councillors' surgeries. Another campaign that developed in Newcastle soon after was Save Elswick Pool, opposing the closure of a swimming pool in one of the poorest areas of the West End of Newcastle. A campaigner in the area described how systematic state neglect of their local area had motivated them to act:

'The area [where] I live … there are a lot of financial problems and low education levels, etc. I think people very much get overlooked. It very much seems like money is more important than people's lives round here. Things like the swimming pool … it's like there's nothing left in this area for people. The council and the government do not care…. You only have to walk ten minutes that way to see how lovely the city centre is. Then, it's just absolute poverty outside the city. There is rubbish everywhere, nobody cares.... I don't think it will get better unless people rise up.... Opinions are changing. More people are getting involved who wouldn't usually touch this kind of thing, but it's nowhere near enough.' (Interview A16)

This expresses the mixture of frustration and optimism among many grass-roots activists in Britain in the current period.

Conclusion

The analysis of the imperialist crisis presented in Chapter 2 helps explain the general character of austerity, its differential effects and the various responses. Overall, austerity can be understood as a shift in the operation of the capitalist state to reduce the availability of resources that are not directly derived from waged labour while increasing social control. This intensifies pressure to submit to work on lower wages, in worse conditions and with less security because the alternative is even worse. It also disrupts resistance by keeping people occupied chasing employment, and it individualises responsibility for each worker to make themselves more attractive to employers. Disabled people have come under particular attack because the allocation of resources based on need, without any future prospect of producing surplus value, is an implicit threat to the hegemony of the law of value. Under conditions of capitalist crisis, previous concessions are being withdrawn, and disabled people are being squeezed to the point that they either perform whatever waged labour is possible, even if this is disastrous for their health, or are thrown into destitution, reliant on charity or pushed to the point where they take their own lives.

Differentiation along racialised lines has intensified as separate welfare regimes provide a useful lever to cut resources across the working class and further the super-exploitation of oppressed sections. Cuts to state welfare have deepened women's oppression because caring work will never be paid for fully by the capitalists, and when the state withdraws, it is often women who take up the burden once more, either on an unpaid basis or as low-waged labour, often performed by migrant workers. Chapter 5 explores how the state interventions discussed in Chapters 3 and 4 come together to structure waged labour, with a focus on the growth of precarity.

Notes

1 See *The Independent*, www.independent.co.uk/news/uk/politics/rachel-reeves-says-labour-does-not-want-to-represent-people-out-of-work-10114614.html

2 See: www.bsa-org.com/

3 See: www.scottishcare.org/

4 See: www.pppforum.com/

5 See: www.cbi.org.uk/business-issues/public-services/

6 See: www.nhspn.org/

7 See: www.careengland.org.uk/about-us

8 See *The Guardian*, www.theguardian.com/politics/2012/sep/06/home-secretary-police-outsourcing-g4s

9 See the *Financial Times*, www.ft.com/content/23883b48-447f-11e8-803a-295c97e6fd0b

10 See: www.gov.uk/report-immigration-crime

11 See the *Huffington Post*, www.huffingtonpost.co.uk/entry/labour-nec-illegal-council-budgets-no-cuts-councillors_uk_57e93fe3e4b004d4d86399f8

12 See *The Independent*, www.independent.co.uk/voices/nhs-funding-pfi-contracts-hospitals-debts-what-is-it-rbs-a7134881.html

13 See *The Independent*, www.independent.co.uk/news/uk/home-news/nhs-british-red-cross-chief-executive-mike-adamson-defends-humanitarian-crisis-remarks-a7516751.html

14 See *The Guardian*, www.theguardian.com/society/2017/nov/30/healthcare-rationing-what-does-nhs-england-intend-to-do

15 Whereby recipients of care are made responsible for a personal budget to buy services.

16 See, for example, *BBC News*, http://news.bbc.co.uk/1/hi/health/3356255.stm

17 See *The Independent*, www.independent.co.uk/news/uk/home-news/pregnant-and-ill-migrants-going-without-medical-care-due-to-hardline-government-immigration-policy-a8011351.html

18 See *Politics.co.uk*, www.politics.co.uk/news/2017/10/25/victory-for-campaigners-as-govt-exempts-school-nurses-from

19 A moneylender charging high fees and often operating illegally.

20 See the *Huffington Post*, www.huffingtonpost.co.uk/entry/dying-migrants-too-scared-to-see-a-doctor-for-fear-of-deportation-mps-are-warned_uk_5a5e1f26e4b0fcbc3a13c963?

21 See *The New York Times*, https://mobile.nytimes.com/2017/11/21/world/europe/nhs-brexit-eu-migrants.html

22 See *iNews*, https://inews.co.uk/news/health/nhs-doctors-blocked-coming-work-uk/

23 See *The Independent*, www.independent.co.uk/news/health/jamaica-nhs-nurse-windrush-theresa-may-amber-rudd-government-india-staff-shortage-a8318121.html

24 See *BBC News*, www.bbc.co.uk/news/health-40442848

25 Including rough sleeping, squatting, hostel/refuge/night shelter accommodation, unsuitable temporary accommodation and 'sofa surfing'.

26 See: www.emptyhomes.com/

27 Based on data from the Nationwide Building Society, adjusted for inflation.

28 See *The Guardian*, www.theguardian.com/society/2017/nov/20/one-in-seven-councillors-in-english-rental-hotspots-are-landlords

[29] See the *Financial Times*, www.ft.com/content/38968766-2c3c-11e8-a34a-7e7563b0b0f4

[30] See: https://insidelambeth1.wordpress.com; www.brixtonbuzz.com/2018/07/lambeth-labour-amends-green-party-motion-calling-for-estate-regeneration-residents-to-be-balloted/; and *The Guardian*, www.theguardian.com/commentisfree/2017/oct/25/labour-council-regeneration-housing-crisis-high-court-judge

[31] See *The Guardian*, www.theguardian.com/commentisfree/2016/dec/20/working-homeless-britain-economy-minimum-wage-zero-hours

[32] See *The Guardian*, www.theguardian.com/commentisfree/2017/sep/01/poverty-ill-health-fast-food-workers-striking-mcdonalds-shareholders

[33] See *The Guardian*, www.theguardian.com/society/2017/dec/15/homelessness-report-working-families-stable-jobs-local-government-ombudsman

[34] See: https://twitter.com/clpsolicitors/status/979299437964091392

[35] See *The Observer*, www.theguardian.com/commentisfree/2007/may/20/comment.politics

[36] See *The Independent*, www.independent.co.uk/news/uk/home-news/i-felt-like-my-life-was-being-taken-away-from-me-a7884576.html

[37] See: https://www.politicshome.com/news/uk/economy/news/63265/david-cameron-speech-making-work-pay

[38] See *Medium*, https://medium.com/@lcelliott2/in-visibility-today-gail-ward-from-disabled-people-against-cuts-501be4bc7e92

[39] See: www.boycottworkfare.org/

[40] See *The Guardian*, www.theguardian.com/society/2015/mar/24/benefit-sanctions-trivial-breaches-and-administrative-errors; see also Lansley and Mack (2015) and http://stupidsanctions.tumblr.com/

[41] See *The Independent*, www.independent.co.uk/news/uk/politics/dwp-benefit-appeals-target-reject-80-per-cent-outrageous-pip-jobseekers-allowance-department-work-a7740101.html

[42] See *The Guardian*, www.theguardian.com/commentisfree/2017/oct/24/jobless-poleaxed-universal-credit-workers-low-income-financial-penalties

[43] *R v The Secretary of State for the Home Office* (2014), http://www.bailii.org/ew/cases/EWHC/Admin/2014/1033.html

[44] See *The Independent*, www.independent.co.uk/news/uk/politics/legal-aid-cuts-benefits-cases-state-help-dla-esa-ministry-justice-disability-living-allowance-a8028936.html

[45] See *The Telegraph*, www.telegraph.co.uk/business/2018/06/13/john-mcdonnell-tells-bankers-bring-government-us/

[46] See: https://focuse15.org/

[47] See: https://radicalhousingnetwork.org/

[48] See: www.defendcouncilhousing.org.uk/

[49] See: *ChronicleLive*, https://www.chroniclelive.co.uk/news/campaigners-protest-against-bedroom-tax-6708736

[50] See: www.facebook.com/groups/668908713178049/about

5

Mobility Power and Labour Power in the Crisis of Imperialism

Introduction: labour exploitation and the crisis of imperialism

Previous chapters argued that the migration crisis and crises of state welfare should be understood in relation to the capitalist crisis. Ideological representations of these crises are facilitating changes to the state in order to shift the costs of the capitalist crisis onto the working class by material and discursive means, and to foreclose possibilities for revolutionary transformation. Increasing restrictions on migration and on state welfare are part of the same process in which the movement of workers is placed under increasingly strict discipline through differential regimes that fraction the working class in order to increase exploitation and contain the contradictions of the imperialist crisis.

This chapter examines the implications of these processes for the exploitation of labour within Britain. To reiterate a point first made in Chapter 1, the extraction of surplus value relies on control over human movement. Capital, labour and commodities must all move to function, but, more fundamentally, the transformative capacity of humans can only be realised through dynamic activity. Directing human activity to the production and capture of value requires control over its dynamism. Taylorism represented a formalisation of this control within the labour process through studies of efficiency that aimed for the elimination of 'unproductive' bodily movements (Braverman, 1998 [1974]: 62). In some types of work, this form of control continues, now enhanced through digital technologies such as the wristbands developed by Amazon that track the precise movements of warehouse employees, down to the placement of their hands, and use vibrations to nudge them in the desired direction (De Lara, 2018). Amazon workers report that those judged to be more 'productive' are given more shifts. The 'gig economy', based on tasks allocated through digital platforms, gives an appearance of workers' autonomy while implementing control and monitoring through digitised systems, and reducing workers' control over their time and mobility by extending the working day indefinitely (Drahokoupil and Jepsen, 2017). Informalised employment and self-employment makes the worker responsible for their own self-control, with material pressure to exercise this in ways that maximise surplus value for the employer/client so that they continue to receive tasks; thus, precarity enforces 'voluntary' compliance.

This chapter draws on concepts that all lie within the Marxist tradition but are rarely combined. Lenin's analysis of imperialism, presented in Chapter 2, connects inherent features of the capital-accumulation process to the development of an international system dominated by monopoly finance capital, with differential regimes of exploitation that are mediated by national states. The autonomy of migration tradition is used to explore how borders extend the differentiation of regimes beyond and across the national divide, and to view capitalist exploitation through the lens of mobility.[1] Finally, the chapter follows Marx's emphasis on the division of the working class into an active labour army (ALA) and three categories of the reserve army of labour (RAL) in order to explore the impact of bordering practices on class fractioning. While the RAL has commonly been understood as a category within which individuals can be grouped (eg Beechey, 1977; Neilson and Stubbs, 2011; Foster et al, 2011), the concept is reinterpreted here to explore differential forms of movement under constraint, not always corresponding neatly to individuals.

The next part of the chapter expands on the idea of differential regimes, and then integrates this approach with a discussion of the RAL. This is applied to empirical data regarding recent migrations to North-East England in order to develop a typology of three 'dynamics of precarity'. These dynamics are both experiential and structural, reflecting a dialectic between structure and agency and offering a reading of human experience that is attentive to immigration categories without reducing migrants to them. The chapter concludes by arguing that the changes to immigration controls and state welfare, discussed in Chapters 3 and 4, are combining with economic geography, employer practices and the balance of class forces to undermine the power of the working class as part of a major shift in class relations.

Regimes of mobility, regimes of exploitation

Jones (2016: 6) emphasises that borders produce geographical territories governed by different regulatory regimes. This has developed historically as part of nation states, using the principle of exclusive territorial authority first established in Europe by the Treaties of Westphalia in 1648 and extended via colonialism to the entire planet. Today, this differentiation does not just occur on a territorial basis. Borders have become disarticulated from national boundaries, as Mezzadra and Neilson (2013) discuss at a global scale and Chapters 3 and 4 of this book examine with regard to Britain. Through contemporary bordering, the divide between oppressed and imperialist countries 'stretches', like an elastic membrane, to cling to some of those who pass through it and maintain their separation through migrant categories. Sometimes, this membrane stretches across generations, as evident on a legal level in the uncertain immigration status of some children born in Britain to migrant parents,[2] and symbolically in the concept of 'second- and third-generation migrants'. Anderson (2010b: 306) points to the capacity of immigration controls to extend the period of 'temporariness' associated with recent arrival. In some cases, this operates directly by including time limits as a visa condition. In other cases, less direct interventions, such as restricted access to English lessons, employment, housing or welfare, sustain the duration of 'migrant-ness' and create distinct temporalities as a form of differential inclusion (Mezzadra and Neilson, 2013: 131–66; Clayton and Vickers, 2018).

As discussed in previous chapters, borders produce differential regimes that take mobility as their defining characteristic through the significance that they attach to past movements across borders, mediated by factors including personal wealth, labour demand and the position of countries of origin within imperialism. 'Mobility' can refer to 'something that moves or is *capable* of movement' (Urry, 2007: 7; emphasis in original) along a continuum of mobility–immobility. Mobility also varies in speed, rate of acceleration, tempo and consistency. Following the connections drawn by Kesserling (2014: 21) between very different types and scales of mobility, 'from the body to the globe', this chapter considers mobility in three interrelated senses: job mobility, representing movement between waged labour roles, which may also involve movement between employers or sectors; geographical mobility, representing movement between places over varying distances and sometimes encountering borders, sometimes not; and mobility within the labour process, representing the dynamic exercise of labour power, discussed previously. Within the autonomy of migration approach, borders represent a:

complex mechanism of biopolitical ordering of populations generating differentiated forms of mobility. This sorting out of people and governing of mobility [is] addressed to locals and foreigners, building a management of economic activities where issues of nationality, administrative documents, and racial politics as well as educational background and skills [are] at play. (Casas-Cortés, 2014: 216)

Borders also frequently feature mobility as part of their disciplinary mechanisms, for example, the enforced immobility of detention centres, the enforced mobility of asylum dispersal, requirements that people in asylum housing return to the property each night and the enforced mobility of deportations. Capitalist state welfare plays a parallel role, overlapping and intersecting with immigration controls as a mechanism to order populations and discipline mobility, as discussed in Chapter 4. Control over mobility in all these forms often takes its most intense and violent forms where workers move from oppressed to imperialist countries because this is the point at which there is the most abrupt disjuncture between regimes of control. The forms of differential inclusion discussed here can therefore be described as 'mobility regimes' (a term also used by Kesserling, 2014).

'Mobility power' conceptualises the ability for people to exercise control over their movement, including its form, direction and speed, offering potential for resistance to the demands of capitalist states and employers, and a way of asserting agency over one's labour power (Alberti, 2014). 'Precarity', associated with the growth of various forms of insecurity, can be understood as a reduction of mobility power, often involving enforced patterns of movement or stasis and leading to increased labour discipline. Casas-Cortés (2014: 220) cites the important influence of feminist perspectives within discussions of precarity, and argues for an approach to precarity in which 'Production and reproduction are so interwoven that it is no longer possible to speak just about precarious labor, but rather precarious life'. While still bearing in mind the strategic centrality of waged labour for capital accumulation, this chapter therefore extends consideration of precarity beyond the waged workplace to also include the relationship to unwaged labour in the home, community support and resources accessed through the state.

Precarity and mobility

Neilson and Rossiter (2008: 52) argue that 'precarity' addresses conditions of 'precarious, contingent or flexible' work, which enable exploitation but also hold potential for 'a new kind of political subject, replete with their own forms of collective organization'. As Jonna and Foster (2016) point out, Marx and Engels viewed precariousness as a fundamental feature of the working class, directly connected to the RAL. Recent changes associated with precarity are both a generalised tendency for growing numbers of people, and cluster for particular groups in particular places (Waite, 2009). Casas-Cortés (2014) traces the origins of the term in its current use to activist collectives and social movements, primarily in Central and Southern Europe, from the late 1980s. She emphasises its multiple and contested uses, understood as process, practice, performance, tendency, category, structural condition and state. Precarity also has figurative power to describe the experience of being off balance, making it difficult to predict or control one's future movements. Butler (2009: ii) makes a useful distinction between precariousness as a fundamental condition of life arising from humans' many interdependencies, and precarity as a 'politically induced condition in which certain populations suffer from failing social and economic networks of support and become differentially exposed to injury, violence, and death'. The approach here combines Butler's distinction between precariousness and precarity with a focus on capitalist exploitation through control over mobility in order to examine how certain populations have their mobility power systematically undermined and are thereby exposed to a process of exploitation that is inherently violent.

Frequent job mobility, or at least the constant threat of it, is a fundamental feature of precarity. Weak commitment by employers towards individual workers, as evident, for example, where an employer avoids investing in training because it is expected that current employees will move on in a short space of time, can contribute to insecurity. In some cases, workers may reciprocate with a lack of commitment to a job or even an entire sector. This can manifest in low levels of intensity and consistency of work, or a lack of investment in the development of job- or sector-specific skills and knowledge. Anderson (2010a: 109) suggests that 'Work which offers no opportunities for career progression may be perceived more opportunistically ... as an opportunity to get a foot on the ladder, while for migrants there may be non-pecuniary returns from work, most importantly the possibility of learning English'. This can lead workers to accept low wages and poor conditions on the basis that they expect them to be temporary (Axelsson et al, 2015). Insecurity can also put pressure on workers to engage in skills development beyond their paid hours and to work more intensively in the hope that this will solicit greater employer investment in the worker (Smith, 2006; Alberti, 2014: 866). The activist group Les Intermittents argue that intermittent work has become a more generalised condition for the working class, interspersed by periods of activity that are productive for employers but unwaged, such as 'self-training, research, non-waged modes of cooperation, productive networking, and social relationships normally associated with reproduction' (Casas-Cortés, 2014: 212). This reproduces labour power and, in cases such as self-training, may increase the productivity of labour, adding to the value produced at no cost to the capitalist. However, job mobility does not inevitably translate into precarity. As Alberti (2014) shows, in practice, the relationship between employer expectations, mobility and workers' agency is highly varied. The outcome of job mobility also depends on the degree of agency afforded to the worker regarding how, when and where to move, and the availability of other sources of support outside the waged relation.

Geographical mobility also features prominently within the literature on precarity, often implicitly, through a focus on international migrants as distinctively precarious subjects (eg Casas-Cortés, 2014; Lewis et al, 2015). Jørgensen (2016) draws on the ideas of the Frassanito network of activists to discuss the political centrality of 'the migrant' within contemporary struggles because it crystallises and foreshadows general developments in contemporary labour towards mobility and diversity. He follows this with the argument that migrants' movements across borders test the limit of capital's control and can thereby inspire and inform wider working-class struggles. The association between precarity and migrants is not necessarily borne of solidarity or sympathy – as Jørgensen (2016) points out, migrants have often been 'scapegoated as carriers of precarity', who threaten to transmit 'Third World' working conditions to imperialist countries.

Multiple factors associated with migration can be understood as contributing to precarity but do not derive inevitably from migration itself. As Anderson (2010b) argues, international structural inequalities combine with state policies to produce conditions of precarity for many migrants as part of the same process that separates workers of different countries and places them within different labour regimes (see also Wills et al, 2010; Jones, 2016). This enables super-exploitation. Paine (1977) argues that the *gasterbeiter* guest worker system, which operated in the Federal Republic of Germany between the 1950s and early 1970s, became unprofitable due to factors including migrants' improved knowledge about their legal rights, the development of organisations capable of upholding those rights and changing demographics as family members joined previously lone workers. The long-term trajectory of migration can thus undermine continued super-exploitation, particularly where there is effective solidarity and organisation.

State interventions that encourage a constant churn in the constituent members of migrant groups and promote divisions on a national basis counter the aforementioned tendencies and help to maintain precarity as a basis for super-exploitation. In some cases, states explicitly restrict the length of stay for specific immigration categories, imposing mobility in jobs and geography. In other cases, precarity emerges as the net result of multiple factors, within which the state often plays a significant role. For example, Anderson (2010b: 308) shows how age demographics and the presence or absence of family members are shaped by immigration controls, with visa requirements and restrictions on access to public funds making it more likely that migrants in some categories will be young and without dependants, increasing their capacity to work long hours, including evenings and weekends. Pemberton et al (2014: 23) survey evidence showing that lack of English proficiency increases vulnerability to exploitation, but that 'migrants' ability to attend English language classes is frequently restricted by the need to work long shifts and overtime in order to earn a living wage', and that access is often further restricted by lack of access to affordable and flexible childcare. In England, government funding for English-language classes was cut by 60 per cent between 2010 and 2016 (Refugee Action, 2017). A Romanian organisation that set up free English classes available to everybody was quickly inundated by people from a wide array of countries, including Romania, Sudan, Iran, Eritrea, Egypt and Venezuela, who had been unable to access classes anywhere else (interview P9). Reduced access to state welfare because of immigration status also contributes to precarity, as discussed in Chapter 4. Precarity is therefore not inherent to migrants, but emerges because of immigration policies and other factors that influence processes of integration.

Within a labour process frame, precarity can be theorised as the net effect of a set of conditions that shift power towards capital in order to 'stretch' labour and increase absolute surplus value through more intensive work and longer hours, and to increase relative surplus value by reducing wages. Within this struggle between labour and capital, mobility represents 'a double terrain of control and resistance against the precarious conditions of life and work' (Alberti, 2014: 878). The decisive question is not whether mobility occurs, but under whose direction and the extent to which it is shaped by the interests of labour or capital. Mobility power may be employed by workers to remain stationary, just as it may be exercised to move. This is consistent with Lewis et al's (2014) definition of precarity through a continuum of unfreedom, but it focuses attention more specifically on freedom to decide whether, how, where and when to move.

Understanding precarity's differential forms calls for a re-coupling of class analysis and labour process analysis (Neilson, 2007). Marx's distinction between the ALA and the categories of the RAL, and their role in shaping the labour process, enables such a re-coupling, as addressed in the next section.

The RAL and the structural conditions of precarity

> One of the peculiarities of post-recession Britain is that there has been significant employment growth without a corresponding growth in pay. While the relationship between pay and productivity is clearly relevant, a further possible factor in this is the extent of hidden 'slack' or unused labour in the economy, partly driven by the growing reserve labour of those in non-standard (often insecure) work, such as the self-employed and over one million people on zero-hour contracts. This makes it relatively easy for companies to add or replace workers to meet production goals, and difficult for workers to request more pay, thereby depressing wages. (Shafique, 2018: 45)

This account illustrates the significance of the RAL for contemporary Britain. Marx (1967 [1890]) argues that capital accumulation necessarily produces a relative surplus population, or RAL. Marx (1967 [1890]: 592) assigns the RAL the importance of 'a condition of existence of the capitalist mode of production', disciplining the ALA through competition, forcing workers 'to submit to overwork and to subjugation under the dictates of capital' (Marx, 1967 [1890]: 595), and determining overall wage levels to the extent that 'the general movements of wages are exclusively regulated ... by the varying proportions in which the working-class is divided into active and reserve army' (Marx, 1967 [1890]: 596). The RAL–ALA composition is thus central to the labour–capital relation. Marx makes these comments with reference to capitalism as a whole, where the imperative to discipline labour operates irrespective of the immediate needs of individual capitalists or the stage of the economic cycle. While Marx's use of the RAL stops at this level of abstraction, Foster et al (2011) and Mandel (1975: 59) link the international distribution of the RAL to differences in national wage rates. The analysis of borders presented earlier in this book suggests that if the RAL–ALA composition can differ between national sections of the working class, then it could also differ according to other divisions across and within territorial boundaries. This can be applied to understand the structural conditions of precarity and its uneven prevalence across the working class.

Historically, the RAL expanded through the internationalisation of capital as new parts of the world and their inhabitants were drawn into capital's 'field of action' (Pradella, 2013). As Foster et al (2011: 5) argue:

> The new imperialism of the late twentieth and twenty-first centuries is ... characterized, at the top of the world system, by the domination of monopoly-finance capital, and, at the bottom, by the emergence of a massive global reserve army of labor. The result of this immense polarization, is an augmentation of the 'imperialist rent' extracted from the South through the integration of low-wage, highly exploited workers into capitalist production. This then becomes a lever for an increase in the reserve army and the rate of exploitation in the North as well.

This connects to the discussion of imperialist super-profits discussed in Chapter 2. The RAL illuminates the relationship between the shift in production to oppressed countries, where the RAL–ALA ratio is much higher, and the lack of investment in Britain, contributing to sluggish productivity growth.[3] There is less incentive to invest in more mechanised production methods in imperialist countries when there is a ready supply of low-waged labour in oppressed countries.

Foster et al (2011) estimate the extent of the RAL globally, including those in the prime working ages of 25–54 who are unemployed, 'vulnerably employed' (informal workers who would be available for regular waged work) or economically inactive, and arrive at a figure of 2.4 billion people, compared to 1.4 billion in the ALA. Using slightly different measures and an age range of 15+, Neilson and Stubbs (2011) estimate 2.9 billion. Such estimates are inevitably approximate given the varying availability and quality of data, but they nevertheless indicate the relative scale of spare capacity in the global workforce. This is one of the great contradictions of capitalism: while so many people's needs go unmet, millions of people's creative potential is wasted. Both of the aforementioned estimates exclude part-time workers, which Marx (1967 [1890]: 593) includes in the RAL as 'half-employed hands'. The World Trade Organisation (WTO), World Bank and International Monetary Fund (IMF) predict further expansions in the global RAL, driven by the expected replacement of more than 3 billion rural unwaged workers by 20 million modern farmers, with the remainder becoming surplus. When Britain went through a similar process between 1820 and 1915, 16 million people emigrated, equivalent to half the net increase each year (Foster et al, 2011: 18–20). This was made possible through colonialism. No such opportunities exist today. Instead, the high RAL–ALA ratio in oppressed countries has enabled special conditions of exploitation, as discussed in Chapter 2.

Foster et al (2011) emphasise that the RAL's impact on wages relates principally to the working class as an organic whole, rather than one section depressing the wages of another section. Migrants from oppressed countries have often been described as an RAL for imperialist countries (eg Castles and Kosack, 1973; Wills et al, 2010). However, as Miles (1986) points out, many of those who migrate were in work prior to migration, contradicting their characterisation as an RAL en masse. A more empirically grounded and nuanced application of the RAL to migration might be achieved by considering the impact of borders in creating class fractions with differing RAL–ALA distributions, and viewing the RAL as representing variations in the worker–capital relation rather than static categories. This approach can be further developed by considering the specific categories of the RAL.

The forms of the RAL

Marx (1967 [1890]: 600–3) outlines different forms of the RAL, which he names 'floating', 'stagnant' and 'latent'. It is interesting to note that the words Marx uses for these categories all evoke a sense of mobility/immobility. These categories are mentioned only in passing, if at all, in many discussions of the RAL, but they offer a useful framework to explore the variety of forms of human mobility in relation to capital. Their relation to one another and to the ALA and capital is outlined in Figure 5.1, and explained further throughout the rest of this chapter.

Floating

Marx (1967 [1890]: 600) defines the floating category as comprising workers 'sometimes repelled, sometimes attracted again', as part of the cycle of capitalist production or because of technological change. Whereas Anthias (1980: 51) defines the RAL as 'synonymous with the unemployed', I follow Foster et al (2011) and Magdoff and Magdoff (2004) in applying

Figure 5.1: The RAL–ALA composition

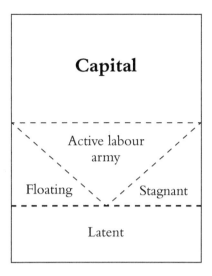

the RAL to a variety of conditions that represent, from the point of view of the capitalist, spare capacity, 'a mass of human material always ready for exploitation' (Marx, 1967 [1890]: 592). As Foster et al (2011: 17–18) say: 'From capital's developmental standpoint, the vulnerably employed are all potential wage workers – grist for the mill of capitalist development'. The floating category can therefore include all those currently looking for work, whatever their reasons, including, for example, temporary workers constantly on the lookout for the next job. In mobility terms, this implies a state of tension, awaiting unpredictable demands to move. In a figurative sense, 'floating' implies the lack of a firm foundation, contrasted to 'standing', and a lack of self-direction, contrasted to 'flying'.

By including those workers who shift between periods of insecure work and unemployment, and who are consequently acutely aware of their 'replaceability' (Wills et al, 2010: 100–1), the floating category can help explain the role of precarious work, as well as unemployment, in shifting the balance of forces against labour. Insecurity can take forms such as those identified by Datta et al (2007a) among migrants in London, where low wages and high costs of living create pressure to take more than one job, and to constantly search for alternative work. Such conditions make it easier for employers to repeatedly reinforce the existing terms of waged labour (Braverman, 1998 [1974]: 96), and to cheapen costs by recruiting new workers on worse terms, removing the need to renegotiate terms with existing employees (Magdoff and Magdoff, 2004). The floating category therefore has relevance for tendencies produced by immigration policies, as discussed in previous chapters, towards concentrations of precarious work among some sections of workers, such as Polish migrants, and high rates of unemployment among others, such as refugees, and highlights connections between their structural locations.

Stagnant

Marx (1967 [1890]: 602) defines the stagnant category of the RAL as:

> part of the active labour-army, but with extremely irregular employment. Hence it furnishes to capital an inexhaustible reservoir of disposable labour power. Its conditions of life sink below the average normal level of the working class; this makes it at once the broad basis of special branches of capitalist exploitation.

The stagnant category is associated with forms of movement that maximise labour time while minimising wage rates. Foster et al (2011) interpret the phrase 'below the average normal level of the working class' to mean wages below the value of labour power. They suggest that, historically, 'This included all sorts of part-time, casual (and what would today be called informal) labor.... The largest part of this stagnant reserve army was to be found in "modern domestic industry", which consisted of "outwork" carried out through the agency of subcontractors' (Foster et al, 2011: 8–9). Such work continues for many people globally, particularly women and especially, though not exclusively, in oppressed countries (Mohanty, 2003: 163). It is accompanied by other forms of 'outwork', such as gang labour (Wilkinson et al, 2009). Within Britain, the stagnant category might also include cash-in-hand or informal work, such as many hand carwashes overwhelmingly staffed by migrants (Clark and Colling, 2018), zero-hours contracts (Grady, 2017), certain kinds of 'self-employment' (Fleming, 2017) or labour within prisons and immigration detention centres (Bales and Mayblin, 2018). In mobility terms, this represents highly constrained movements that offer a disproportionately small reward (for workers) relative to the expended effort. Figuratively, 'stagnant' recalls a swamp, implying both unpleasant conditions and a sense of restricted and exhausting conditions for movement.

The conditions described by the stagnant category may result at the extreme of contemporary trends, discussed in Chapter 2, which involve 'the intensification of labour processes and the tendency for work to colonise the time of life' (Mezzadra and Neilson, 2013: 21). Farris argues that the RAL is not applicable to migrant women in EU15 countries because of their high employment levels, based on the same identification Anthias makes between the RAL and the unemployed. Yet, the 'unsafe contexts' that Farris (2015: 19) describes for migrant women in the care and domestic sector, 'without contract regulations, health and social benefits, and ... very exploitative working conditions', are reminiscent of the 'extremely irregular' conditions ascribed by Marx to the stagnant category. Farris (2015: 18) argues that migrants who perform 'labour-intensive and non-relocatable human services' are 'less classically "disposable"', but this is contradicted by the high rates of staff turnover, estimated at 27.8 per cent for England's adult social care workforce in 2016/17 (Skills for Care, 2017). From capital's perspective, workers may be simultaneously disposable as individuals and indispensable as a collective pool of labour power. The existence of the RAL creates conditions for individual disposability despite structural reliance by providing replacements for individuals, and the RAL–ALA distribution shapes the extent of their disposability. This is modified by subjective factors, the most important of which is collective organisation to resist the expulsion of individuals from jobs or territories.

Latent

Marx (1967 [1890]: 602) includes in the latent category those distanced from waged work but potentially available, representing 'a constant latent surplus population, the extent of which becomes evident only when its channels of outlet open to exceptional width'. Marx gives the example of those forced off the land due to increasingly centralised private ownership. Today, the latent category might include the 'economically inactive',[4] prisoners not undertaking waged work and those excluded from employment because of immigration status. It is distinct from the other categories of the RAL in that there are no expectations of imminent engagement in waged labour, and is therefore a 'reserve' in the fullest sense. This means that it is not immediately interchangeable with the ALA, does not compete directly for work and therefore can be expected to exert a less direct pressure on wages. However, its boundaries are changeable, and variations in the latent category can have important implications for labour–capital relations. Anthias (1980: 51; emphasis in original) limits the RAL to workers who are socially constituted as part of the labour force, rather than 'merely *physiologically available* labour'. Yet, the separation of the latent category from the ALA, to a greater degree than the floating or stagnant categories, suggests that we could include in the latent category labour that is currently outside the socially constituted labour force, such as those excused from waged work due to social conventions around age or disability but who could be made to work if these norms changed.[5] In mobility terms, the latent category is characterised by stasis with regard to the labour process, although it may involve other forms of productive mobility outside the wage relation. Figuratively, it implies a limp passivity and a removal from the public realm that reflects the primacy given to waged labour under capitalism.

The latent category has been widely applied to women's unpaid caring and domestic work on the basis that such reproductive labour stands outside the wage relationship, and so from the perspective of capital, represents spare labour capacity (Adamson et al, 1976). Humphries (1983: 13) reflects on agricultural labourers as part of the latent army, and their periodic usefulness to capital, with significant implications for migration:

> Agricultural migrants initially are perfect members of the latent reserve since not only are they attracted to industrial employment without any increase in existing wages (i.e. available in elastic supply) but also during periods of reduced demand for labour they can be persuaded to drift back to their native villages thus reducing the cost of recession to capital, which one way or another is partially responsible for the otherwise bloated welfare rolls and escalated costs of maintaining urban law and order in the face of high unemployment and mass deprivation. But over time rural migrant labour loses these happy qualities. Migration becomes increasingly permanent for larger numbers of people and extends intergenerationally.

This demonstrates: (1) the potential for movement back and forth between categories of the RAL–ALA over time; (2) the benefits for capitalism of mechanisms to induce such movements according to changing labour demand; and (3) the problems facing the state in accommodating the RAL within Britain.

The categories of the RAL–ALA are not static, but rather represent an underlying structure of labour interacting with capital. More than one category may apply to the same individual simultaneously, across different parts of the time of life. The categories of the RAL–ALA are characterised by different forms of movement and their overall composition sets the objective conditions for mobility power. A diversity of mobility regimes, associated with RAL–ALA distributions that vary between class fractions, creates conditions for a multitude of conditions of labour whose concrete form must be empirically established. In the next section, a case study of new migrants in North-East England is used to further explore varieties of precarity, and the interaction between borders, regional and local characteristics, and individual subjectivities.

The role of (im)mobility in everyday precarity in North-East England

North-East England, as defined by the Office for National Statistics, includes the significant urban areas of Newcastle, Sunderland and Middlesbrough, smaller yet historically important centres like Durham, coastal settlements, and considerable rural areas. Regional characteristics include relative geographic isolation from other urban centres, a history of distinctive work-based identities, socio-economic peripheralisation (Tomaney and Ward, 2001) and intra-regional inequalities (Hudson, 2005). There is a long history of migration to and from the region, as well as racialised-minority communities, although limited in numbers compared to some parts of Britain and often concentrated around the region's ports and some industries built on migration (Renton, 2007; Vickers, 2012). Despite these histories, the North-East has often been portrayed as England's quintessential 'white highlands' (Nayak, 2003).

Since the late 1990s, the region has become more diverse by ethnicity and country of origin. For example, the number of residents recorded in the Census as born in Eastern Europe increased by 359 per cent between 2001 and 2011, and the number of residents born in Africa increased by 112 per cent, arriving through a variety of migration routes, including the forced dispersal of asylum seekers since 1999. Our survey of 402 migrants arriving since 1999 found people from 57 different countries. Altogether, people born outside Britain and the North of Ireland accounted for around 5.2 per cent of the region's population by 2014 (ONS, 2015a). Migrant settlement has been unevenly spread, with major urban areas such as Newcastle and Middlesbrough receiving larger numbers, while some smaller centres such as the town of Berwick have become home to significant numbers relative to their total population.

Former industries associated with shipbuilding and coalmining have experienced long-term decline, leading to a low-waged economy dominated by service sector and public sector employment, alongside high-tech industries and a shortage of highly qualified workers (Stenning and Dawley, 2009). In recent years, the region has experienced the economic crisis and austerity more severely than many other parts of Britain (Jarvis et al, 2013; Clayton et al, 2016). The employment rate for the region between February and April 2015 was 4.4 per cent below the average for Britain and the North of Ireland, and the official unemployment rate in November 2015 was the highest of any region, at 8.8 per cent (ONS, 2016b). In 2014, the region had the lowest average gross disposable household income in Britain, at £15,189 a year (ONS, 2016a).

The intersection of this regional context with migrant categories associated with low-paid precarious work suggests the possibility for particularly severe forms of precarity. Regional data on refugee employment are sparse (Crossley and Fletcher, 2013), and administrative data and sources, such as the Labour Force Survey (LFS), do not identify refugees with leave to remain and tend to under-represent migrants due to housing patterns. Research on European Union (EU) migrants' employment in the region has focused largely on Polish workers (eg Fitzgerald, 2005; Stenning and Dawley, 2009; Fitzgerald and Smoczynski, 2017), and identifies widespread low pay and insecurity.

Labour-related (in)security as an indicator of precarity

The International Labour Organisation (ILO) conceptualises seven forms of labour-related security, outlined by Standing (2011: 17). These offer useful indicators of precarity, and thereby of mobility power; each of its forms is discussed in the following and our data from North-East England are used to indicate differences associated with migration histories and categories.

Labour market security refers to the availability of work that is within a person's abilities and viable given other commitments, that is, not only formally available, but accessible in practice. Among survey respondents who were not prohibited from working, rates of sustained worklessness varied widely, as shown in Figure 5.2.

The figures shown in Figure 5.2 are comparable to previous research.[6] The LFS for 2014–15 shows 32 per cent of the region's general workforce not in work in the survey week, although these figures are not directly comparable because our survey represents people out of work for at least a year. A total of 89 per cent (*n* = 196) of our survey respondents who were currently out of work said that they would like a paid job. This suggests that the relatively low levels of employment within parts of the sample indicate a lack of available work, or weak labour market security, rather than a preference not to work.

Employment security represents protections against dismissal, with indicators including levels of agency and self-employment, which are often associated with weaker protection (Fitzgerald, 2005; Sporton, 2013). A total of 14 per cent (*n* = 14) of UK jobs reported in the survey were paid

Figure 5.2: Not in paid work in Britain in the previous 12 months

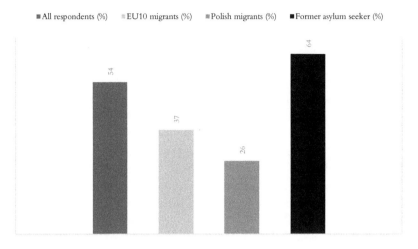

via an agency. This may be an under-reporting given that some agency work is classified as self-employment (Anderson, 2010b), and taking into account Fitzgerald's (2005) findings that many migrants in the region were uncertain about who their employer actually was. A total of 23 per cent (*n* = 38) of respondents' jobs in Britain were self-employed, compared to 11 per cent of the general North-East workforce (LFS), and these were overwhelmingly lower-paid and lower-status roles, such as cleaning, washing cars, painting and decorating, and various types of kitchen work.

Job security indicates the ability to retain a niche in employment through a recognition of distinctive skills, and to progress in status and income. The most common UK work roles reported by survey respondents are shown in Figure 5.3.

Figure 5.3: Most common reported work roles

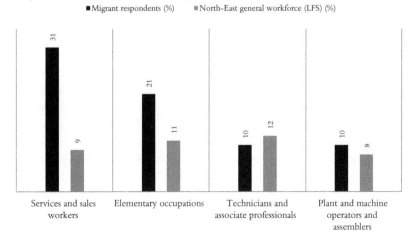

Roles taken disproportionately by migrant respondents are typically described as 'unskilled', and therefore constitute a weak basis for job security. While there were indications that some were able to progress over time, many remained 'stuck' in these same roles.

Skill reproduction security refers to opportunities to gain and maintain skills. In our survey, a lack of recognition for skills and qualifications gained outside Britain or difficulties accessing British qualifications was the second most frequently reported barrier to work among those not prohibited from working due to their immigration status (13 per cent, $n = 17$).[7] The National Recognition Information Centre (NARIC) identifies and validates British equivalents for qualifications gained in another country, but people must apply individually and practitioners reported that high fees were a significant barrier for many, if they were even aware that NARIC existed. Many respondents reported barriers to accessing education, including a lack of childcare, long working hours and, for refugees with limited leave to remain, a lack of access to student loans.

Income security represents the assurance of an adequate stable income. A total of 73 per cent ($n = 82$) of the jobs that respondents reported paid below the 2015 living wage of £7.85 an hour. Late payment of wages was also an issue, with 23 per cent ($n = 30$) of people who answered this question saying that they had been paid late at least once in the last year. There was also evidence of deductions by employers such that the money that workers received was below the minimum wage. Unpredictability of hours was a concern for some, often linked to agency work, adding to the unpredictability of income. A total of 60 per cent ($n = 221$) of respondents said that their income was not enough to cover necessities. There was evidence of limitations in access to state welfare that went beyond formal restrictions. This was particularly acute for some countries of origin, for example, 46 per cent ($n = 39$) of EU10 migrants reported having welfare applications refused and 49 per cent ($n = 43$) reported delayed payments. A welfare rights worker suggested that these figures for support being refused were "probably just the tip of the iceberg", with "a lot of maladministration, misinformation, bad decision-making" (interview P8).

Representation security encompasses trade union rights and membership, and other forms of collective representation. A total of 12 per cent ($n = 39$) of respondents had been members of a trade union before moving to Britain, and 13 per cent ($n = 16$) of those who had been in paid employment/self-employment in the last year reported currently belonging to a trade union, compared to 33 per cent of all North-East employees (BIS, 2015). Interviews identified voluntary sector organisations playing a role in collective representation (see also Holgate et al, 2012; Fitzgerald et al, 2013), including two organisations staffed by individuals with trade union experience. However, their resources were very limited, and 54 per cent (*n* = 183) of survey respondents said that they were not aware of any organisation that could offer advice or support relating to employment or self-employment.

Work security refers to protection against accidents and illness at work. We did not include questions on this in our survey, but qualitative interviews provided examples of work practices that contributed to poor health, leading to worklessness and poor levels of protection. For example, a community worker with a Romanian organisation described people working in takeaways on a 'self-employed' basis without health and safety training, and receiving burns and other injuries with no rights to compensation (interview P9). In another part of the region, a Polish migrant, Henryk, described a previous job working with chemicals without a mask or adequate ventilation, which left him with lasting health problems. In many other cases, interviewees reported poor mental health, often connected directly to immigration policies and/or experiences at work. The impact of unsafe conditions is compounded by restrictions in accessing disability benefits, discussed in Chapter 4, leading to weak work security.

Together, these findings indicate low levels of labour-related security among new migrants who participated in the survey, in some respects, significantly worse than the general workforce of the region. Practitioners with extensive experience working with migrants suggested that these findings reflected patterns they had witnessed, suggesting relevance beyond those who participated in the survey. This supports an association between these migrant categories and precarity.

These findings can be partly explained by the motivations for migration and the differential rights and restrictions determined by immigration status, which combine to influence the point of entry to the labour market. For example, Lewis et al (2014) identify multiple and overlapping 'pathways to precarity' among refugees and asylum seekers at a micro level, involving varying combinations of socio-legal status, family obligations that may be transnational, vulnerabilities that pre-dated refugees' arrival in Britain, their social position as a migrant within Britain, limited social networks, gendered divisions of labour in waged and unwaged settings, insecure accommodation, lack of access to money and state welfare, fear of deportation, and language barriers. In addition, the compulsory dispersal of asylum seekers to areas chosen because of the availability of low-cost housing, discussed in Chapter 4, means that, in many cases, refugees who secure leave to remain enter the labour market resident in poor localities with limited employment opportunities. Long waits for asylum also have an impact on skill depreciation and mental health, and mean that many refugees enter the labour market as long-term unemployed. The difficulties that this creates are compounded by the abrupt change in entitlements and expectations after securing status, also discussed in Chapter 4. EU citizens enjoy greater formal freedom of movement, but respondents' accounts showed that this can also be constrained by formal and informal networks. Instances were identified in which recruitment agencies and social contacts channelled migrants geographically and occupationally, in some cases, replicating the disadvantaged positions of previous migrants. Cases were also encountered where EU migrants felt that returning to their country of origin was not an option, further calling into question assumptions that EU citizens' migrations are entirely voluntary.

Difficulties accessing language classes contributed to precarity for many migrants who were not already fluent in English. This cut across immigration categories, although it was influenced to some extent by differences in funding entitlements associated with status. Limited confidence in English both led to concentrations in types of work where language was not important, which tended to be lower paid and less secure, and limited workers' knowledge about their rights. An experienced trade union organiser described companies asking workers to sign documents without checking that they understood what they were signing (interview P2). Another worker with a voluntary sector organisation supporting migrants at work described some employers as showing a preference for workers with more limited knowledge of English because they were thought to be less likely to know their rights and therefore easier to manage (interview P12).

Some respondents managed to make a positive and strategic use of their mobility and temporariness, particularly among EU migrants, but for others, mobility was severely constrained. Self-employment was often seen as a route away from precarity, but for the majority, this was more aspirational than actual. There was some evidence of more collective strategies, including workplace organisation and strategies to combat discrimination. However, in most cases, mobility power was exercised more narrowly, at the level of the individual or the family, to move on occupationally and sometimes geographically in search of better conditions or perceived opportunities. This is consistent with Lewis et al's (2014) research, which found widespread reports of resistance to exploitative conditions, particularly in the form of workers demanding money that had been withheld, but also found that resistance was usually individualised, organising was actively discouraged and threatened, and, in many cases, the final act of resistance was to leave the job, often resulting in lost pay and movement to another job that may be just as exploitative. They identified nascent forms of solidarity, but operating in extremely difficult conditions.

Social relations and precarity

The conditions of labour-related insecurity described in this chapter cannot be understood in isolation. As Shafique (2018: 17) says:

> economic insecurity relates to more than an individuals' experience of work. It can impact and be impacted by a broad range of factors, from health through to family relationships and financial wealth. Insecurity is mediated through our household circumstances ... and the premise of many public services is to in effect moderate insecurity through both service provision and financial transfers. (See also Standing, 2011: 19–20)

Wider social relations can influence how particular working conditions are experienced, as well as the pressures on individuals to accept poor conditions. Precaritisation is thus 'linked to work and working conditions, but somehow going far beyond the field of work', connecting with diverse fields, including 'housing, women's rights, education, health, social rights, culture, mobility and migration' (Trimikliniotis et al, 2016: 1038). For example, Lewis et al's (2014: 70) research found that a 'lack of family or trusted social contacts, and limited knowledge of UK systems, rights and protections ... contributed to [some refugees and asylum seekers] feeling they had no choice but to agree to substandard work'. This isolation was deepened further for some by long working hours that left little time and energy to form relationships outside work. In our research, we found that the relatively small numbers of recent migrants within the region limited support networks based on shared ethnicity or country of origin; however, where such networks did exist, they played an important role. Other sources of support were limited, in some cases, by restrictions on state support and by informal discrimination.

Reports of discrimination were widespread among respondents, adding to their precarity through increased isolation and informal barriers to action against employers. Out of those who had been in paid employment in the last 12 months, 127 answered a question about workplace discrimination connected with their country of origin or immigration status. The results are shown in Figure 5.4.

Such a high prevalence of experiences of discrimination is supported by the Race at Work survey (Ashe and Nazroo, 2016), which included 24,457 responses and found that 30 per cent of those surveyed had witnessed or experienced racist harassment or bullying from managers, colleagues, customers or suppliers in the previous year. In our survey,

Figure 5.4: Experiences of discrimination in the UK in the previous 12 months

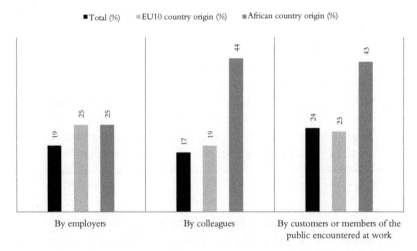

Note: Other country-groups are not given due to small numbers.

the differences between the proportion of migrants from EU10 and African countries who experienced discrimination raise questions about how different forms of racism are at play in interactions with employers, colleagues and customers, which cannot be fully explored using our data. Although perceptions of discrimination varied widely among interviewees, some gave powerful accounts of discrimination operating formally and informally within the workplace:

> 'you can see it by the type of contract or agreement that they are given, the people from outside the UK would be given temporary contracts or work for an agency, while people from the UK would get an agreement with the company much easier. Also ... you could just see it from the other ways of treatment, so if she [a migrant] would just stand about a little [having a rest], then she would be told off for it, also by other British employees, whereas the British employees could do the same, stand for a while, have a coffee for example and ... it would not be commented.' (Julia, 30s, arrived from Poland in 2010)

This suggests differing expectations of sustained productive mobility within the labour process. Some other respondents described the workplace as a source of solidarity against discrimination encountered outside work.

A trade union organiser suggested that some perceived discrimination is due to misunderstandings (interview P2); while it is impossible to be sure about the motivations of people who are perceived as discriminating, it seems likely that the wider climate of hostility to migrants, discussed in Chapters 3 and 6, influence interpersonal interactions and interpretations in multiple ways, contributing to isolation.

Variations in the concrete forms of precarity have important implications for how the general tendencies described earlier are experienced and responded to, and what they represent in terms of RAL–ALA composition. This is explored in the next section.

Dynamics of precarity

The concentrations of labour-related and social insecurity described earlier in this chapter suggest low levels of mobility power within the labour process. 'Mobility differentials' (Alberti, 2014) were also evident, depending on respondents' social position. State policy, and the immigration categories that it assigned to individuals, had a major influence on respondents' mobility power and their relationship to the categories of the RAL–ALA, but was not the sole determinant. For example, there were indications that success in turning down 'bad jobs' and finding a 'better' job differed according to factors that also included employment status, age, 'race', gender, educational background, responsibility to family members and access to local and transnational support networks (also Alberti, 2014; Bloch and McKay, 2016). Lewis et al (2014) argue that these differences produce extremes of unfreedom that cannot be captured by 'precarity', and use the term 'hyper-precarity'. Precarity certainly varies by degree, and also qualitatively.

In this section, qualitative differences are considered through three 'dynamics of precarity': (1) the surplus worker; (2) the rooted worker; and (3) the hyper-flexible worker. This typology is not intended to encompass all forms of precarity, to correspond perfectly to any individual or to imply a uniformity of experience, but rather to make sense of emerging trends. Key influences within each dynamic can be identified in interactions of state and employer policies and practices, social relations within and beyond the workplace, and individual agency, within a context that has international, national, regional and local dimensions.

The surplus worker

'Surplus' movements are those currently unneeded by capital *as labour*, leading to a disconnect from the labour process that is often accompanied by a subjective experience of feeling 'unwanted' or unable to 'contribute'. This dynamic is characterised by severely restricted mobility power, in terms of geography, jobs and the labour process, leading to a state of subjection that can result in immobility but also contains the potential for rapid enforced mobility: today's unwanted labour is also a reserve for the possible needs of tomorrow. This dynamic is emblematic of the situation for many asylum seekers, having experienced forced migration across borders followed by forced dispersal within Britain, and legally prohibited from moving into work or moving geographically away from their assigned housing. In our research, there were also many reports of migrants, across all immigration categories, finding it impossible to continue with their previous career, or, indeed, to access any work at all, because of a lack of recognition of skills, experience and/or qualifications gained outside Britain. Even skilled workers can thus be rendered surplus within the regional labour market. This dynamic can also result from health conditions that severely limit job mobility and consequently deny the financial resources necessary for further geographical mobility. Restricted access to out-of-work or disability benefits because of immigration status can intensify the impact of worklessness. Limited employment opportunities within the region compound limited geographical mobility's impact on job mobility.

The frustration felt by many asylum seekers at being prohibited from working was expressed by Amina, who arrived in Britain from Pakistan in 2010:

> 'It was really hard because a person who used to work and who never asked for anything … it becomes really very difficult when you suddenly realise that now you just have to ask for help…. If I need to buy clothes for my daughter, for example, I'll just think, "Oh my god how I will save some money…. I'm just getting five pounds a day". It's so hard.'

Amina reported engaging in voluntary activities, including highly skilled work and long hours, which represent a mobilisation of labour power. Yet, because it is unwaged, this mobilisation of labour power does not grant an entitlement to resources that could directly reduce precarity or confer equivalent status to if the same work was paid. Practitioners and activists described multiple cases of refused asylum seekers working for as little as

£1 an hour in restaurants as a necessity for survival (interviews P5, A5). This represents a clandestine mobilisation of labour power that may be an economic necessity but comes at the price of an even more precarious legal situation that can make it difficult to challenge exploitation due to the risk of discovery and deportation (Lewis et al, 2014). As De Genova (2010: 38–9) argues, 'deportability' can create conditions for extremes of exploitation.

This dynamic leaves people heavily reliant on non-waged forms of support. Depending on their immigration status, access to state support may be limited, and universal services such as libraries and children's services have been severely curtailed by public and voluntary sector cuts, discussed in Chapter 4. Social support is often limited, as discussed earlier in this chapter. Bloch (2014) found that the fear of deportation led many refused asylum seekers to rely heavily on family, faith or community contacts for support, rather than seeking support from the state or even charities. In some cases, this included non-monetary exchanges of domestic labour for food and accommodation, which enabled people to survive but could lead to exploitation. The dynamic of the surplus worker corresponds closely to the latent and stagnant categories of the RAL, and shows the interplay between them, as people are positioned into states of subjection involving extremely exploitative forms of work, both waged and unwaged.

The rooted worker

'Rooted' forms of movement arose from social or cultural attachments outweighing the demands of the labour market to move geographically. This dynamic is characterised by participation in waged labour but with limited geographical mobility. In some cases, this resulted from mobility power exercised to remain stationary to pursue non-economic goals. In other cases, caring responsibilities or other non-waged commitments constrained geographical mobility. For some, further geographical mobility would have improved employment opportunities but posed other costs, such as the loss of support networks and community.

Leaving North-East England was seen by many interviewees as a precondition for accessing better-paid, higher-status and less precarious work, or, in some cases, any work. For some, this also promised benefits such as moving to a city with larger national, cultural or religious populations and associated services, or closer to family members. However, interviewees reported a range of non-economic attachments influencing a decision to remain in the region. Similarly, in Sporton's (2013: 454) survey of A8 migrants in Doncaster, where there were limited employment opportunities, 56 per cent declared an intention to stay in Doncaster and a further 11 per cent said that they planned to stay in Britain. Participants in our study gave many reasons for choosing to stay, framed sometimes by the region and sometimes by a more local area. This was explained in various ways, including staying close to social support networks for themselves and/or family members, aesthetic attachments to the region, or lifestyle factors, such as a slower pace of life compared to elsewhere. The variety of non-economic attachments is illustrated by the following accounts:

> 'it's beautiful, I like it. Of course, it has problems, as any other part of the country.... And by the sea, I like that.... Every time that I go to London ... I see everyone running up and down ... I said, "Oh my God, really, you really want to move here?".' (May, arrived from Angola in 2008 and secured refugee status)

> '[For] a job, career, I would probably move away.... But ... I have got a two-year-old [child], and then a new baby coming.... I am just aware of how important it is, the environment where you are growing up. So, it's not much pollution ... and for kids growing, I think it's a perfect place to live.' (Aleksy, arrived from Poland in 2005)

This was connected for some to what Tyler (2013: 12) calls the desire for 'anchorage ... to lay down roots, to feel safe, to create a family and home, to belong to a community and to have some sense of a (better) future'. A welfare rights worker suggested that in their experience, single people tended to move on to other cities more than families (interview P8), reinforcing the importance of familial connections in developing the kind of 'roots' described here.

Beyond a simple preference to stay, some respondents described the prospect of moving *again* as traumatic. For example, Marie, who arrived from the Gambia in 2013 and claimed asylum, suggested:

> 'I think people are just ... scared of moving.... This is the only place I know.... If you should move me from here today, that's when you are killing me. I'll be starting from zero again because it will be very hard. So, people are running away from that now.'

The meaning of this is context dependent. It is not a tremendous physical journey to move outside the region, but for some respondents with very limited control over their previous migration and who had established support networks and become comfortable with their local knowledge, further movement was an unwelcome prospect.

While there is a lack of comparative data on which to base firm conclusions about the distinctiveness of the North-East region, the importance of non-economic attachments to the region and/or localities may be distinctive in that it appears to contradict previous research that focused on larger metropolitan areas. For example, Alberti's (2014) study of the hospitality sector in London found migrants valuing their temporariness and viewing their employment in London as part of a longer-term migratory plan (also Anderson, 2010b). In our research, place-based attachments contributed to some individuals' acceptance of precarious conditions, just as a lack of attachment did in Alberti's (2014) study. While this book has discussed the coercive role of borders in maintaining differential regimes of exploitation, this suggests that, in some cases, subjective attachments to place, which may be emotional, familial, social and future-orientated, can both contribute to precarity and make the experience more bearable.

The hyper-flexible worker

'Hyper-flexibility' refers to movements that are highly responsive to labour market demands. This dynamic is characterised by a high degree of geographical and job mobility, constrained by the economic geography of the region. Sometimes, this takes the form of forced movements between work sites and jobs, and sometimes the juggling of multiple jobs, cyclically or sequentially. This follows the association that Anderson (2010b: 300) notes between migrant labour and 'hyperflexible labour, working under many types of arrangements (not always "employment"), available when required, undemanding when not'. Welfare systems play a major role in shaping such hyper-flexibility by creating pressure to find any work at all as quickly as possible, which is particularly intense for some migrants due to the differential entitlements to welfare discussed in Chapter 4.

Frequent movement from one job to another, sequentially, was a routine part of work for some respondents due to temporary contracts or agency employment. Henryk, a Polish man in his early 40s who moved to Britain in 2007, gave a typical account:

> 'When I arrived, I went to [a] factory because I had a job
> through the agency.... I was cleaning toilets.... I was supposed
> to work about two to three months and then I [was promised

I would] be placed in a different sector [welding]. I'd been waiting ten months and then I asked [the] agency ... shouldn't they change my sector.... The next day, I was told that they don't need me anymore. They got rid of me, they booted me out.... Then, over the Internet, I have found this cleaning firm, where I was working not so long because [of the economic] crisis.... [Since then,] I was working sometimes in [a] printing house, sometimes in recycling and I'm looking for something stable, but for now, I can't find any[thing] stable.'

A sequence of low-paid and insecure jobs thereby emerged through a combination of agency work, limited sectoral options within the region and worsening economic conditions because of the economic crisis.

Sequential movement between jobs was often connected to experiences of discrimination in migrants' accounts, as discussed earlier in this chapter. The most common response reported by participants was to leave the job and seek an alternative. This is illustrated by Natalia, who arrived from Zimbabwe in 2002, claimed asylum and later secured British citizenship:

'I am opting to leave [my job] next week because, to me, I feel the place has got a lot of racism.... We even complained to the manager ... you are working with two people, you are the third one, and they will be talking, talking, and once you get there, they go into silence.... Or the work ... they don't want to do, they will always throw it at you, "Can you do that?", "Can you do that?", "Can you do that?".... When they know it's you who is coming for a night shift, they will just leave things scattered.'

Such accounts suggest a direct connection between experiences of discrimination and forced job mobility. This had a regional dimension: while some respondents described North-East England as exceptionally welcoming, others saw it as particularly discriminatory, and linked this to lower levels of ethnic diversity compared to some other parts of Britain (eg Clayton, 2012). In some cases, people responded by leaving the region for another part of Britain that they considered more multicultural, although a refugee charity worker also described refugees securing leave to remain and then moving to the North-East in an attempt to escape discrimination in other parts of England (interview P7). In both cases, this represents geographical mobility under duress.

Job mobility also took cyclical forms, and was sometimes combined with considerable geographical mobility within the region. In a pronounced example of this, in an area encompassing the northern part of the region and extending into Scotland, there was a pattern of temporary, low-paid employment across multiple sectors, summarised in the following account by an experienced worker with a voluntary sector organisation:

> 'many migrants have remained here for many, many years, on these precarious contracts.... Come December ... they are laid off [from Food Processing Site 1] ... and some of them may go to [Food Processing Site 2] for a bit.... Come the holiday season, many people in the winter vegetable processing firms go to [caravan parks] to clean the caravans.... So they work all the time with various jobs.' (Interview P3)

Migrants with experience working in these sectors verified this account. Over the years, some of these workers moved onto permanent contracts in food processing but the majority either remained in this situation of precarious cyclical mobility or moved away.

Some participants reported working multiple jobs at the same time, representing job mobility over a shorter temporal scale that often also involved significant geographical mobility within the region. Prudence, a refugee arriving from Zimbabwe in 2001, described such experiences as widespread: "I remember when we [were] first granted refugee status ... you would work as a care worker during the day and do some cleaning as well and only be home briefly to have a sleep and pick up my daughter from school". Many respondents viewed this negatively, particularly where travel times and costs combined with caring responsibilities and a lack of informal support networks. For example, Gabi, a man in his 50s from Hungary, described working long hours and split shifts in the care sector across a wide geographical area, which sometimes led to having to sleep in his car between shifts and disrupting family relationships:

> 'It's too much because I'm a family man. My son is that age when I would like to spend as much time as possible with him. But there are weeks when from Friday evening until Tuesday afternoon, I don't see him.... One day, my wife phoned me and said, "Your son asked if you're coming home". She said, "He was home every day, but he came after you went to bed, and left before you get up". There are weeks when I was working 70, 76 hours was the maximum lately. And that is too much.'

Such work patterns also have clear implications for the balance of domestic labour within the family. Negative assessments of day-to-day geographical mobility suggest that this is not a 'free' choice, but reflects limited mobility power. In some cases, hyper-flexibility was maintained but at the cost of impaired family relationships, revealing a tension between some forms of non-economic attachments discussed as part of the rooted worker dynamic and the demands of hyper-flexibility. In other cases, such conditions made paid work impossible, showing how the hyper-flexible worker dynamic can rapidly slip into the surplus worker dynamic.

Thus, the hyper-flexible dynamic requires constant movement between places and jobs, with limited mobility power in either a geographical or employment sense. Lack of control about the location, timing and nature of work contributes to a state of subjection, limits the ability to direct one's mobility to escape conditions of exploitation and consequently leaves workers with little power within the labour process. This is characteristic of the floating category of the RAL.

Resisting exploitation through mobility power

Control over movement between places enables tighter control over movement within the labour process by making labour available to capital at specific times and places, and restricting options for escape. The extension of the labour–capital relation to the total time of life, discussed in Chapter 2, blurs the distinction between 'work' and 'not work', and this strengthens the continuity between mobility within the labour process and other forms of mobility, such as movement between jobs and places. This suggests that the state interventions discussed in Chapters 3 and 4 should be considered as part of a continuous system together with the managers, supervisors and 'human relations' departments of specific companies. The concept of the 'social factory', developed within autonomous Marxism, has relevance here (Gill and Pratt, 2008). Indeed, because the British state represents the general interest of British capital, and consequently is concerned with the mobility of labour in its totality, the state is arguably more pivotal to the class struggle than any particular employer.

Mezzadra and Neilson (2013: 20) highlight labour power's distinctive character as a commodity that is essential for capitalism but inseparable from living bodies, 'socially constructed within multiple systems of domination'. This inseparability means that the potential for resistance is always present, but also means that forms of subjection vary, calling for different responses and creating challenges for unity among the oppressed. Casas-Cortés (2014: 214) proposes that precarity can form a singularity despite differences through 'a series of shared subjective experiences and practices', and that this offers a basis for collective organising. Yet, realising that potential faces inherent challenges arising from the multiplicity of precarity's forms. Indeed, Trimikliniotis et al (2016: 1038) argue that multiplicity is one of the defining features of precarious labour, existing 'only in the plural, as a multiplicity of experiences variously positioned, exploited, and lived in the system of embodied capitalism'. Focusing on mobility power might help to navigate this multiplicity by providing both a common denominator that links different types of precarity, and a lens to make sense of their differences. Examining precarity through arrangements of mobility/immobility can help to identify strategic demands that are appropriate to precarious workers' varying situations.

The application of this analysis can be demonstrated by considering the specificities of each dynamic of precarity described in this chapter. The precarity of the surplus worker might require a range of measures to increase mobility power in geographical and job terms, according to the concrete factors limiting mobility power for different groups:

- for asylum seekers, ending compulsory dispersal, which strips geographical mobility power, and ending the prohibition of paid work, which severely constrains job mobility;
- increasing state welfare provision, regardless of immigration status, so that an inability to sell one's labour power does not lead to a precarious existence; and
- improving the recognition of skills and experience gained outside Britain, without prohibitive fees.

The precarity of the rooted worker might be reduced by:

- developing the number and range of employment opportunities locally, and their security and pay, so that these workers can increase their labour security while maintaining their non–economic attachments; and
- increasing childcare provision and flexible working hours to fit with caring commitments in order to prevent caring roles restricting the ability to travel and do paid work.

Improving the hyper-flexible worker's situation relies on:

- improvements to job security, pay and hours; and
- effective action against discrimination in order to reduce the pressure for such frequent movements.

These measures may seem utopian in the current international context of economic crisis and the regional context of deindustrialisation and austerity. They are nevertheless the logical implications arising from the findings discussed in this chapter, and can help to inform consideration of the kinds of changes that would be necessary to make them achievable, discussed later in this chapter and in Chapter 7. Organising around these kinds of specific demands can build organisation, consciousness and confidence, contributing towards systemic critiques and structural transformation.

Beyond the migrant categories discussed here, and other visa categories, with their attendant restrictions, there are those rendered 'illegal' through the denial of any recognised immigration status. Anderson (2010b: 311–12; see also Hanieh, 2018) discusses the active production of illegality, with state interventions that are often justified on the basis of combatting exploitation but actually deepen it through 'institutionalised uncertainty ... [and] enforced temporariness'. The legal insecurity of people who are prohibited from waged work makes it almost impossible to secure basic employment rights or contest pay or conditions, producing a direct connection between state categories and vulnerability to exploitation. It also produces tendencies for such workers to be concentrated in types of employment where papers are not checked, on the fringes of the economy (Bloch, 2014: 1513). These conditions of illegality have implications for all migrants because they serve as a threat that rights may be withdrawn and, as we have seen with the 'Windrush Generation' (see Chapter 2), can also affect racialised-minority citizens.

Mobility power as an issue for the whole working class

To conclude, precarity can be understood as fundamentally a reduction of various forms of mobility power for growing sections of the working class. Commonalities might be identified between the interests of precarious migrants and other sections of the working class who also lack mobility power, for example, as manifested in the disempowering experiences of moving cyclically between jobs and welfare statuses (McCollum, 2013; Greer, 2016), and enforced relocations within Britain that some have described as 'social cleansing' (Elmer and Dening, 2016; Paton and Cooper, 2016). Balaram and Wallace-Stephens (2018: 10) highlight increasingly widespread experiences of 'chronic precariousness', accounting for around 15 per cent of the workforce, describing those 'employed on typical contracts [but who] still worry about job security because of wider trends in the labour market ... the pace of technology and the possibility of their job succumbing to automation. They report low autonomy and excessive monitoring'. The proliferation of borders and increasing conditionality in state welfare are leading more of the working class to move in ways consistent with the RAL. The diversity of forms that this takes obscures its scale and undermines the development of resistance. Identifying the common denominator of mobility power offers one way to understand connected interests despite these differences. Acting on these connected interests also calls for a direct attack on hierarchical fractioning within the working class (James, 2012 [1983]: 156–7), situating struggles against racism, sexism and other forms of discrimination as central to the class struggle.

While immigration controls produce tendencies towards class fractioning to the detriment of the working class, migration itself offers opportunities for international alliances and solidarity. Although some have suggested that the presence of immigrants weakens worker solidarity and radicalism, Strikwerda and Guerin-Gonzales (1998: 24–5) argue that the evidence for this comes 'almost exclusively from the pre-World War I United States or contemporary Western Europe – both periods of apparent "failure" or "conservatism" of the labor movement as a whole'. The authors cite other examples where unions have included, and, in some cases, been led by, migrants. Virdee (2014) gives other examples of migrants who have been part of working-class leaderships in Britain, and Alberti and Però (2018) discuss more recent examples (see also Oliveri, 2012, 2018; Vickers, 2014). Writing about the exploitation of Russian migrant workers in Europe in an earlier period of imperialist crisis, Lenin (1977 [1913]: 454–7) points to mutual learning and class development through international migration, both taking workers 'out of their semi-feudal conditions and ... putting them in the ranks of the advanced, international army of the proletariat', and introducing new methods, for example, 'Workers who had participated in various strikes in Russia introduced into America the bolder and more aggressive spirit of the mass strike'. This reflects the potential for special kinds of exploitation to produce special forms of resistance and for international migration to strengthen the working class.

Peutz and Genova (2010: 3; emphasis in original) situate the struggle against deportations in relation to '*freedom*, in one of its most basic and meaningful senses: the freedom to traverse space and to make a place for oneself in the world'. Yet, under capitalism, just as 'free' waged labour means systematic exploitation (see Chapter 1), freedom to move may operate within, and fail to challenge, relations of oppression and exploitation. Equally, permanence, or the right to *not move*, does not necessarily come with equality of social and political rights (Latham et al,

2014: 4). The question is not whether mobility occurs, but on whose terms and in whose interests. As Tyler (2013) shows, relationships between forced displacement, capture, oppression and resistance can take many forms. Taking control of our mobility and directing it towards social goods rather than private profits, or developing a 'mobile commons' (Trimikliniotis et al, 2016), calls for conscious collective action, and the freedom to move and work must be coupled with social and civil rights.

Mobility power creates possibilities for resistance to exploitation, but whether those possibilities are realised is also influenced by consciousness and collective organisation. As Rogaly (2009: 1984) points out, 'incremental and sometimes highly-significant changes in microspaces of work and living' may occur in such a way that the domination of capital and the exploitation of labour remain unchallenged or increase. The tendency to prioritise 'getting by' or 'getting ahead', on an individual basis, may be increased where precarity makes organising difficult, as Berntsen (2016) finds in research with migrant construction workers. This highlights the importance of political consciousness. Jones (2016: 180) suggests that 'The movements of migrants are tactics that repoliticize the concepts of states, borders, and nations. [But] [t]his repoliticization does not necessarily mean the concepts are rejected; it could result in a further hardening of borders and more extreme systems of migrant capture and control'. The response to this repoliticisation is an open question, where the subjective agency of the working class comes into play. Capitalist control of workers' mobility can only be effectively resisted, and ultimately transcended, through workers' control of their mobility, requiring collective action. This, in turn, requires the reclaiming of control over land and the means of production, the dispossession of which enables the ruling classes to enforce waged labour (see Chapter 2). Such collective action requires an independent working-class perspective, and that requires critical engagement to develop alternative narratives that challenge capitalist hegemony. This is addressed in Chapter 6 through an analysis of media representations.

Notes

[1] The approach taken here also differs from the autonomy of migration perspective in not viewing migration as *necessarily* constituting resistance.

[2] See, for example, *The Independent*, www.independent.co.uk/news/uk/british-born-eu-nationals-children-gain-citizenship-after-brexit-negotiations-passport-channel-4-a7807386.html

[3] See the *Financial Times*, www.ft.com/content/02da4ef0-ebe6-11e7-bd17-521324c81e23

[4] Those currently not in waged employment but not considered to be 'actively seeking work'.

5   Thus, increases to the pension age and reduced access to disability benefits shift labour from the latent to the floating and stagnant categories.
6   LFS figures for 2014–15 show 24 per cent of Polish migrants in the region not in paid work. The Survey of New Refugees during 2005–09 found 56 per cent of North-East respondents not in paid employment/self-employment, and Bloch (2002) found 71 per cent of refugees not in work.
7   The most frequently reported barrier was language.

6

Deconstructing Migrant/Worker Categories in Britain

Introduction: ideological categories in an age of crisis

Hegemonic discourse supplements physical means of differentiation with ideological categories of workers divided along multiple lines. Racism facilitates capitalist exploitation by increasing pressure to accept lower wages, undermining solidarity from other sections of the working class and further reducing access to state welfare (Miles, 1986). Hegemonic cultural processes are therefore part of systems of material exploitation, and discursive challenges are a necessary part of struggles to transform them.

Oliveri (2012: 796–7) suggests that 'In relation to human mobility ... [neoliberal hegemony] produces a trend towards the radical commodification of migrants as pure labour-power: their rights to leave, to entry or to stay in a country depend preponderantly on their economic usefulness according to market rules'. This ideological trend has emerged as part of ruling-class responses to the capitalist crisis, intensifying labour discipline, and leads to dehumanisation that normalises state violence and discourages solidarity. Ideological figures such as 'migrants', 'newcomers', 'Romanians', 'illegals', 'residents' and 'British workers' play the role of 'exemplary bodies' (Rajaram and Grundy-Warr, 2007: xv; see also Philo et al, 2013), which mark out terms of belonging and non-belonging within the national territory. In doing so, they reveal important characteristics of wider social structures, with significance for systems of domination and exploitation that affect the entire working class, though differentially.

Chapter 6 examines discursive reflections and reinforcements of the class divisions discussed in previous chapters. This analysis is developed through a 'close reading' of three British television documentaries, together with academic literature which suggests that these documentaries are representative of wider trends. The chapter concludes by arguing for the need to shift the discursive focus from migrants to borders, and to question how both are constructed and connected to systems of exploitation and oppression.

Migrant/worker categories in three television documentaries

Documentaries often claim to present a direct, unmediated and therefore 'authentic' image of reality (Nichols, 2010). Santa Ana (2013: 202) argues that such claims are always false because the construction of a narrative inevitably involves choices about what to include and what to leave out, and the act of telling a story about 'the facts' necessarily transforms them. Documentary television is therefore not just representational, but 'authorial' in its presentation of a particular 'vision' of society (Corner, 1996: 14). This is also true of reality television, which, as Skeggs and Wood (2011: 7–8) show, crafts 'dramas through real people' and attaches 'value to certain modes of performance and behaviour over others'. Historically, documentaries in Britain have had strong attachments to the political establishment, 'frequently subject to considerable circumscription through a mixture of straightforward censorship and an unwillingness to offend senior political figures' (Corner, 1996: 23). They therefore offer insights regarding the contours of hegemonic national discourse.

Three television documentaries were selected for analysis: 'The truth about immigration in the UK' (TIUK), 'The hidden world of Britain's immigrants' (HWBI) and Episode 2 of 'Benefits Street' (BS). All three were broadcast on terrestrial British television in January 2014, TIUK and HWBI on BBC Two and BS on Channel Four. This was an important juncture in national discussions of migration, indicated by a spike in media coverage of migration (Allen, 2016), following the lifting of restrictions on Romanian and Bulgarian migrants.[1] While social media may have potential to decentralise discourse, an extensive study of British Twitter discussions about migration during the same period (Shah et al, 2016) found that a large proportion of tweets by individuals simply shared mainstream media headlines without additional comment. This suggests that mainstream media remains influential. Television continues to be a significant medium across Britain's population, with 94.2 per cent of individuals watching some television each week (BARB, 2014: 4). Television's wealth of multi-sensory data, consumed in normal viewing practices at a pace unregulated by the viewer/listener, increases the influence of implicit messages and makes critical engagement more difficult (Selby and Cowdery, 1995: 3); this increases its significance in perpetuating hegemonic discourse.

All three documentaries were shown during, or immediately after, the national viewing peak of 9–10 pm (Ofcom, 2013), suggesting that they were prioritised by broadcasters. BS has been subject to considerable public and academic debate (eg MacDonald et al, 2014). The British Broadcasting Corporation (BBC) documentaries attracted smaller audiences, but the BBC carries additional hegemonic significance as Britain's only state-funded broadcaster. While Channel Four and BBC Two have similar UK audience shares, 6.1 per cent and 6.5 per cent in 2011/12, respectively, BBC Two attracts an older, more male demographic (Ofcom, 2013: 200–1). Considering these documentaries together therefore enables a breadth of audience, and consequently a broader perspective on hegemonic discourses at that point in time. Other characteristics of the documentaries are provided in the Appendix.

The documentaries vary in style. A significant proportion of BS and HWBI takes the form of what Corner (1996: 28) terms 'reactive observationalism', positioning the viewer as vicarious witness to apparently 'naturally occurring' events, interspersed with segments of 'proactive observationalism' in the form of interviews. TIUK relies more on structured presentations, sometimes to the point of overlaying statistics and other images on top of video, alongside interviews, direct address to the camera by the presenter and only occasional reactive observational clips used for scene setting. All three documentaries are weighted towards a 'multivocal' approach, combining many voices and complicating the task of establishing which perspectives are privileged (Corner, 1996: 23). BS adopts a reality television format. Although HWBI and TIUK present themselves as investigative journalism, they exhibit pronounced influences from reality television, consistent with a broader trend in documentary television (Skeggs and Wood, 2011: 6).

Migrants are constructed in all three documentaries as exclusively from oppressed countries in Africa, Asia and Eastern and Central Europe, and are consequently racialised. None of the documentaries show migrants from other imperialist countries, such as the US, France or Australia, despite significant numbers within Britain (ONS, 2014: 25). This reflects the invisibility of 'whiteness' as an unspoken ideological centre that identifies racialised minorities as problematic outsiders, legitimising special measures of control (Virdee, 2014). The documentaries exemplify a discourse in which migrants are set apart from a British working class that is implicitly white, except when racialised-minority British workers are explicitly highlighted to present hostility to migrants as non-racial.

Through a process of analysis described in the Appendix, three discursive 'roles' emerged for working-class migrants:

- disposable labour;
- passive victim; and
- active threat.

These encapsulate multiple subsidiary roles, and, at times, overlap. They represent particular configurations of long-standing 'topoi', argumentative strategies that construct migrants in terms of usefulness/uselessness, burden, danger and threat (Reisigl and Wodak, 2001: 75–80; see also Shah et al, 2016). Other categorisations would be possible, but these proved most helpful in making sense of the data. Together, these roles indicate a hegemonic view that limits what is considered possible for those framed as 'migrants', and positions them in relation to other parts of the population. A fourth role, the migrant as capitalist entrepreneur, is used at times as a contrast to working-class migrants, but it is associated almost exclusively with earlier periods of migration. The persistent absence of more affluent businesspeople from representations of 'the migrant' is consistent with their very different relationship to the state, experiencing it as an enabler rather than a barrier to migration, 'moving frictionlessly across borders, failing to trigger the scrutiny of border guards or media' (Andrejevic, 2011: 60). This is another form of differential inclusion. Each of these three roles is explored in the following.

Migrants as disposable labour

This section explores the implications of defining migrants through their work: as 'disposable labour' whose presence in Britain is conditional on their usefulness to employers. In TIUK and HWBI, the word 'work' is the second most frequent verb. The documentaries' depiction of migrants through their work reflects and justifies conditions of precarity, through a heroised narrative of sturdy self-reliance and self-sacrifice. For example, TIUK portrays a Kent farmer's difficulties in finding fruit-pickers, counterpoising British workers' refusal to do work that is 'a bit hard, a bit uncomfortable' with migrants' smiling enthusiasm. The portrayal of Romanians in BS offers another pronounced example:

[Cut from a shot of unemployed British parents.]

Narrator: 'George's family isn't claiming a penny off the social.' [Images of people loading scrap metal onto a van.] 'They're hard at work.' [Cut back to unemployed British man standing watching.]... 'Building a business out of scrap metal.'... [Scene inside house, a Romanian woman cooks on a portable electric hob.]

Unnamed Romanian [subtitles]: 'We're not interested in hand-outs, we can manage on our own. We don't need money or food. We just need permits to work. So we can live like regular citizens.'

Scenes are shown portraying this family as active, serious, hardworking and struggling to provide for themselves with limited means. 'The Romanians' represent the ideal worker from the capitalist perspective, taking care of the reproduction of their labour power privately, without making demands on the state, but could also be interpreted as asserting agency and independence despite a limited range of options. Yet, despite their hard work, the family are shown to be ultimately unable to pay their rent. Amid these ambiguities is a clear warning to British workers that if they are not prepared to work on whatever terms employers choose to offer, somebody else will. The juxtaposed portrayals of British benefit claimants in the same programme as 'work-shy' (MacDonald et al, 2014), typically lounging on sofas or aimlessly socialising on the doorstep, underlines this warning.

Providing such examples of the 'good worker' follows reality television's pedagogic role in lecturing the working class on how to improve their situation through 'self-work and self-development', using the personal immediacy of the individual to obscure historical context and structural constraints, and to explain social problems as the result of individual failings (Skeggs and Wood, 2011: 15). The focus on work in these documentaries contrasts with the focus in other contemporary media on cultural characteristics, particularly in relation to Islam, ignoring class and other differences (Macdonald, 2011). This difference reflects the contours of hegemonic discourse, with different groups of migrants defined in different terms, within a limited range.

Defining migrants through their work combines with the focus on movement across a border as their defining characteristic (their 'migrant-ness') to present migrants as workers characterised by movement and change. This alternately elevates and denigrates migrants and British workers: in some places, portraying migrants as transient, disconnected and selfish, using a negative tone, versus British workers as consistent and responsible; while in others, portraying migrants as dynamic and flexible, using a positive tone, versus British workers as stagnant and stubborn. The implied individualism or self-sufficiency of migrants justifies the abdication of responsibility on the part of society and the state. The logical conclusion is to blame migrants if they 'fail' to make themselves sufficiently useful as workers, and to legitimate conditional welfare policies to push British workers into waged labour, both consistent with capital's demand for 'flexible' labour with limited social rights (Standing, 2011). In other words, such othering enables conditions for the exploitation of those positioned on both sides of the divide, while simultaneously encouraging each to blame the other for their resulting hardships.

Migrants' supposed transience emphasises their conditional position. Repeated oppositions are created between a settled and rooted British population and new migrants whose presence as individuals is always under question and insecure, although their presence en masse is permanent. This is consistent with the systematic 'disposability' of migrants across Europe, 'providing labor markets permanently with new manpower' (Karakayali and Rigo, 2010: 132). In the documentaries we analysed, explicit expressions of migrants' transience are backed by metaphorical associations. For example, images of rubbish are repeatedly juxtaposed with migrants in all three documentaries (eg TIUK 06:38; BS 07:15; HWBI 15:44), creating second-order meanings of disposability and dirt through association (Corner, 1996: 29). In BS, the word 'rubbish' is mentioned 13 times, the fifth most frequent noun in the programme. A central plot line involves a Romanian family who the presenter claims rip apart the bin bags of 'the residents' looking for scrap metal and leave rubbish strewn across the street – the 'dark side' of the portrayal of migrants' resourcefulness discussed earlier. This is presented as leading the council to refuse to collect rubbish from the street, with mounting piles of refuse threatening children (BS 08:46). The signifiers of 'the Romanians' and 'the residents' again emphasise migrants' transience: migrants cannot be 'resident' because they are defined by their movement. In the same programme, Britain in Bloom[2] is used to contrast white–British continuity and cleanliness. Emphasis is placed on rubbish trucks frequently sweeping the area on the day of the competition. This produces implicit meanings through the combination of elements (Selby and Cowdery, 1995: 58–9), playing on long-standing dichotomies within discourses linking migration to poverty and disease, including stability–transience, dirt–cleanliness and familial care–neglect (Andrejevic, 2011). The events regarding the split rubbish bags appear to have a dubious factual basis – Birmingham City Council denies them and a detailed viewing of the footage suggests that events portrayed as happening within a few weeks were filmed in different seasons. There are also significant silences: it is not mentioned that in April 2013, as part of its programme of service cuts, Birmingham City Council withdrew its provision of free bin bags to households[3]; and there is only a brief, unexplained reference to the state restrictions which meant that selling scrap metal was one of the only legal means of livelihood for many Romanians in Britain at that time.

Where migrants' labour is no longer needed, all three documentaries suggest that they are individually responsible for the problems they face. The following example from HWBI focuses on a young single male who initially found work in construction but was subsequently unable to get work and turned to hard drugs and theft:

[Shots of the outside of Shanki's house, then inside, the dirty state of which had been a focus earlier in the programme.]

Presenter: 'Shanki didn't blame anybody else for his situation, he clearly felt embarrassed he'd come to Britain, and ended up a failure.'

[Interview in a car park.]

Shanki: 'I am ashamed to go home, you know why? I am spending fucking nine years in this country, I have fucking zero.'

Morley (2009: 490) suggests that there is a strong tendency in reality television 'to melodramatise all "fates" as ultimately a matter of individual responsibility, while obscuring the structural factors that still largely determine them' (see also Redden, 2011; Skeggs and Wood, 2011). The two BBC documentaries also exhibit this quality. In the passage quoted earlier, Shanki takes responsibility and thus absolves the state. Representing migrants' poverty as caused by individual failure silences the role of immigration controls in producing conditions for exploitation and destitution, as discussed throughout previous chapters. Andrejevic (2011) suggests that this is typical of reality television concerned with border enforcement, which makes pedagogical examples of those who are supposed to have fallen destitute because of failures in self-management and thus require intervention by the state, marking out 'borderlands' between classes as well as nations. Migrants who are portrayed as failing to make themselves sufficiently useful to capital may be relegated to the second role we identified, that of passive victim.

Migrants as passive victim

This section discusses the promotion of a passive victim role through the idea that Britain is an alien environment for migrants, through portrayals of migrants as childlike and through a dichotomy of 'successful' and 'failing' migrants. Across all three documentaries, migrants not fitting the role of successful middle-class entrepreneur or hardworking and compliant worker are overwhelmingly portrayed as helpless and passive, or if active, then criminal. This resonates with longer histories of helplessness as a condition for receiving state or charitable resources, with marginalised groups presented as either victim or problem (Gilroy, 1998: 11). For example, in HWBI, we are shown a couple who the presenter tells us were brought from Lithuania by an agent who then abandoned them, leading to homelessness and dependency on charity while they applied for state support. A history of heroin addiction is provided as further evidence of their inability to 'cope'. The HWBI presenter suggests that migrants whose labour is unwanted and who face such problems would be better off leaving Britain: '[Interviewing charity manager.] "If you're here and you're destitute, dependent on drink or drugs, or frequently trying to get work that isn't there, you'd be much better off going home wouldn't you?"'. He follows this with the suggestion that such people should be forced to return whether or not they consent, providing a 'humanitarian' justification for deportation.

In some places, migrants' helplessness is associated with urban British environments. In BS, we are told a group of Romanian men were 'trucked in from their village and promised a job' by a faceless 'boss' who makes them work 17 hours per day and withholds their wages. After fleeing their house, some of them sleep in a park, which the group's main spokesperson assesses positively: '[Standing next to a park at night, under street lights.] "I like this lifestyle. It represents me, a bit of adrenaline, a fight for survival." [Pans to other Romanian men who are smiling.]… "It's how we were brought up. This is our environment, we're used to it."' This resonates with the orientalist idea of migrants from oppressed countries as 'backward' or 'primitive' (Said, 2003: 40), more at home in the open air. Similarly, in TIUK, positive representations of European Union (EU) workers in the fields of Kent (TIUK 06:14) shift, with the help of some dramatic guitar music, to the streets of Sheffield (TIUK 06:25), where a story is told of groups of Roma disrespecting English people, urinating in the street and dumping rubbish, suggesting an inability to meet the expectations of a modern urban environment. This is consistent with narratives portraying immigrants as 'uncivilised', which were prevalent on Twitter during the same period (Shah et al, 2016). These portrayals silence the ways in which government policies have deliberately transformed Britain into a 'hostile environment', discussed in Chapter 3.

Migrants' apparent helplessness within Britain is contrasted with romanticised depictions of their countries of origin. In HWBI, Satpal is followed making the return from Britain – where he is unemployed, sleeping on the streets, drinking heavily and with only a single friend – to India, where he is surrounded by caring family. The colours of each scene further emphasise this contrast, from the grey backstreets of London, with many scenes shot at night (eg HWBI 20:28, 39:30), to images of sunshine, communal eating and brightly coloured fabrics in India (eg HWBI 55:21, 56:21). Although Satpal travels under the 'Voluntary Returns' programme, his conditions of destitution in Britain make the voluntary character of his return questionable. The documentaries are all silent about less positive consequences of forced return, including difficulties reintegrating and pressures to migrate again (Miller, 2012).

Across the three documentaries, there are persistent references to a 'British dream', implicitly and explicitly, which migrants apparently believe but is then dashed by reality. For example, HWBI's presenter describes in melancholic tones migrants 'battling to survive in a hidden world of poverty, crime, and broken dreams', having 'fallen so far from the path of normal life that it's almost impossible to imagine what the way back for them is going to be'. In BS, the presenter melodramatically sums up the experience of a group of Romanian men:

> 'The 14 Romanians came to James Turner Street with hopes of the good life.' [Street shots of children in the sun change to images inside the house – a picture of Jesus on the wall, a narrow corridor, a room with mattresses on the floor.] 'But they found only slave labour. They left in fear.' [Final shot outside the house, window ajar.]

This contributes to an impression of childlike naivety, resonating with long-standing portrayals of the inhabitants of oppressed countries as justification for colonialism and imperialism (Young, 2001: 40).

As detailed earlier, the passive victim role suggests that migrants whose labour is not needed within Britain must submit to becoming charitable objects, and ultimately to return 'home' under the justification that their migration has rendered them helpless. Those who refuse to accept such a passive role and leave Britain are portrayed as a threat, justifying the use of force against them.

Migrants as active threat

This section discusses the various forms of threat attributed to migrants, from competing for jobs to burdening public services, and the subjects of this threat, including 'successful' migrants, British workers and the rule of law (themes that also emerge in Shah et al's [2016] study of Twitter during the same period). This is part of a wider trend within European media, with frequent portrayals of migrants posing a threat via 'economic competition, erosion of national identity and culture or security risks' (Caviedes, 2015: 5; see also Bleich et al, 2015). The alternative roles of passive victim or active threat parallel EU border authorities' 'dual coding of travellers', described by Feldman (2012: 93). This illustrates the capacity for media discourse to reflect and legitimate state practices. The analysis presented here adds to this picture by identifying additional criteria for differentiation among those who have already arrived in British territory. In the documentaries we analysed, threat levels are implicitly associated with how poorly migrants 'fit in' as compliant waged workers, and if their labour is not needed, then how compliant they are with their removal from Britain. This is consistent with the focus on economic considerations in recent media representations of migration in Britain, compared to other Western European countries (Caviedes, 2015), and to earlier periods in Britain (Allen, 2016).

In some places, the documentaries portray migrants as threatening British workers. This is part of what Moore and Forkert (2014: 500) describe as 'an emerging populist media consensus ... that working-class people are not only anti-immigration, but also that immigration is fundamentally bad for working-class people'. The suggestion that migrants threaten 'British' workers is particularly pronounced in TIUK through a narrative that presents immigration as beneficial for more privileged sections of society, but harmful to poorer sections. The presenter positions himself as an advocate for 'the worst off', complaining indignantly:

> [Presenter walking towards the camera down an ornate stone staircase.] 'Immigration was supposed to benefit us all, and the better-off certainly noticed, they noticed that cheaper Polish plumber or decorator, they enjoyed that nice new delicatessen down the road, but the worst off in society ... thought that their job was at risk, they thought their wages were being undercut, they often thought that their identity was being threatened.'

As Sohoni and Mendez (2014) identify in local media representations of migration in the US, such representations draw on anti-corporate and anti-government discourses to undermine solidarity between non-migrant and migrant workers against the kind of class offensive described in previous chapters.

All three documentaries suggest that recent migration is fundamentally unlike previous migration, not only quantitatively, but qualitatively, and this supposed difference is used to construct further forms of threat. In TIUK, contemporary migration is described as 'unprecedented', and in BS, as a 'new wave from the East'. In TIUK and HWBI, new migrants are portrayed not merely as different to earlier migrants and their descendants, but as an active threat to them, as in the case of a robbery in HWBI carried out by a recent migrant on a shop owned by an earlier migrant. A more general sense of economic threat is expressed by an unnamed South Asian man in TIUK: '[Interviewed against the backdrop of a cultural festival.] "The frustrating thing about it is our communities, our British-born, cannot get the job, and the Eastern communities, the European communities, can get a job."' The presenter does not question the implied causal relationship between unemployment among British South Asian people and Eastern European migration. Suggestions that migrants are harming longer-established racialised-minority communities emphasise and legitimate defensive responses to migration by these communities and downplay inclusive responses (Kymlicka, 2001), thereby discouraging solidarity and helping to neutralise anti-racist critiques of immigration controls.

Depictions of different periods of migration are strongly classed in these documentaries. The dependency of destitute migrants is contrasted to the self-reliance of successful entrepreneurs in both BBC documentaries: each category of migrant is produced through the other. In HWBI, migrants with a background in construction work, currently unemployed and with irregular immigration status are introduced by the presenter through contrast with migrants whose professional qualifications enable a more stable employment and immigration status:

> [Shanki walking along residential streets, snapping something in his hands and throwing the bits away, kicking a can.] 'While Kamal [a solicitor] represents successful, legal immigration from India, further down the road ... it's illegal immigrants, a group whose presence causes most public concern. We wanted to gain access to their underworld.'

This accommodates the historical contribution of migrants to Britain (Virdee, 2014) with the narrative of migrants as a burden (Kundnani, 2007) by suggesting that while migration may have 'worked' in the past, this is no longer the case. This is an example of Morley's (2009: 491) characterisation of television as a 'pedagogic medium' through which 'the "bad citizens" [or non-citizens] will be identified, shamed and then reformed (or, at least, they can perform a valuable function by providing a negative point of reference against which the 'good' can then measure their success)'. All three documentaries are silent on the agency exercised by working-class migrants in Britain to wage collective struggles.

Beyond the supposed threat that they pose to particular groups, the documentaries present migrants as threatening law and order. As Sohoni and Mendez (2014: 512) identify in the US context, 'the "master frame" of criminality [is mobilised] to link diverse issues and discourses in constructing anti-immigrant positions'. In HWBI and TIUK, migration is repeatedly associated with crime, both through what is said and through visual imagery, such as police vans with flashing lights, criminal drug use and spotlights shining on migrants. This is reflected in different ways in the opening imagery of each programme: HWBI opens with migrants scaling a wall into a boarded-up house; TIUK opens in the darkened cockpit of a patrol boat; and BS opens with a series of short clips, including a police car with flashing lights eight seconds in. As with Andrejevic's (2011) study in Australia, irregular immigration status is ascribed to an individual failure to 'abide by the rules' rather than a consequence of state policy, and this individual culpability is used to justify repression. In HWBI, the word 'illegals' is used 11 times as a noun to describe migrants, presenting illegality as their defining characteristic. In BS, criminality is mainly associated with working-class British people, othered through their contrast with law-abiding, if helpless, migrants. The exception is the Romanian 'boss' who is never seen, but who we are told is exploiting migrants who fear him. The focus on crime within documentaries nominally about immigration contributes to the criminalisation of migration itself. The state is portrayed as weak and ineffective, as expressed by the presenter of HWBI when he concludes 'how difficult the authorities find it to deport illegals'. Similarly, in TIUK, the presenter emphasises that there is 'so much beyond the government's control', and in BS, the presenter tells the audience that 'There's no hard evidence against the boss, so the police leave the street'. Such portrayals of a weak state help build a case for increased repressive powers.

Portrayals of threat are used to justify the criminalisation of certain categories of migrants, which can increase vulnerability to exploitation as well as deportation (Lewis et al, 2014; Vickers, 2015). The possibility of lifting restrictions in order to enable people to gain a measure of protection from exploitation through equal rights is a further silence in these documentaries.

Declassing migrants

The discourses emerging from these documentaries are multiple, complex and contradictory, but among them, a coherent narrative emerges: where migrants' labour is needed, they might be tolerated; where their labour is unwanted, they will inevitably degenerate and would be better off back in their country of origin; if they refuse to leave, they pose a threat that justifies further restrictions. Moore and Forkert (2014: 499) suggest that 'Work, for British citizens, is a moral duty; but for migrants it is seen as morally wrong to come to the UK and work, and indeed, immigrant workers are seen to be depriving British citizens of a moral duty to work'. Complicating this picture, our analysis shows migrants discursively constructed in multiple and shifting ways, sometimes as morally superior and sometimes as inferior. However, migrants are consistently portrayed as separate, reinforcing Moore and Forkert's overall argument that depictions of migrants disidentify them from the working class, thereby masking their exploitation and undermining the potential for class-based solidarity. Additionally, migrants and workers are constructed as categories that are antagonistic to one another, a portrayal that reality television is well suited to (Skeggs and Wood, 2011: 2). An example of how such declassing can be challenged is offered by the refugees who organised in the 'Lampedusa in Hamburg' (LiHH) movement in Germany from 2013. Jørgensen (2016) describes how the group's statements placed great significance on questions of access to work, working conditions and refugees' identity as workers, extending their political claims far beyond the demand for asylum. LiHH's political platform also made connections to the international operations of imperialism that influenced their crossing of borders, summed up in a banner reading: 'We did not survive the NATO [North Atlantic Treaty Organisation] war in Libya to come and die in the streets of Hamburg'. These politics formed the basis for an alliance that included 'churches, the leftist St Pauli football club, local schools, the university, the theatre, alternative social movements and to various degrees trade unions such as Ver.di and IG Metall' (Jørgensen, 2016: 10; see also Oliveri, 2018).

Restrictions on migrants' rights are portrayed in the documentaries we analysed as a question of 'common sense', hiding their active role in constructing sections of super-exploited labour. Montali et al (2013: 245) identify a similar process in Italian media, whereby migration is presented as fundamentally problematic in order to justify the exclusion of migrants as 'reasonable, natural or obvious'. TIUK claims that an 'adult debate' about immigration has been impossible for decades because anybody raising the issue was associated with politician Enoch Powell's 'Rivers of Blood' speech in 1968 and accused of racism. Such a claim is contradicted by the many immigration Acts passed, and the extensive coverage of migration in the media, over the intervening decades. The claim that no debate has been allowed may therefore represent a form of 'entitlement racism' (Essed, 2013), and a justification for anti-migrant hostility regardless of anti-racist critiques. Perhaps ironically, the BBC went on to broadcast Powell's speech again, in full for the first time, in 2018 as part of another documentary.

Migrants are used as a mutable 'other' against which categories of 'deserving' and 'undeserving' British workers can be constructed (see also Philo et al, 2013). This contributes to what Anderson (2013) calls a 'community of value', where depictions of the 'failed citizen' and the 'non-citizen' mark out the conditions for inclusion as someone of worth within the nation, and is part of a wider European trend (Holzberg et al, 2018). This aids the ruling classes in controlling workers' mobility through differential regimes, with the net effect of an increase in exploitation. For example, the unemployed are stigmatised as 'shirkers', despite evidence to the contrary (MacDonald et al, 2014), through contrast with hard-working and self-sacrificing migrants, and this increases pressure to accept jobs however terrible the pay and conditions. In other cases, migrants are presented as a threat to settled British workers; this is used to justify restrictions on the rights of some groups of migrants, removing protections from exploitation, for example by limiting their ability to change employer (Strauss, 2015). In a different but complementary way, pressure is placed on earlier migrants and their descendants to distance themselves from more recent migrants lest they become associated with 'immigrant failure'. As members of established, yet still marginalised, racialised minorities are threatened with increased exploitation, they might respond with solidarity with recent migrants, or by distancing themselves and reaffirming their loyalty to the British state; the narratives of othering described here encourage the latter, promoting opportunism (see Chapter 2).

Shifting the focus from migrants to borders

This chapter has called commonplace categorisations into question and has examined the role that they play in undermining solidarity and legitimating exploitation. As highlighted throughout this book, critiques and counter-hegemonic understandings are present among activists. The kind of critique of hegemonic discourses presented earlier can further develop such discursive challenges by informing an approach to informal education that focuses on highlighting the contradictions and exposing the silences.

Confusion, with multiple contradictory depictions of migrants contained within hegemonic discourse, can be functional for the ruling classes because it creates a sense of anxiety, with people not quite knowing what to believe – some people might feel that they do not understand migration, but within the bounds of hegemonic discourse, they 'know' that migrants are different to them and in competition. Given this confusion, additional explanations may simply be lost. One response was suggested by an activist (interview A12), who argued for people to be involved in actively developing their own understandings, a process they described as 'horizontal demystification':

> '[It is] longer and more sustaining because actual genuine human creative effort on the part of the people who are engaging with it has been exerted … whereas if it's just being informed, it's an outside influence and it's being viewed as an outside influence because it's not arisen or doesn't seem like it's arisen organically from that position as working-class people. So, I think we need to find a way in which we get horizontal propaganda to work in campaigns … because until people are undergoing a process of political education, they're not really acting as protagonists within the struggle because they aren't informing their own decisions....
>
> And I think from my experience growing up as a working-class person … when you get told it, it doesn't make sense to you. The reason that I came to my politics is because I saw politics in action and saw which ones were working [laughs] and which ones were going to actually challenge the people I wanted to challenge. And involving yourself in it is what really steels you against other influences as well. You can determine what their political character is and what they're attempting to achieve and make you do.'

As part of such a process, identifying the contradictions within dominant discourses can help develop more critical perspectives in order to make sense of the confusing array of messages in circulation. In some cases, this can involve identifying contradictions between people's own experiences and media depictions; in other cases, it might involve identifying contradictions between what the media say at different times.

Our analysis also highlights the value of studying the silences, such as those highlighted throughout this book, to question the paradigmatic decisions made by media producers about what to include and what not to include in media products (Selby and Cowdery, 1995: 58–9). What is not being said by the media about the reasons that people come to Britain, and the reasons for the problems that they and other working-class people face? Silences often include the hidden histories of marginalised groups, who are represented in the media in a limited range of roles, denying their agency (Gilroy, 1998: 11). The structural factors that shape patterns of migration and the targeting of racism represent a further, overarching silence within hegemonic discourse. Addressing this silence may require an approach that is both analytical and informed by a commitment to social and economic justice, enabling a shift in focus 'to systems and structures leading to inequality, and not to individuals as objects for blame' (Redden, 2011: 839). Exploring hidden histories, hidden aspects of the present and the ways in which they have been silenced offers a way to unmask the roots of oppression and identify points of commonality and connection. These can form the basis for counter-hegemonic understandings as part of a deep, engaged solidarity spanning people who are differently positioned within economic and discursive structures but have in common their subjection to the same capitalist system.

Notes

[1] From 2007 to 2014, employment was restricted to skilled roles and the agricultural and food-processing sectors (MAC, 2011).
[2] Britain in Bloom is an annual competition organised by the Royal Horticultural Society, see: www.rhs.org.uk/get-involved/britain-in-bloom
[3] See: www.birmingham.gov.uk/refusecollection

7

Conclusion

Introduction: mobility struggles in an age of crisis

This book has argued that capitalism is inherently violent in its reliance on the coercion of millions of people to produce according to the demands of capital, on pain of destitution. This process relies on control over mobility, and struggles by workers to assert their needs often necessitate challenging that control, or exercising mobility power (see Chapters 1 and 5). Capitalism is organised according to national divisions in the control and operation of capital (see Chapter 2). States have arisen on this basis, and continue to play a central role in defending national fractions of capital and maintaining conditions for continued capital accumulation (see Chapters 2, 3 and 4).

The capitalist crisis shows no sign of ending. As Shafique (2018: 16–17) points out, 'GDP [gross domestic product] growth in the UK is being driven by consumer spending enabled by borrowing, rather than business investment, stronger productivity and higher wages'; in other words, the apparent 'recovery' is built on sand. Accumulated consumer debt is projected to reach 47 per cent of household income by 2021, beyond the 45 per cent that preceded the crash in 2008. Brexit seems likely to intensify the capitalist crisis for Britain by undermining the international position of the city of London and the share of global surplus value that it captures for the ruling classes (see Chapter 2). The imperative to increase surplus value, intensified by the severity of the crisis, is driving new forms of exploitation, internationally and domestically, supported by the growth of precarity. Precarity represents a hidden labour reserve, and disciplines workers through insecurity (see Chapter 5). Increasing numbers of precarious workers face pressure to make the entirety of their time and mobility subject to the demands of capital, while also finding themselves responsible for their own reproduction and, in some cases, their own management. This precaritisation takes many forms, calling for a range of responses, but the struggle for mobility power is a common thread.

The sense of crisis is deeply felt among large sections of Britain's population, what Bauman (2016: 23) describes as 'floating insecurity in search of an anchor', and has been channelled by the ruling classes to adapt their systems of domination. Immigration controls and state welfare employ categories that result in differential inclusion, within a national system of citizenship that is also exclusionary. In recent years, these categorisations, and the violent interventions that they help to structure, have been given the appearance of urgent necessity, and have been intensified, through narratives of crisis (see Chapters 3 and 4). Control over labour and the protection of imperialist profits are thereby presented as a defence of British citizens in general. Under these conditions, Jones' (2016: 170) proposal that a reconstructed global immigration system, 'at the very least ... should embrace the ideal of all people ... having a right to work and reside within the boundaries of any nation-state' is wholly inadequate because it allows a separation between the right to move geographically and sell one's labour power, and social and civil rights. The logical consequence would be the continuation of differential inclusion as a basis for diverse forms of exploitation.

As the state plays such a central role in structuring the working class and disciplining mobility, asserting mobility power requires struggle against the state. As domination and exploitation are normalised by hegemonic discourse (see Chapter 6), these struggles must also rearticulate the nature of the crisis, challenge the divisive categories used to structure exploitation and identify new points of connection among the working class. This is already evident in the perspectives of campaigners discussed throughout this book; such perspectives currently lack influence and are embodied in campaigns that are small scale and fragmented, but show that it is possible to combine systemic critique and demands for change with short-term victories. Examples from other imperialist countries show that such struggles are also possible on a larger scale (eg De Lara, 2018; Oliveri, 2018).

Possible trajectories for Britain

Capitalism's internal contradictions constrain the possible responses to its crisis. Furthermore, the analysis presented here suggests that borders are central to capitalism, and the imperialist division of labour relies on exclusionary and differentially inclusive forms of national citizenship.

Within capitalism, the only response to the crisis is to continue to open up new areas for profitable exploitation, driving ever sharper differentiation. This means that Britain faces two possible futures: remaining within capitalism, with an increasingly fractioned working class, living standards driven down for the majority and antagonistic relations around the migrant–native divide enforced with increasing violence; or a radical break from capitalism in order to find a social form that can move beyond capitalism's endemic crises and divisions. A third course, involving concessions to some sections of the working class alongside continued division and exploitation in some form of revived social democracy, seems highly unlikely given the depth of the capitalist crisis and the absence of the kind of conditions that enabled previous social-democratic settlements.

Today, the end of capitalism is alternately considered unthinkable or already underway (eg Mason, 2015). To argue for an active struggle to destroy capitalism is distinctly unfashionable yet is necessary if the current trajectory of society is to be changed. Rather than more equitable forms of inclusion, liberation is called for. This requires new articulations of the hope for progress, the loss of which Kyriakides and Torres (2014) argue characterises the current period. It is important not to be overly prescriptive about what an alternative mode of production might look like. The mass movements that would be necessary to bring about such a transformation will inevitably develop new ideas and learn lessons through practice that cannot be anticipated. Nevertheless, in Marx and Engels' (1969 [1848]) sense of a mode of production involving common ownership of the means of production and the rational use of resources to meet human needs, it seems reasonable to describe the necessary alternative as socialist. Such a transformation would not solve everything overnight, and the histories of previous socialist revolutions, including all their errors and accomplishments, provide a rich store of lessons if we take them seriously and apply them in today's context (eg Carr, 1969; Yaffe, 2009, 2019). Socialism would open possibilities to begin to address problems that remain intractable today, necessarily including a reorganisation of Britain's relationship with other parts of the world, from relations based on exploitation to ones based on voluntary cooperation.

Pursuing a break from capitalism might be supported by retrieving the concept of the general interest of the working class, arising from a position of exploitation that manifests in multiple forms. This would require an ongoing struggle for independence from the institutional apparatus and governing ideas of the capitalist state, and against the influence of opportunism (see Chapter 2). Arguments that adopt a narrow focus on economic issues – concerning wages, jobs or services – correspond to a trend that Lenin (1978 [1902]) called 'economism'. Such approaches cannot effectively tackle racism within the working class because they do not engage with either subjective identities or the possibility for working-class liberation, and are easily subverted by concessions that may benefit one section of the working class while selling out others. A sense of cultural threat has been an important part of discussions about migration in Britain (Macdonald, 2011), and needs to be accounted for in building class solidarity. It can be understood as the dominance of national consciousness over international class consciousness. The national basis and international operations of British capitalism lend its hegemonic ideas a strongly nationalist character. This also applies to their Left variants, such as the Labour Party's commitments under Jeremy Corbyn to increase the number of border guards, maintain defence spending and sustain Britain's role in NATO (Labour Party, 2017). Challenging hostility to migrants therefore requires the development of radical class-based and internationalist subjectivities, which can enable more effective challenges to the ruling classes.

Establishing a general class interest through multiplicity

Mezzadra and Neilson (2013) point out that, today, the essential unity of the working class is both more concrete and more complex and obscured in everyday experience because labour is simultaneously globally interconnected and highly differentiated by its concrete forms and conditions. Consistent with this, points of connection that show the way towards an independent working-class standpoint are both emergent within many grass-roots struggles and require rigorous analysis and elaboration. This book has aimed to contribute to such an analysis.

The irreducible heterogeneity of the working class does not invalidate the idea of a general interest, rooted ultimately in shared humanity, and more immediately in alienation resulting from a lack of mobility power. Neither does this heterogeneity invalidate the potential for the working class to act as a revolutionary agent in the destruction of capitalism. Mezzadra and Neilson (2013: 93) suggest that class fractioning is both a means of subjugation and a catalyst for resistance:

> in [one] sense, [labour's] multiplication plays the role of 'divide and rule'. On the other hand, living labour has still the chance to refuse to subordinate itself.… It is from this point of view that multiplication can become an incalculable element in the

relations between capital and labor, giving rise to unforeseeable tensions, movements, and struggles.

A general class interest as a basis for collective action, necessarily embracing the multiplicity of the working class, can only be established concretely through practice. As Oliveri (2018) demonstrates in the case of Italy, struggles around issues such as migrant rights, employment and housing can all provide opportunities to challenge racialised divides and build action around connected interests.

Forming alliances between differently positioned groups and individuals raises difficult questions of trust. Bloch and McKay (2016: 13) point out that trust 'does not necessarily indicate relationships of equality or even of choice ... there may be no alternative but to "trust" or perhaps more accurately to "hope" that the individual or organisation in whom trust has been placed will not betray'. Building trust across the multiple cleavages within the working class, which have been discussed throughout this book, calls for practices of solidarity defined by:

> mutuality, accountability, and the recognition of common interests as the basis for relationships among diverse communities. Rather than assuming an enforced commonality of oppression, the practice of solidarity foregrounds communities of people who have chosen to work and fight together. Diversity and difference are central values here – to be acknowledged and respected, not erased in the building of alliances. (Mohanty, 2003: 7)

Openness and democracy are therefore essential, as is the *time* necessary to develop an understanding of objective connections between differently positioned sections of society and their lived experiences.

In charting a way forward, from the imperialist crisis towards socialist transformation, Marx's (1943 [1852]) and Lenin's (1978 [1902]) ideas remain relevant. Both emphasise the convergence of objective and subjective conditions that make a revolution possible, such that: (1) the ruling classes are unable to continue their rule in the old way; (2) the working class, or at least significant sections of it, face a significant deterioration in their living conditions; (3) as a consequence of the first two conditions, there is an increase in collective action among oppressed classes. Where these objective conditions combine with a working-class leadership that is able to develop a counter-hegemonic perspective and draw wider sections of oppressed classes around it in a mass movement to break the control of the ruling classes, revolution becomes possible. Today the first of those conditions is already fulfilled: the ruling classes are being forced to rapidly adapt their strategies of governance, by increasing the disciplinary character of the state, attacking formerly privileged sections of the working class, and extending exploitation to new areas. The second condition is also clearly evident, but so far, instead of collective action, deteriorating conditions have largely led to individual responses, such as those who take their own life following welfare cuts, or individuals evading border controls. Where people have responded collectively this has often taken isolated forms, for example in campaigns that focus on employment, or housing, or migrant rights, each important in themselves but so far lacking strong connections between them, even if the same individuals are sometimes part of multiple campaigns. These limitations in the development of collective action are part of a decades-long 'political stultification of labor' (Carbonella and Kasmir, 2018: 2), although it is by no means absolute and history suggests that it will not last. As Carbonella and Kasmir (2018: 24–5) say when commenting on Arundhati Roy's essay on Maoist rebellions in Central India:

> In the one instance, impoverished, indebted peasants and proletarians appear as surplus populations whose way out is to end their lives. In the next, they rise up against their misery and command the attention and resources of the state and capital that furiously try to put them down. And they make history.

Such confidence in oppressed people to transform the world is an important part of any hope for socialist transformation.

Today, where counter-hegemonic understandings exist, they generally lack any organisational expression. Most organisations that seek to address the issues discussed in this book operate well within the capitalist horizon and limit their demands to concessions that seem possible under current political and economic conditions. That is why the critical activist perspectives discussed throughout this book are important, particularly where they push beyond the limited options available within capitalism while remaining rooted in concrete struggles. Their existence points towards the practical possibility of developing working-class standpoints that are attentive to differential conditions of inclusion and exploitation and look beyond the capitalist horizon. Realising the potential of such work calls for the centre of theoretical development to move out of the university, as hooks (2014) suggests, and to make use of approaches such as small group meetings in the community, where personal experiences can be discussed together with theory, and hierarchies of knowledge that arise from capitalism can be challenged.

In translating these ideas into practice, the form of organisation is important. A black and minority ethnic (BME) voluntary sector worker described a process by which community activists had moved into the statutory sector and become 'compromised':

> 'the VCS [voluntary and community] sector and the BME sector was good at training people up, and what you found was then people moved on ... to the statutory sector.... And that's why then that strength of ... activism hasn't continued because people have gone on to do policy jobs or any other jobs ... or race equality officer. So, then, that pool of knowledge and expertise is, not totally lost, but is compromised, because then that worker ... feels that they are not in a position to speak up sometimes because their paymaster is, is the local authority.' (Interview P1)

Similar issues have been identified in previous research (Vickers, 2012, 2016), as well as the potential for alternative forms of independent organisation (Vickers, 2014). Yet, formal independence is no guarantee that an organisation will give expression to the general interest of the working class. As James (2012 [1983]: 78) argues, organisations that have emerged from within struggle can become some of the most dangerous enemies of the working class:

> Precisely because they are not grafted onto the class but have come from struggle, it is they who have become the most efficient agency to buttress and reinforce the working class as capital, to discipline us to work, and to work us so we will be disciplined. As the working class becomes stronger ... the more do the agencies of capital reach into the fabric of the working class itself, more difficult to identify, more mystified in their function by their working-class mantle, vocabulary, accent – more dangerous.

Building new organisations also faces many challenges. The BME voluntary sector worker quoted earlier suggested that there is currently a lack of self-organisation among migrants in North-East England. They explained this partly through funding cuts for organisations that had previously helped people to organise, and partly through the desperation of people's personal situations, such that concerns over "food, shelter, employment" dominated, "and before you get to that stage of helping others, it's about helping yourself". This was echoed by many of the campaigners interviewed, and emphasises the importance of alliances between people who are differently positioned within the system, facing varying barriers and with varying resources, experience and skills.

Today, there is an urgent need to strengthen connections between campaigns that already exist, to expand their reach through open and democratic organising, and to deepen the connection between struggle around immediate issues and systemic analysis. Forms of organising need to be developed that are simultaneously sensitive to the kind of local attachments and specificities discussed in Chapter 5, and extend beyond them, recognising that 'the local' is actively produced, and can be both 'a site of solidarity, shared suffering, and common struggle', and 'a central feature of dispossession', undermining working-class power by breaking it into disconnected geographical units (Carbonella and Kasmir, 2018: 21). Alternatives need to be worked out in practice, tailored to specific conditions:

> 'we need to both fight for the rights of the Windrush Generation but, at the same time, show how what is happening to them is not happening in isolation, but rather is linked to this very colonial, imperial regime of mobility and citizenship which is both external and internal.... There needs to be both the specificity and the direct actions that in the meantime are creating conditions of allowing people to survive. Whether that's opening squats to house refuges because the state is shutting them down, whether that's grounding flights that are deporting people, whether that's calling on people to boycott the Schools Census.... At the same time, there also needs to be a broader coalition building that breaks down a lot of the racist discourses in society. And really, I don't really see how we can move much more forwards without that. All we're gonna get is these tiny little wins which are the odd resignation in the government and an apology. I don't want an apology; I want every detention prison to get shut down.' (Interview A14)

The critical distinction is to begin from people's needs, rather than limiting ourselves to what is possible within capitalism; arguably, this is the meaning of a revolutionary approach.

Appendix: Methodology

Amid the diverse activity that informed the writing of this book, described in Chapter 1, three more bounded areas of empirical research warrant more detailed explanation.

Researching 'new migrants' in the North-East England workforce

This project took place during 2013–16 and adopted a mixed-methods approach, drawing on Bloch (2002) and Phillimore and Goodson (2006). It included a survey ($n = 402$), qualitative interviews with migrants ($n = 40$) and practitioners ($n = 12$), and a policy seminar ($n = 50$).

In the absence of a reliable sampling frame for the target population, the survey used non-probability methods, similar to Bloch and McKay (2016), with purposive sampling from multiple starting points. Sampling aimed for diversity by locality, gender, age, immigration status and country of origin. Responses were collected face-to-face via support agencies, drop-ins, migrant community organisations, ESOL classes, workplaces and a small number online. The sample composition is shown in Table A1.

A total of 40 migrants participated in qualitative interviews, 27 of whom volunteered following completion of the survey and 13 of whom were recruited via referrals. The sample composition is shown in Table A2. Six of the 40 interviews used an interpreter, and a second translator checked these transcripts for accuracy.

A total of 12 voluntary and statutory sector practitioners were recruited through a snowball approach, aiming for diversity in sector and migrant user groups. They included representatives of migrant organisations, voluntary and statutory service providers, a trade union, and an employers' association.

SPSS software was used to produce descriptive statistics from survey data. Thematic coding of interview transcripts used Nvivo software. Biographical summaries were also produced for each of the 40 migrants interviewed and this informed consideration of how different themes interacted within individuals' lives (for further details, see Clayton and Vickers, 2017).

Table A1: Survey sample

Sub-region	
Tyneside and Northumberland (NE postcodes)	31% (*n* = 126)
Sunderland and Durham (SR and DH postcodes)	24% (*n* = 98)
Teesside and Darlington (TS and DL postcodes)	35% (*n* = 139)
Unknown (no postcode provided)	10% (*n* = 39)
Gender	
Male	51% (*n* = 194)
Female	49% (*n* = 184)
Age	
Under 16	1% (*n* = 3)
16–24	14% (*n* = 55)
25–34	36% (*n* = 143)
35–44	33% (*n* = 128)
45–54	14% (*n* = 55)
55–64	3% (*n* = 10)
Immigration status	
EU10 migrants	28% (*n* = 112)
Refugees with leave to remain[a]	24% (*n* = 98)
Asylum seekers[b]	22% (*n* = 88)
Other status/unknown[c]	26% (*n* = 104)

Notes: [a] Includes British citizens who previously claimed asylum. [b] Includes refused asylum seekers. [c] Includes EU15 migrants, spouse visas and work permits.

Table A2: Migrant qualitative interviews sample

Sub-region	
Tyneside and Northumberland	37% ($n = 15$)
Sunderland and Durham	40% ($n = 16$)
Teesside and Darlington	18% ($n = 7$)
Unknown	5% ($n = 2$)
Gender	
Male	38% ($n = 15$)
Female	62% ($n = 25$)
Age	
Under 16[a]	0% ($n = 0$)
16–24	5% ($n = 2$)
25–34	20% ($n = 8$)
35–44	33% ($n = 13$)
45–54	10% ($n = 4$)
55–64	3% ($n = 1$)
Unknown	30% ($n = 12$)
Immigration status	
EU10 migrants	35% ($n = 14$)
Refugees with leave to remain[b]	43% ($n = 17$)
Asylum seekers[c]	20% ($n = 8$)
Other status[d]	3% ($n = 1$)

Notes: [a] The survey targeted people aged 16 years and older. Three self-completed responses were received from people describing themselves as under the age of 16 but these were excluded from the analysis. [b] Includes British citizens who previously claimed asylum. [c] Includes refused asylum seekers. [d] A non-EU spouse of an EU migrant.

Analysing hegemonic discourse via media products

Key characteristics of the television documentaries discussed in Chapter 6 are shown in Table A3.

Table A3: Documentary characteristics

Documentary	Viewers	Audience share	Broadcast date	Time	Channel
BS Episode 2	5.1 million	20.8%	13 January 2014	9 pm	Channel Four
HWBI	1.5 million	6.9%	8 January 2014	10 pm	BBC Two
TIUK	1.37 million	6.3%	7 January 2014	9.30 pm	BBC Two

Source: www.digitalspy.co.uk

The documentaries were analysed thematically using the transcription of spoken words, images and sounds, combined with repeat viewing at various speeds. Corner (1996: 11) notes the importance of analysing documentaries in the context of their wider 'political, economic and social orders, within different landscapes of public knowledge'. Responding to this, our analysis moved from the documentaries as concrete media products, to abstractions, such as discourses of race and systems of capitalist exploitation, and back from there to a more informed understanding of the documentaries (following Marx, 1973 [1857]: 100–2). This produced an interpretation of the documentaries in the context of wider representations of class, race and migration, and in relation to different class interests (Wayne, 2003: 222).

Activist perspectives

A total of 17 campaigners were interviewed during 2018 about their views on the policies and the practices of the British state, as well as the perspectives on society that informed their own political practice. This aimed for insights that McDermott and Raley (2011: 372) suggest are available by listening to people engaged in action in and on the world:

> People figuring out what to do next are a boon to researchers. In the work people do to make their versions of the world available to each other, researchers can find the organising principles of social life.... Even if the underlying dynamics of the social world are obscured, this condition, too, is a systematic result of people distorting their vision and repressing their interpretations of each other under difficult circumstances.

Interviewees were selected using criteria that included coverage of a range of contemporary struggles over migration and welfare, a variety of places and a focus on campaigners who were independent in the sense that they were not paid to campaign, although some had jobs that were closely related. The sample did not aim to cover the full range of perspectives among campaigners, but rather to seek out people questioning the fundamental structures of society that could be brought into conversation with the ideas presented in this book. Characteristics of the interviewees are shown in Table A4. Due to the small size of the campaigns under discussion, specific countries of origin are not given because this would threaten anonymity.

Two of the participants who were born in the UK described being the children of migrants and suggested that this was important for their perspective. Nine spoke about being directly affected by the issues that they were campaigning on, and five were also engaged in some form of professional practice relating to the issue. Some of these participants were recruited through long-standing relationships, while others were recruited by contacting campaigns online.

All research conformed to the ethical guidelines of the British Sociological Association and was approved by ethics committees at Northumbria and Nottingham Trent universities.

Table A4: Activist sample

Location[a]	
London	5
Worcester	1
Birmingham	1
Nottingham	4
Newcastle-upon-Tyne	7
Gender	
Male	7
Female	9
Campaigning focus[b]	
Housing	10
Deportations	6
Immigration detention	9
Council cuts	7
Health care	5
Education	4
Country of origin	
UK	14
Non-UK	3

Notes: [a] Where an individual reported living in more than one location during the course of their activism, both are indicated. [b] Where a participant reported significant involvement in more than one area of campaigning, all are indicated.

References

Aburish, S.K. (1997) *A brutal friendship: The West and the Arab elite*, New York, NY: St. Martin's Press.

Adamson, O., Brown, C., Harrison, J. and Price, J. (1976) 'Women's oppression under capitalism', *Revolutionary Communist*, 5: 1–48, http://www.revolutionarycommunist.org/britain/women-s-oppression/2850-women-s-oppression-under-capitalism

ADS (2017) 'Industry facts and figures: a guide to the UK's aerospace, defence, security, and space sectors', https://www.adsgroup.org.uk/wp-content/uploads/sites/21/2017/06/ADS-Annual-Facts-2017.pdf

Agostinone-Wilson, F. (2013) *Dialectical research methods in the classical Marxist tradition*, New York, NY: Peter Lang.

Alberti, G. (2014) 'Mobility strategies, "mobility differentials" and "transnational exit": the experiences of precarious migrants in London's hospitality jobs', *Work, Employment and Society*, 28(6): 865–81.

Alberti, G. (2017) 'The government of migration through workfare in the UK: towards a shrinking space of mobility and social rights?', *Movements*, https://movements-journal.org/issues/04.bewegungen/08.alberti--government-migration-workfare-uk-mobility-social-rights.html

Alberti, G. and Però, D. (2018) 'Migrating industrial relations: migrant workers' initiative within and outside trade unions', *British Journal of Industrial Relations*, 56(4): 693–715.

Allen, W.L. (2016) *A decade of immigration in the British press, Migration Observatory report*, Oxford: COMPAS, University of Oxford.

Alonso, J.M., Clifton, J. and Díaz-Fuentes, D. (2013) 'Did new public management matter? An empirical analysis of the outsourcing and decentralization effects on public sector size', *Public Management Review*, 17(5): 643–60.

Anderson, B. (2010a) 'British jobs for British workers? Understanding demand for migrant workers in a recession', *The Whitehead Journal of Diplomacy and International Relations*, Winter/Spring: 103–14.

Anderson, B. (2010b) 'Migration, immigration controls and the fashioning of precarious workers', *Work, Employment and Society*, 24(2): 300–17.

Anderson, B. (2013) *Us and them? The dangerous politics of immigration control*, Oxford: Oxford University Press.

Anderson, K. (2010) *Marx at the margins*, Chicago, IL: University of Chicago Press.

Andrejevic, M. (2011) 'Managing the borders: classed mobility on security-themed reality TV', in H. Wood and B. Skeggs (eds) *Reality television and class*, London: Palgrave MacMillan/BFI, pp 60–72.

Anthias, F. (1980) 'Women and the reserve army of labour: a critique of Veronica Beechey', *Capital and Class*, 4(1): 50–63.

Ashe, S. (2018) 'Increasing economic opportunity or bolstering racial neoliberalism?', *Discover Society*, https://discoversociety.org/2018/05/01/increasing-economic-opportunity-or-bolstering-racial-neoliberalism/

Ashe, S.D. and Nazroo, J. (2016) *Equality, diversity and racism in the workplace: A qualitative analysis of the 2015 race at work survey*, Manchester: ESRC Centre on Dynamics of Ethnicity, University of Manchester.

ASYL (Informationsverbund Asyl und Migration) (2017) 'Dublin: Germany', Asylum Information Database, www.asylumineurope.org/reports/country/germany/asylum-procedure/procedures/dublin

Axelsson, L., Malmberg, B. and Zhang, Q. (2015) 'On waiting, work-time and imagined futures: theorising temporal precariousness among Chinese chefs in Sweden's restaurant industry', *Geoforum*, 78: 169–78.

Bakewell, O. (2011) 'Migration and development in sub-Saharan Africa', in N. Phillips (ed) *Migration in the global political economy*, Boulder, CO: Lynne Rienner Publishers, pp 121–41.

Balaram, B. and Wallace-Stephens, F. (2018) *Thriving, striving, or just about surviving? Seven portraits of economic security and modern work in the UK*, London: RSA Future Work Centre.

Balch, A. (2015) 'Understanding and evaluating UK efforts to tackle forced labour', in L. Waite, G. Craig, H. Lewis and K. Skrivankova (eds) *Vulnerability, exploitation and migrants: Insecure work in a globalised economy*, Basingstoke: Palgrave MacMillan, pp 86–98.

Bale, T. (2016) 'Corbyn's labour: survey of post-2015 Labour members and supporters', QMUL Blog, www.qmul.ac.uk/media/news/2016/items/corbyns-labour-survey-of-post-2015-labour-members-and-supporters.html

Bales, K. (2017) 'Immigration raids, employer collusion and the Immigration Act 2016', *Industrial Law Journal*, 46(2): 279–88.

Bales, K. and Mayblin, L. (2018) 'Unfree labour in immigration detention: exploitation and coercion of a captive immigrant workforce', *Economy and Society*, 47(2): 191–213.

Bandeira, L.A.M. (2017) *The second Cold War: Geopolitics and the strategic dimensions of the USA*, Cham: Springer.

Banks, A., Hamroush, S., Taylor, C. and Hardie, M. (2014) *An international perspective on the UK – Gross domestic product*, London: Office for National Statistics.

BARB (Broadcasters' Audience Research Board) (2014) 'Trends in television viewing: 2013', https://www.barb.co.uk/download/?file=/ wp-content/uploads/2015/12/BARB-Trends-in-Television-Viewing-2013.pdf

Bassel, L. and Emejulu, A. (2017) *Minority women and austerity: Survival and resistance in France and Britain*, Bristol: The Policy Press.

Bauman, Z. (2016) *Strangers at our door*, Cambridge: Polity.

Beatty, C. and Fothergill, S. (2011) 'The prospects for worklessness in Britain's weaker local economies', *Cambridge Journal of Regions, Economy and Society*, 4(3): 401–17.

Beatty, C. and Fothergill, S. (2013) *Hitting the poorest places hardest: The local and regional impact of welfare reform*, Sheffield: Sheffield Hallam University Centre for Regional Economic and Social Research.

Beechey, V. (1977) 'Some notes on female wage labour in capitalist production', *Capital and Class*, 1(3): 45–66.

Bell, E. (2016) 'Soft power and corporate imperialism: maintaining British influence', *Race and Class*, 57(4): 75–86.

Bell, J. (2014) 'Newcastle council's attempted bribery', Revolutionary Communist Group, www.revolutionarycommunist.org/branches/ north-east-england/3469-newcastle-council-bribery

Berntsen, L. (2016) 'Reworking labour practices: on the agency of unorganized mobile migrant construction workers', *Work, Employment and Society*, 30(3): 472–88.

BIS (Department for Business, Innovation and Skills) (2017) *Trade union membership 2016: Statistical bulletin*, London: Department for Business, Innovation and Skills.

Black Women's Rape Action Project and Women Against Rape (2015) 'Rape and sexual abuse in Yarl's Wood immigration removal centre', www.womenagainstrape.net/sites/default/files/dossier_rape_in_ yarls_woodfinaljuly15.pdf

Blagg, H. and Derricourt, N. (1982) 'Why we need to reconstruct a theory of the state for community work', in G. Craig, N. Derricourt and M. Loney (eds) *Community work and the state: Towards a radical practice*, London: Routledge and Kegan Paul, pp 11–23.

Bleich, E., Bloemraad, I. and Graauw, E.D. (2015) 'Migrants, minorities and the media: information, representations and participation in the public sphere', *Ethnic and Migration Studies*, 41(6): 857–73.

Blinder, S. (2017) *Deportations, removals and voluntary departures from the UK*, Oxford: The Migration Observatory.

Bloch, A. (2002) *Refugees' opportunities and barriers in employment and training*, London: Department for Work and Pensions.

Bloch, A. (2014) 'Living in fear: rejected asylum seekers living as irregular migrants in England', *Journal of Ethnic and Migration Studies*, 40(10): 1507–25.

Bloch, A. and McKay, S. (2016) *Living on the margins: Undocumented migrants in a global city*, Bristol: The Policy Press.

Blyth, M. (2013) *Austerity: The history of a dangerous idea*, Oxford: Oxford University Press.

Boleat, M. (2018) *Brexit and the financial services industry: The story so far*, London: Centre for European Reform.

Bonell, C., McKee, M. and Fletcher, A. (2016) 'Troubled families, troubled policy making', *BMJ*, 10.1136/bmj.i5879(355).

Boswell, C. (2003) 'Burden-sharing in the European Union: lessons from the German and UK experience', *Journal of Refugee Studies*, 16(3): 316–35.

Braedley, S. and Luxton, M. (2015) 'Foreword', in K. Meehan and K. Strauss (eds) *Precarious worlds: Contested geographies of social reproduction*, Athens, GA: University of Georgia Press, pp vii–xv.

Bramley, G. (2017) *Homelessness projections: Core homelessness in Great Britain*, London: Crisis and Heriot Watt University.

Braverman, H. (1998 [1974]) *Labor and monopoly capital: The degradation of work in the twentieth century*, New York, NY: Monthly Review Press.

Brewer, M., Finch, D. and Tomlinson, D. (2017) *Universal remedy: Ensuring Universal Credit is fit for purpose*, London: Resolution Foundation.

Briskman, L. and Cemlyn, S. (2005) 'Reclaiming humanity for asylum-seekers: a social work response', *International Social Work*, 48(6): 714–24.

British Red Cross (2010) 'Not gone, but forgotten: the urgent need for a more humane asylum system', http://lastradainternational.org/lsidocs/not%20gone.pdf

British Red Cross and Boaz Trust (2013) 'A decade of destitution: time to make a change', https://www.redcross.org.uk/-/media/documents/about-us/research-publications/refugee-support/greater-manchester-destitution-report.pdf

Bromma (2013) *The worker elite: Notes on the 'labor aristocracy'*, Montreal: Kersplebedeb Publishing.

Brown, H.A. (2012) *Marx on gender and the family: A critical study*, Leiden: Brill.

Butler, J. (2009) 'Performativity, precarity and sexual politics', *AIBR Revista De Antropologia Iberoamericana*, 4(3): 321–36.

Cabinet Office (2018) 'Race disparity audit', https://assets.publishing. service.gov.uk/government/uploads/system/uploads/attachment_ data/file/686071/Revised_RDA_report_March_2018.pdf

Cabral, A. (1964) 'Brief analysis of the social structure in Guinea', Marxist Internet Archive, www.marxists.org/subject/africa/ cabral/1964/bassg.htm

Callinicos, A., Rees, J., Harman, C. and Haynes, M. (1994) *Marxism and the new imperialism*, London: Bookmarks.

Campesi, G. (2018) 'Crisis, migration and the consolidation of the EU border control regime', *International Journal of Migration and Border Studies*, 4(3): 196–221.

Capita Asset Services (2014) 'FTSE 100 net cash piles soar as firms find few opportunities to invest', findings available at: https://www. newbusiness.co.uk/articles/banking-finance/ftse-100-net-cash-piles- soar-firms-find-few-opportunities-invest

Carbonella, A. and Kasmir, S. (2018) 'Introduction', in S. Kasmir and A. Carbonella (eds) *Blood and fire: Toward a global anthropology of labor*, New York: Berghahn, pp 1–29.

Carey, M. (2008) 'Everything must go? The privatization of state social work', *British Journal of Social Work*, 38(5): 918–35.

Carling, J. and Hagen-Zanker, J. (2018) 'Record deaths at sea: will "regional disembarkation" help save lives?', PRIO Blogs, https:// blogs.prio.org/2018/07/record-deaths-at-sea-will-regional- disembarkation-help-save-lives/

Carmel, E. and Cerami, A. (2011) 'Governing migration and welfare: institutions and emotions in the production of differential integration', in E. Carmel, A. Cerami and T. Papadopoulos (eds) *Migration and welfare in the new Europe: Social protection and the challenges of integration*, Bristol: The Policy Press, pp 1–20.

Carr, E.H. (1969) *The Bolshevik Revolution 1917–1923*, London: Penguin.

Casas-Cortés, M. (2014) 'A genealogy of precarity: a toolbox for rearticulating fragmented social realities in and out of the workplace', *Rethinking Marxism*, 26(2): 206–26.

Casey, L. (2016) *The Casey review: A review into opportunity and integration*, London: Department for Communities and Local Government.

Cassidy, K. (2018) 'Everyday bordering, healthcare and the politics of belonging in contemporary Britain', in A. Paasi, J. Saarinen, K. Zimmerbauer and E.-K. Prokkola (eds) *Borderless worlds – For whom? Ethics, moralities and mobilities*, Abingdon: Routledge.

Castells, M., Bouin, O., Caraça, J., Cardosa, G., Thompson, J.B. and Wieviorka, M. (eds) (2018) *Europe's crises*, Cambridge: Polity.

Castles, S. and Kosack, G. (1973) *Immigrant workers and class structure in Western Europe*, London: Oxford University Press.

Caviedes, A. (2015) 'An emerging "European" news portrayal of immigration?', *Journal of Ethnic and Migration Studies*, 41(6): 897–917.

Chahal, K. (2007) *Racist harassment and housing services*, London: Race Equality Foundation.

Charnock, G. and Starosta, G. (2016) 'Introduction: the new international division of labour and the critique of political economy today', in G. Charnock and G. Starosta (eds) *The new international division of labour: Global transformation and uneven development*, London: Palgrave MacMillan, pp 1–22.

CIPD (Chartered Institute of Personnel and Development) (2013) 'The state of migration: employing migrant workers', https://www.cipd.co.uk/knowledge/fundamentals/emp-law/recruitment/migrant-workers-report

Clark, I. and Colling, T. (2018) 'Work in Britain's informal economy: learning from road-side hand car washes', *British Journal of Industrial Relations*, 56(2): 320–41.

Clarke, J. and Newman, J. (2012) 'The alchemy of austerity', *Critical Social Policy*, 32(3): 299–319.

Clayton, J. (2012) 'Living the multicultural city: acceptance, belonging and young identities in the city of Leicester, England', *Ethnic and Racial Studies*, 35(9): 1673–93.

Clayton, J. and Vickers, T. (2017) 'The contingent challenges of purposeful co-production: researching new migrant employment experiences in the north east of England', *Area*, 10.1111/area.12409.

Clayton, J. and Vickers, T. (2018) 'Temporal tensions: European Union citizen migrants, asylum seekers and refugees navigating dominant temporalities of work in England', *Time & Society*, 10.1177/0961463X18778466.

Clayton, J., Donovan, C. and Merchant, J. (2016) 'Distancing and limited resourcefulness: third sector service provision under austerity localism in the north east of England', *Urban Studies*, 53(4): 723–40.

Clough, R. (2010) 'Trade unions in Britain: unparalleled stagnation and decay', *Fight Racism! Fight Imperialism!*, 217, http://www.revolutionarycommunist.org/britain/labourtrade-unions/3378-trade-unions-in-britain-unparalleled-stagnation-and-decay-frfi-217-octnov-2010

Clough, R. (2014) *Labour: A party fit for imperialism* (2nd edn), London: Larkin Publications.

Clough, R., Davidson, S., Mulgrew, D., Palmer, S., Rayne, T. and Wiener, C. (2018) *Whose land is it anyway? Housing, the capitalist crisis and the working class*, London: Larkin Publications.

Cockburn, P. (2015) *The rise of the Islamic State: Isis and the new Sunni revolution*, London: Verso.

Collett, E. (2011) *Immigrant integration in Europe in a time of austerity*, Washington, DC: Migration Policy Institute.

Collett, E. (2016) 'The paradox of the EU–turkey refugee deal', www.migrationpolicy.org/news/paradox-eu-turkey-refugee-deal

Collinson, S. (1996) 'Visa requirements, carrier sanctions, "safe third countries" and "readmission": the development of an asylum "buffer zone" in Europe', *Transactions of the Institute of British Geographers*, 21(1): 76–90.

Corner, J. (1996) *The art of record*, Manchester: Manchester University Press.

Corporate Watch (2018) 'The UK border regime: a critical guide', https://corporatewatch.org/new-book-the-uk-border-regime/

Coulter, J., Miller, S. and Walker, M. (1984) *State of siege: Miners' strike 1984*, London: Canary Press.

Craig, G. (2007) '"Cunning, unprincipled, loathsome": the racist tail wags the welfare dog', *Journal of Social Policy*, 36(4): 605–23.

Craig, G. (2011) 'Forward to the past: can the UK black and minority ethnic third sector survive?', *Voluntary Sector Review*, 2(3): 367–89.

Craig, G. (2012) 'The history and pattern of settlement of the UK's black and minority ethnic population', in G. Craig, K. Atkin, S. Chattoo and R. Flynn (eds) *Understanding 'race' and ethnicity: Theory, history, policy, practice*, Bristol: The Policy Press, pp 41–70.

Crawley, H. and Skleparis, D. (2018) 'Refugees, migrants, neither, both: categorical fetishism and the politics of bounding in Europe's "migration crisis"', *Journal of Ethnic and Migration Studies*, 44(1): 48–64.

Crawley, H., Düvell, F., Jones, K., McMahon, S. and Sigona, N. (2018) *Unravelling Europe's 'migration crisis': Journeys over land and sea*, Bristol: The Policy Press.

Crenshaw, K. (2018) 'From shattered ceilings to a broken democracy: the post-racial condition of Trump's America', paper presented at the British Sociological Association Annual Conference, Newcastle upon Tyne.

Cross, H. (2013) *Migrants, borders and global capitalism: West African labour mobility and EU borders*, Abingdon: Routledge.

Crossley, S. (2018) '"Telling it like it is?" A critical perspective on the Casey review into opportunity and integration', Discover Society, https://discoversociety.org/2018/05/01/telling-it-like-it-is-a-critical-perspective-on-the-casey-review-into-opportunity-and-integration/

Crossley, S. and Fletcher, G. (2013) *Written out of the picture? The role of local services in tackling child poverty amongst asylum seekers and refugees*, Durham and Gateshead: North East Child Poverty Commission and Regional Refugee Forum North East.

Curtis, M. (2016) 'The new colonialism: Britain's scramble for Africa's energy and mineral resources', War on Want, https://waronwant.org/resources/new-colonialism-britains-scramble-africas-energy-and-mineral-resources

D'Arcy, C. (2017) 'Low pay Britain 2017', Resolution Foundation, www.resolutionfoundation.org/publications/low-pay-britain-2017/

Darling, J. (2016) 'Privatising asylum: neoliberalisation, depoliticisation and the governance of forced migration', *Transactions*, 41(3): 230–43.

Datta, K. (2011) 'Last hired and first fired? The impact of the economic downturn on low-paid Bulgarian migrant workers in London', *Journal of International Development*, 23: 565–82.

Datta, K., McIlwaine, C., Evans, Y., Herbert, J., May, J. and Wills, J. (2007a) 'From coping strategies to tactics: London's low-pay economy and migrant labour', *British Journal of Industrial Relations*, 45(2): 404–32.

Datta, K., McIlwaine, C., Wills, J., Evans, Y., Herbert, J. and May, J. (2007b) 'The new development finance or exploiting migrant labour? Remittance sending among low-paid migrant workers in London', *International Development Planning Review*, 29(1): 43–67.

Day, R.B. and Gaido, D. (eds) (2012) *Discovering imperialism: Social democracy to World War I*, Chicago, IL: Haymarket Books.

DCLG (Department for Communities and Local Government) (2015) 'Land value estimates for policy appraisal', https://www.gov.uk/government/publications/land-value-estimates-for-policy-appraisal-2015

DCLG (2017a) 'English housing survey headline report, 2015–16', https://www.gov.uk/government/statistics/english-housing-survey-2015-to-2016-headline-report

DCLG (2017b) *Fixing our broken housing market*, Cm 9352, London: HMSO.

Deeming, C. (2015) 'Foundations of the workfare state – reflections on the political transformation of the welfare state in Britain', *Social Policy & Administration*, 49(7): 862–86.

De Genova, N. (2010) 'The deportation regime: sovereignty, space, and the freedom of movement', in N. De Genova and N. Peutz (eds) *The deportation regime: Sovereignty, space, and the freedom of movement*, Durham, NC: Duke University Press, pp 33–68.

De Genova, N. (ed) (2017) *The borders of 'Europe': Autonomy of migration, tactics of bordering*, Durham, NC: Duke University Press.

De Lara, J. (2018) *Inland shift: Race, space, and capital in Southern California*, Oakland, CA: University of California Press.

De Stefano, V. (2016) *The rise of the 'just-in-time workforce': On-demand work, crowdwork and labour protection in the 'gig economy'*, Geneva: International Labour Office.

DH (Department of Health) (2004) 'Implementing the overseas visitors hospital charging regulations: guidance for NHS trust hospitals in England', https://assets.publishing.service.gov.uk/government/uploads/system/uploads/attachment_data/file/474278/Implementing_overseas_charging_regulations_2015.pdf

Dhesi, S., Isakjee, A. and Davies, T. (2015) *An environmental health assessment of the new migrant camp in Calais*, Birmingham: University of Birmingham.

DHSC (Department of Health and Social Care) (2018) 'Guidance on implementing the overseas visitor charging regulations', https://www.gov.uk/government/publications/overseas-nhs-visitors-implementing-the-charging-regulations

Dickenson, V. and Grayson, J. (2018) 'UK migration rules make children homeless', Open Democracy, www.opendemocracy.net/john-grayson-violet-dickenson/children-made-homeless-by-migration-rules

Dines, N., Montagna, N. and Vacchelli, E. (2018) 'Beyond crisis talk: interrogating migration and crises in Europe', *Sociology*, 52(3): 439–47.

Donaghy, R. (2009) *One death is too many: Inquiry into the underlying causes of construction fatal accidents*, London: Secretary of State for Work and Pensions.

Donovan, C., Clayton, J. and Merchant, J. (2012) *Localism or pulling the plug on public services? Consequences of austerity for the third sector in the North East: Second year report*, Sunderland: Centre for Children, Young People and Families, University of Sunderland.

Drahokoupil, J. and Jepsen, M. (2017) 'The digital economy and its implications for labour. 1. The platform economy', *Transfer: European Review of Labour and Research*, 23(2): 103–19.

Dustmann, C. and Frattini, T. (2014) 'The fiscal effects of immigration to the UK', *The Economic Journal*, 124(580): F593-F643.

Dwyer, P. and Scullion, L. (2014) *Conditionality briefing: Migrants*, York: JRF.

EEAS (European External Action Service) (2016) 'Eunavfor med op sophia – six monthly report 22 June–31 December 2015', https://wikileaks.org/eu-military-refugees/EEAS/EEAS-2016-126.pdf

Elmer, S. and Dening, G. (2016) 'The London clearances', *City*, 20(2): 271–7.

Engels, F. (1987 [1887]) *The condition of the working class in England in 1844*, London: Penguin Classics.

Essed, P. (2013) 'Entitlement racism: license to humiliate', in S. Pfohman and L. Fekete (eds) *Recycling hatred: Racism(s) in Europe today*, Brussels: European Network Against Racism aisbl (ENAR), pp 62–76.

EUMC (European Union Military Committee) (2015) 'Military advice on the draft crisis management concept for a possible CSDP operation to disrupt human smuggling networks in the southern central Mediterranean', www.statewatch.org/news/2015/may/eu-military-refugee-plan-EUMC.pdf

European Commission (2016) 'On establishing a new partnership framework with third countries under the European agenda on migration', www.europarl.europa.eu/RegData/docs_autres_institutions/commission_europeenne/com/2016/0385/COM_COM(2016)0385_EN.pdf

European Commission (2017) 'Central Mediterranean route: commission proposes action plan to support Italy, reduce pressure and increase solidarity', http://europa.eu/rapid/press-release_IP-17-1882_en.htm

European Commission (2018) 'Smart Borders', https://ec.europa.eu/home-affairs/what-we-do/policies/borders-and-visas/smart-borders_en

European Parliament (2016) 'Serbia's role in dealing with the migration crisis', www.europarl.europa.eu/RegData/etudes/BRIE/2016/589819/EPRS_BRI(2016)589819_EN.pdf

Faist, T., Fauser, M. and Reisenauer, E. (2013) *Transnational migration*, Cambridge: Polity.

Farris, S.R. (2015) 'Migrants' regular army of labour: gender dimensions of the impact of the global economic crisis on migrant labor in Western Europe', *The Sociological Review*, 63(1): 121–43.

Feldman, G. (2012) *The migration apparatus: Security, labor, and policymaking in the European Union*, Stanford, CA: Stanford University Press.

Finch, D. (2017) *Still just about managing? Pre-election briefing on the main political parties' welfare policies*, London: Resolution Foundation.

Fitzgerald, I. (2005) *Migrant workers in the North East of England*, Newcastle: Northern TUC and Northumbria University.

Fitzgerald, I. and Smoczynski, R. (2017) 'Central and Eastern European accession: changing perspectives on migrant workers', *Social Policy & Society*, 16(4): 659–68.

Fitzgerald, I., Hardy, J. and Lucio, M.M. (2013) 'The Internet, employment and Polish migrant workers: communication, activism and competition in the new organisational spaces', *New Technology, Work and Employment*, 27(2): 93–105.

Fitzpatrick, S., Bramley, G., Sosenko, F. and Blenkinsopp, J. (2018) *Destitution in the UK 2018*, York: JRF.

Fleming, P. (2015) *The mythology of work: How capitalism persists despite itself*, London: Pluto.

Fleming, P. (2017) 'The human capital hoax: work, debt and insecurity in the era of Uberization', *Organization Studies*, 38(5): 691–709.

Foster, J. (2010) 'The aristocracy of labour and working-class consciousness revisited', *Labour History Review*, 75(3): 245.

Foster, J.B., McChesney, R.W. and Jonna, R.J. (2011) 'The global reserve army of labor and the new imperialism', *Monthly Review*, 11(1): 1–31.

FRFI (Fight Racism! Fight Imperialism!) (2011) *No cuts – Full stop! Capitalist crisis and the public sector debt*, London: Larkin Publications.

Friman, H.R. (2011) 'The illegal "migration industry"', in N. Phillips (ed) *Migration in the global political economy*, Boulder, CO: Lynne Rienner Publishers, pp 83–99.

Fukuyama, F. (1992) *The end of history and the last man*, New York, NY: Free Press.

Gall, G. (2009) 'The engineering construction strikes in Britain, 2009', *Capital and Class*, 36(3): 411–31.

Geddes, A. (2011) 'Borders and migration in the European Union', in N. Phillips (ed) *Migration in the global political economy*, Boulder, CO: Lynne Rienner Publishers, pp 193–208.

Gill, R. and Pratt, A. (2008) 'In the social factory? Immaterial labour, precariousness and cultural work', *Theory, Culture & Society*, 25(7/8): 1–30.

Gilroy, P. (1998) *There ain't no black in the Union Jack*, London: Routledge.

GLA (Greater London Authority) (2017) 'CHAIN annual report Greater London April 2016–March 2017', https://files.datapress.com/london/dataset/chain-reports/2017-06-30T09:03:07.84/Greater%20London%20full%202016-17.pdf

Glazebrook, D. (2013) *Divide and ruin: The West's imperial strategy in an age of crisis*, San Francisco, CA: Liberation Media.

GMB (2009) 'GMB accuse senior managers of provoking the unofficial dispute at Lindsey by the layoff of original 51 workers in breach of agreements', press release, 22 March.

Gordon, D., Mack, J., Lansley, S., Main, G., Nandy, S., Patsios, D. and Pomati, M. (2013) 'The impoverishment of the UK – PSE UK first results: living standards: poverty and Social Exclusion UK', http://www.poverty.ac.uk/sites/default/files/attachments/The_Impoverishment_of_the_UK_PSE_UK_first_results_summary_report_March_28.pdf

Gosling, P. (2011) 'The rise of the "public services industry"', Unison, www.cheshireeastunison.org.uk/files/resources/19.pdf

Grady, J. (2017) 'The state, employment, and regulation: making work not pay', *Employee Relations*, 39(3): 274–90.

Grady, J. and Simms, M. (2018) 'Trade unions and the challenge of fostering solidarities in an era of financialisation', *Economic and Industrial Democracy*, 10.1177/0143831X18759792.

Gramsci, A. (1982 [1929–35]) *Selections from the prison notebooks*, London: Lawrence and Wishart.

Grayson, J. (2012) 'Forced evictions, racist attacks. Meet the new landlord, security company G4S', openDemocracy, www.opendemocracy.net/shinealight/john-grayson/forced-evictions-racist-attacks-meet-new-landlord-security-company-g4s

Grayson, J. (2013) 'After Mubenga unlawful killing verdict: could asylum seekers have a worse landlord than G4S?', OurKindom, www.opendemocracy.net/ourkingdom/john-grayson/after-mubenga-unlawful-killing-verdict-could-asylum-seekers-have-worse-landl

Grayson, J. (2017) 'Fail, fail, and have another government contract', openDemocracy, www.opendemocracy.net/uk/shinealight/john-grayson/fail-fail-and-have-another-government-contract

Greer, I. (2016) 'Welfare reform, precarity and the re-commodification of labour', *Work, Employment and Society*, 30(1): 162–73.

Griffiths, M. (2017) 'Foreign, criminal: a doubly damned modern British folk-devil', *Citizenship Studies*, 21(5): 527–46.

Grossmann, H. (1992 [1929]) *The law of accumulation and breakdown of the capitalist system*, London: Pluto.

Hall, S., Critcher, C., Jefferson, T., Clarke, J. and Roberts, B. (1978) *Policing the crisis: Mugging, the state and law and order*, London: Macmillan.

Hall, S.-M., McIntosh, K., Neitzert, E., Pottinger, L., Sandhu, K., Stephenson, M.-A., Reed, H. and Taylor, L. (2017) *Intersecting inequalities: The impact of austerity on black and minority ethnic women in the UK*, London: Women's Budget Group and Runnymede Trust.

Hanieh, A. (2018) 'The contradictions of global migration', *Socialist Register*, 55(Socialist Register 2019: A world turned upside down?), https://socialistregister.com/index.php/srv/article/view/30927

Hannington, W. (1973) *Unemployed struggles, 1919–1936: My life and struggles amongst the unemployed*, London: Barnes and Noble.

Hardy, J. (2008) 'Polish–UK migration: institutions, capital and the response of organised labour', paper presented at the EAEPE Conference 'Labour, Institutions and Growth in a Global Knowledge Economy', Rome.

Harling, P. (2001) *The modern British state: An historical introduction*, Cambridge: Polity.

Harvey, D. (2003) *The new imperialism*, Oxford: Oxford University Press.

Harvey, G., Rhodes, C., Vachhani, S.J. and Williams, K. (2017) 'Neo-villeiny and the service sector: the case of hyper flexible and precarious work in fitness centres', *Work, Employment and Society*, 3(1): 19–35.

Hastings, A., Bailey, N., Bramley, G., Gannon, M. and Watkins, D. (2015) *The cost of the cuts: The impact on local government and poorer communities*, York: JRF.

Hewitt, R.L. (2002) 'Asylum-seeker dispersal and community relations: an analysis of developmental strategies', Centre for Urban and Community Research, Goldsmiths College, London.

Hill Collins, P. (2009) 'Foreword: emerging intersections – building knowledge and transforming institutions', in B.T. Dill and R.E. Zambrana (eds) *Emerging intersections: Race, class, and gender in theory, policy, and practice*, New Brunswick: Rutgers University Press, pp vii–xiii.

Hillmann, F., Van Naerssen, T. and Spaan, E. (eds) (2018) *Trajectories and imaginaries in migration: The migrant actor in transnational space*, Abingdon: Routledge.

HM Chief Inspector of Prisons (2018) 'Report on an unannounced inspection of Heathrow Immigration Removal Centre: Harmondsworth site', www.justiceinspectorates.gov.uk/hmiprisons/wp-content/uploads/sites/4/2018/03/Harmondsworth-Web-2017.pdf

Holgate, J., Pollert, A., Keles, J. and Kumarappan, L. (2012) 'De-collectivization and employment problems: the experiences of minority ethnic workers seeking help through citizens advice', *Work, Employment and Society*, 26(5): 772–88.

Holzberg, B., Kolbe, K. and Zaborowski, R. (2018) 'Figures of crisis: the delineation of (un)deserving refugees in the German media', *Sociology*, 52(3): 534–50.

Home Affairs Committee (2017) 'Asylum accommodation', https://publications.parliament.uk/pa/cm201617/cmselect/cmhaff/637/637.pdf

Homeless Link (2017) 'Support for single homeless people in England annual review 2017', www.homeless.org.uk/sites/default/files/site-attachments/Annual%20Review%202017_0.pdf

Home Office (2017) 'Immigration statistics, April to June 2017', www.gov.uk/government/statistics/immigration-statistics-april-to-june-2017

hooks, b. (2014) *Talking back: Thinking feminist, thinking black* (2nd edn), New York, NY: Routledge.

Howell, P. (1975) 'Once again on productive and unproductive labour', *Revolutionary Communist*, 3/4, https://www.marxists.org/subject/economy/authors/howell/produnprod.htm

Hudson, B. (2016) *The failure of privatised adult social care in England: What is to be done?*, London: Centre for Health and the Public Interest.

Hudson, R. (2005) 'Rethinking change in old industrial regions: reflecting on the experiences of North East England', *Environment and Planning A*, 37(4): 581–96.

Humphries, J. (1983) 'The "emancipation" of women in the 1970s and 1980s: from the latent to the floating', *Capital and Class*, 7(6): 6–28.

ICIBI (Independent Chief Inspector of Borders and Immigration) (2016) 'An inspection of the "hostile environment" measures relating to driving licences and bank accounts, https://assets.publishing.service.gov.uk/government/uploads/system/uploads/attachment_data/file/567652/ICIBI-hostile-environment-driving-licences-and-bank-accounts-January-to-July-2016.pdf

ICIBI (2018) 'An inspection of the "right to rent" scheme, www.gov.uk/government/publications/an-inspection-of-the-right-to-rent-scheme

IMB (Independent Monitoring Boards) (2018) *Annual Report of the Independent Monitoring Boards' Charter Flight Monitoring Team for reporting year 2017*, Independent Monitoring Boards.

Ipsos MORI (2018) 'March 2018 Ipsos MORI issues index', www.ipsos.com/ipsos-mori/en-uk/brexit-and-nhs-top-britons-concerns-worry-about-housing-rising

James, S. (2012 [1983]) 'Marx and feminism', in S. James (ed) *Sex, race and class – The perspective of winning a selection of writings 1952–2011*, Chicago, IL: PM Press, pp 92–101.

Jameson, N. (2005) 'The reality of capitalism's immigration policy', *Fight Racism! Fight Imperialism!*, 185, http://www.revolutionarycommunist.org/britain/fight-racism/1219-the-reality-of-capitalisms-immigration-policy-frfi-185-june-july-2005

Janmyr, M. (2016) 'Precarity in exile: the legal status of Syrian refugees in Lebanon', *Refugee Survey Quarterly*, 35(4): 58–78.

Jarvis, A., Crow, R., Crawshaw, P., Shaw, K., Irving, A., Edwards, P. and Whisker, A. (2013) *The impact of welfare reform in the North East*, Durham: Institute of Local Governance.

Jones, H., Gunaratnam, Y., Bhattacharyya, G., Davies, W., Dhaliwal, S., Forkert, K., Jackson, E. and Saltus, R. (2017) *Go home? The politics of immigration controversies*, Manchester: Manchester University Press.

Jones, R. (2016) *Violent borders: Refugees and the right to move*, London: Verso.

Jonna, R.J. and Foster, J.B. (2016) 'Marx's theory of working-class precariousness: its relevance today', *Monthly Review*, 67(11), https://monthlyreview.org/2016/04/01/marxs-theory-of-working-class-precariousness/

Jørgensen, M.B. (2016) 'Precariat – what it is and isn't – towards an understanding of what it does', *Critical Sociology*, 42(7/8): 959–74.

Juncker, J.-C. (2015) 'State of the Union 2015', European Commission, https://ec.europa.eu/commission/sites/beta-political/files/state_of_the_union_2015_en.pdf

Kar, D., Schjelderup, G., Salomon, M. and Baker, R. (2016) *Financial flows and tax havens: Combining to limit the lives of billions of people*, Washington, DC: Global Financial Integrity.

Karakayali, S. and Rigo, E. (2010) 'Mapping the European space of circulation', in N.D. Genova and N. Peutz (eds) *The deportation regime: Sovereignty, space, and the freedom of movement*, Durham, NC: Duke University Press, pp 123–44.

Kasparek, B. and Speer, M. (2015) 'Of hope. Hungary and the long summer of migration', http://bordermonitoring.eu/ungarn/2015/09/of-hope-en/

Kesserling, S. (2014) 'Mobility, power and the emerging new mobilities regimes', *Sociologica*, (1) 10.2383/77047.

King, N. (2016) *No borders: The politics of immigration control and resistance*, London: Zed.

Kitson, F. (1973) *Low intensity operations: Subversion, insurgency and peacekeeping*, London: Faber and Faber.

Kitson, M., Martin, R. and Tyler, P. (2011) 'The geographies of austerity', *Cambridge Journal of Regions, Economy and Society*, 4(3): 289–302.

Kmak, M. (2015) 'Between citizen and bogus asylum seeker: management of migration in the EU through the technology of morality', *Social Identities*, 21(4): 395–409.

Kundnani, A. (2007) *The end of tolerance: Racism in 21st century Britain*, London: Pluto.

Kundnani, A. (2015) *The Muslims are coming! Islamophobia, extremism, and the domestic war on terror*, London: Verso.

Kuperman, A.J. (2013) 'A model humanitarian intervention? Reassessing NATO's Libya campaign', *International Security*, 38(1): 105–36.

Kymlicka, W. (2001) *Politics in the vernacular, nationalism, multiculturalism, and citizenship*, Oxford: Oxford University Press.

Kyriakides, C. (2017) 'Words don't come easy: Al Jazeera's migrant–refugee distinction and the European culture of (mis)trust', *Current Sociology*, 65(7): 933–52.

Kyriakides, C. and Torres, R. (2014) *Race defaced: Paradigms of pessimism, politics of possibility*, Stanford, CA: Stanford University Press.

Kyriakides, C. and Virdee, S. (2003) 'Migrant labour, racism and the British National Health Service', *Ethnicity and Health*, 8(4): 283–305.

LabourList (2015a) 'Corbyn urges Labour councils not to set illegal budgets', https://labourlist.org/2015/12/corbyn-urges-labour-councils-not-to-set-illegal-budgets/

LabourList (2015b) '"These things are not dreams." Jeremy Corbyn's full speech to the TUC', https://labourlist.org/2015/09/these-are-not-just-dreams-full-text-of-jeremy-corbyns-tuc-speech/

Labour Party (2017) 'For the many not the few: the Labour Party manifesto 2017', https://labour.org.uk/wp-content/uploads/2017/10/labour-manifesto-2017.pdf

Lafleur, J.-M. and Mescoli, E. (2018) 'Creating undocumented EU migrants through welfare: a conceptualization of undeserving and precarious citizenship', *Sociology*, 52(3): 480–96.

Lansley, S. and Mack, J. (2015) *Breadline Britain: The rise of mass poverty*, London: Oneworld.

Latham, R., Vosko, L.F., Preston, V. and Bretón, M. (2014) 'Introduction: liberating temporariness? Imagining alternatives to permanence as a pathway for social inclusion', in L.F. Vosko, V. Preston and R. Latham (eds) *Liberating temporariness? Migration, work, and citizenship in an age of insecurity*, Montreal and Kingston: McGill-Queen's University Press, pp 3–31.

Lees, L. and Ferreri, M. (2016) 'Resisting gentrification on its final frontiers: learning from the Heygate Estate in London (1974–2013)', *Cities*, 57: 14–24.

Lenin, V.I. (1972 [1895–1916]) *Philosophical notebooks* (vol 38), London: Lawrence and Wishart.

Lenin, V.I. (1972 [1917]) *The state and revolution*, Moscow: Progress.

Lenin, V.I. (1975 [1916]) *Imperialism, the highest stage of capitalism*, Moscow: Progress.

Lenin, V.I. (1977 [1913]) 'Capitalism and workers' immigration', in *Lenin collected works* (vol 19), Moscow: Progress, pp 454–57, Marxist Internet Archive, https://www.marxists.org/archive/lenin/works/1913/oct/29.htm

Lenin, V.I. (1978 [1902]) *What is to be done?*, Peking: Foreign Language Press.

Lenin, V.I. (2000 [1916]) 'The discussion on self-determination summed up', Marxists Internet Archive, www.marxists.org/archive/lenin/works/1916/jul/x01.htm

Lenin, V.I. (2005 [1915]) 'Opportunism, and the collapse of the second international', Marxists Internet Archive, www.marxists.org/archive/lenin/works/1915/dec/x01.htm

Lewis, H., Dwyer, P., Hodkinson, S. and Waite, L. (2014) *Precarious lives: Forced labour, exploitation and asylum*, Bristol: The Policy Press.

Lewis, H., Dwyer, P., Hodkinson, S. and Waite, L. (2015) 'Hyper-precarious lives: migrants, work and forced labour in the Global North', *Progress in Human Geography*, 39(5): 580–600.

LEWRG (London Edinburgh Weekend Return Group) (1980) *In and against the state*, London: London Edinburgh Weekend Return Group and Pluto.

LGSCO (Local Government and Social Care Ombudsman) (2017) 'Still no place like home? Councils' continuing use of unsuitable bed and breakfast accommodation for families', https://www.lgo.org.uk/assets/attach/4235/FINAL1.pdf

Liberty (2018) 'A guide to the hostile environment', www.libertyhumanrights.org.uk/sites/default/files/HE%20web.pdf

Lonergan, G. (2015) 'Migrant women and social reproduction under austerity', *Feminist Review*, 109: 124–45.

Lovett, A., Whelan, C. and Rendón, R. (2017) *The reality of the EU–turkey statement: How Greece has become a testing ground for policies that erode protection for refugees*, IRC, NRC and Oxfam International.

MAC (Migration Advisory Committee) (2011) 'Review of the transitional restrictions on access of Bulgarian and Romanian nationals to the UK labour market', https://www-cdn.oxfam.org/s3fs-public/bn-eu-turkey-statement-migration-170317-en.pdf

Macdonald, M. (2011) 'British Muslims, memory and identity: representations in British film and television documentary', *European Journal of Cultural Studies*, 14(4): 411–27.

MacDonald, R., Shildrick, T. and Furlong, A. (2014) '"Benefits Street" and the myth of workless communities', *Sociological Research Online*, 19(3), doi: 10.5153/sro.3438

Machin, R. (2018) 'The two-child limit for benefits: a move away from a "needs based" system', *Discover Society*, 54, https://discoversociety.org/2018/03/06/the-two-child-limit-for-benefits-a-move-away-from-a-needs-based-system/

Magdoff, F. and Magdoff, H. (2004) 'Today's reserve army of labor', *Monthly Review*, 4(1), http://monthlyreview.org/2004/04/01/disposable-workers-todays-reserve-army-of-labor

Maló, M. (2001) 'Sobre la feminizacion del trabajo', *Contrapoder*, 4/5: 75–8.

Malpass, P. (1990) *Reshaping housing policy: Subsidies, rents and residualisation*, London: Routledge.

Mandel, E. (1975) *Late capitalism*, London: NLB.

Marx, K. (1943 [1852]) *The eighteenth brumaire of Louis Bonaparte*, London: George Allen and Unwin.

Marx, K. (1959 [1844]) *Economic & philosophic manuscripts of 1844*, Moscow: Progress and Marxists Internet Archive.

Marx, K. (1967 [1890]) *Capital, volume 1*, London: Lawrence and Wishart.

Marx, K. (1971 [1859]) *A contribution to the critique of political economy*, London: Lawrence and Wishart.

Marx, K. (1973 [1857]) *Grundrisse*, London: Penguin.

Marx, K. (1991 [1894]) *Capital, volume 3* (3rd edn), London: Penguin.

Marx, K. and Engels, F. (1969 [1848]) *Manifesto of the Communist Party*, Moscow: Progress.

Marx, K. and Engels, F. (1991 [1845]) *The German ideology*, London: Lawrence and Wishart.

Mason, P. (2015) *Postcapitalism: A guide to our future*, London: Penguin.

McCollum, D. (2013) 'Investigating A8 migration using data from the worker registration scheme: temporal, spatial and sectoral trends', *Local Economy*, 28(1): 35–50.

McDermott, R. and Raley, J. (2011) 'Looking closely: toward a natural history of human ingenuity', in E. Margolis and L. Pauwels (eds) *The sage handbook of visual research methods*, London: SAGE, pp 372–91.

Meardi, G., Martin, A. and Riera, M.L. (2012) 'Constructing uncertainty: unions and migrant labour in construction in Spain and the UK', *Journal of Industrial Relations*, 54(1): 5–21.

Meehan, L. (2017) 'Universal Credit – bleeding the poor', *Fight Racism! Fight Imperialism!*, 261, http://www.revolutionarycommunist.org/britain/housing-and-welfare/5013-uc011217

Meek, J. (2018) 'NHS SOS', *London Review of Books*, 40(7): 17–30.

Meiksins Wood, E. (2005) *Empire of capital*, London: Verso.

Mezzadra, S. and Neilson, B. (2013) *Border as method, or, the multiplication of labour*, Durham, NC: Duke University Press.

MHCLG (Ministry of Housing, Communities & Local Government) (2012) 'Major clampdown launched on "beds in sheds"', www.gov.uk/government/news/major-clampdown-launched-on-beds-in-sheds

MHCLG (2016) 'Press release: Casey calls for integration plan to bind communities together', www.gov.uk/government/news/casey-calls-for-integration-plan-to-bind-communities-together

Miles, R. (1986) 'Labour migration, racism and capital accumulation in Western Europe since 1945: an overview', *Capital and Class*, 10: 49–86.

Miller, O.A. (2012) 'Deportation as a process of irreversible transformation', *Journal of Ethnic and Migration Studies*, 38(1): 131–46.

Mills, C.W. (2000 [1959]) *The sociological imagination*, New York, NY: Oxford University Press.

Mir, G. and Tovey, P. (2003) 'Asian carers' experiences of medical and social care: the case of cerebral palsy', *British Journal of Social Work*, 33(4): 465–79.

Mishra, P. (2018) *Age of anger: A history of the present*, London: Penguin.

Mitropoulos, A. (2006) 'Precari-us?', *Mute*, 2(0), http://www.metamute.org/editorial/articles/precari-us

Mohanty, C.T. (2003) *Feminism without borders*, Durham, NC: Duke University Press.

Mohanty, C.T. (2013) 'Transnational feminist crossings: on neoliberalism and radical critique', *Signs*, 38(4): 967–91.

Momani, B. (2008) 'Gulf Cooperation Council oil exporters and the future of the dollar', *New Political Economy*, 13(3): 293–314.

Montali, L., Riva, P., Frigerio, A. and Mele, S. (2013) 'The representation of migrants in the Italian press: a study on the corriere della sera (1992–2009)', *Journal of Language and Politics*, 12(2): 226–50.

Moore, P. and Forkert, K. (2014) 'Class and panic in British immigration', *Capital and Class*, 38(3): 497–505.

Mori, A. (2017) 'The impact of public services outsourcing on work and employment conditions in different national regimes', *European Journal of Industrial Relations*, 23(4): 347–64.

Morley, D. (2009) 'Mediated class-ifications: representations of class and culture in contemporary British television', *European Journal of Cultural Studies*, 12(4): 487–508.

Morris, M. (2017) *Striking the right deal: UK–EU migration and the Brexit negotiations*, London: IPPR.

Morrissens, A. and Sainsbury, D. (2005) 'Migrants' social rights, ethnicity and welfare regimes', *Journal of Social Policy*, 34(4): 637–60.

Murray, R., Jabbal, J., Maguire, D. and Ward, D. (2018) *How is the NHS performing? March 2018 quarterly monitoring report*, London: King's Fund.

National Audit Office (2018) 'Rolling out Universal Credit', www.nao.org.uk/wp-content/uploads/2018/06/Rolling-out-Universal-Credit.pdf

National Black Carers and Workers Network (2008) 'Beyond we care too: Putting black carers in the picture', London.

Nayak, A. (2003) *Race, place and globalization: Youth cultures in a changing world*, London: Bloomsbury.

Neilson, B. and Rossiter, N. (2008) 'Precarity as a political concept, or, Fordism as exception', *Theory, Culture & Society*, 25(7/8): 51–72.

Neilson, D. (2007) 'Formal and real subordination and the contemporary proletariat: re-coupling Marxist class theory and labour-process analysis', *Capital and Class*, 31(1): 89–123.

Neilson, D. and Stubbs, T. (2011) 'Relative surplus population and uneven development in the neoliberal era: theory and empirical application', *Capital and Class*, 35(3): 435–53.

Newbigging, K., McKeown, M., Hunkins-Hutchinson, E.A. and French, D.B. (2007) *Mtetezi: developing mental health advocacy with African and Caribbean men*, in *Knowledge Review*, vol 15, London: Social Care Institute for Excellence.

Newman, J., Glendinning, C. and Hughes, M. (2008) 'Beyond modernisation? Social care and the transformation of welfare governance', *Journal of Social Policy*, 37(4): 531–57.

Ngai, P., Yuan, S., Yuhua, G., Huilin, L., Chan, J. and Selden, M. (2014) 'Worker–intellectual unity: trans-border sociological intervention in Foxconn', *Current Sociology*, 62(2): 209–22.

Nichols, B. (2010) *Introduction to documentary* (2nd edn), Bloomington, IN: Indiana University Press.

Nkrumah, K. (1965) *Neo-colonialism: The last stage of imperialism*, London: Thomas Nelson and Sons.

Norfield, T. (2016) *The city: London and the global power of finance*, London: Verso.

Ofcom (Office of Communications) (2013) 'Communications market report 2013', https://www.ofcom.org.uk/__data/assets/pdf_file/0021/19731/2013_uk_cmr.pdf

Oliveri, F. (2012) 'Migrants as activist citizens in Italy: understanding the new cycle of struggles', *Citizenship Studies*, 16(5/6): 793–806.

Oliveri, F. (2018) 'Racialization and counter-racialization in times of crisis: taking migrant struggles in Italy as a critical standpoint on race', *Ethnic and Racial Studies*, 41(10): 1855–73.

ONS (Office for National Statistics) (2014) 'Migration statistics quarterly report, February 2014', https://webarchive.nationalarchives.gov.uk/20140912101749/http://www.ons.gov.uk/ons/rel/migration1/migration-statistics-quarterly-report/february-2014/index.html

ONS (2015a) 'Population by country of birth and nationality report: August 2015', https://www.ons.gov.uk/peoplepopulationandcommunity/populationandmigration/internationalmigration/articles/populationbycountryofbirthandnationalityreport/2015-09-27

ONS (2015b) 'United Kingdom balance of payments: the pink book 2015', https://www.ons.gov.uk/economy/nationalaccounts/balanceofpayments/compendium/unitedkingdombalanceofpaymentsthepinkbook/2015-10-30

ONS (2016a) 'Regional gross disposable household income (GDHI): 1997 to 2014', https://www.ons.gov.uk/economy/regionalaccounts/grossdisposablehouseholdincome/bulletins/regionalgrossdisposablehouseholdincomegdhi/2014

ONS (2016b) 'Regional labour market: March 2016', https://www.ons.gov.uk/employmentandlabourmarket/peopleinwork/employmentandemployeetypes/bulletins/regionallabourmarket/march2016

Paine, S. (1977) 'The changing role of migrant workers in the advanced capitalist economies of Western Europe', in R.T. Griffiths (ed) *Government, business and labour in European capitalism*, London: Europotentials Press, pp 199–225.

Paton, K. and Cooper, V. (2016) 'It's the state, stupid: 21st gentrification and state-led evictions', *Sociological Research Online*, 21(3): 1–7.

Pearson, R., Anitha, S. and McDowell, L. (2010) 'Striking issues: from labour process to industrial dispute at Grunwick and Gate Gourmet', *Industrial Relations Journal*, 41(5): 408–28.

Pemberton, S., Phillimore, J. and Robinson, D. (2014) *Causes and experiences of poverty among economic migrants in the UK*, IRIS Working Paper Series, Birmingham: University of Birmingham.

Pensiero, N. (2017) 'In-house or outsourced public services? A social and economic analysis of the impact of spending policy on the private wage share in OECD countries', *International Journal of Comparative Sociology*, 58(4): 333–51.

Petras, J. (2012) 'The Western welfare state: its rise and demise and the Soviet bloc', http://petras.lahaine.org/?p=1902

Petras, J. and Veltmeyer, H. (2013) *Imperialism and capitalism in the twenty-first century*, Farnham: Ashgate.

Peutz, N. and Genova, N.D. (2010) 'Introduction', in N.D. Genova and N. Peutz (eds) *The deportation regime: Sovereignty, space, and the freedom of movement*, Durham, NC: Duke University Press, pp 1–32.

Phillimore, J. (2012) 'Implementing integration in the UK: lessons for integration theory, policy and practice', *Policy & Politics*, 40(4): 525–45.

Phillimore, J. and Goodson, L. (2006) 'Problem or opportunity? Asylum seekers, refugees, employment and social exclusion in deprived urban areas', *Urban Studies*, 43(10): 1715–36.

Phillimore, J. and Sigona, N. (2018) 'The government's hostile environment and its consequences on integration', Discover Society, https://discoversociety.org/2018/05/01/the-governments-hostile-environment-and-its-consequences-on-integration/

Philo, G., Briant, E. and Donald, P. (2013) *Bad news for refugees*, London: Pluto.

Phizacklea, A. and Miles, R. (1980) *Labour and racism*, London: Routledge and Kegan Paul.

Piper, N. (2011) 'Toward a gendered political economy of migration', in N. Phillips (ed) *Migration in the global political economy*, Boulder, CO: Lynne Rienner Publishers, pp 61–81.

Pollock, A.M. (2005) *NHS plc: The privatisation of our health care*, London: Verso.

Portes, J. (2018) 'The economic impacts of immigration to the UK', CEPR Policy Portal, https://voxeu.org/article/economic-impacts-immigration-uk

Potter, J. (2018) 'Who has to pay for the NHS and when?', *The Conversation*, https://theconversation.com/who-has-to-pay-for-the-nhs-and-when-91344

Pradella, L. (2013) 'Imperialism and capitalist development in Marx's Capital', *Historical Materialism*, 21(2): 117–47.

Pradella, L. and Cillo, R. (2015) 'Labour, exploitation and migration in Western Europe: an international political economy perspective', in L. Waite, G. Craig, H. Lewis and K. Skrivankova (eds) *Vulnerability, exploitation and migrants: Insecure work in a globalised economy*, Basingstoke: Palgrave MacMillan, pp 43–56.

Prederi (2013) 'Quantitative assessment of visitor and migrant use of the NHS in England, exploring the data: main report', https://assets.publishing.service.gov.uk/government/uploads/system/uploads/attachment_data/file/251909/Quantitative_Assessment_of_Visitor_and_Migrant_Use_of_the_NHS_in_England_-_Exploring_the_Data_-_FULL_REPORT.pdf

Prentis, D. (2017) 'The scandal of 15-minute social care visits must end', Unison Blog, www.unison.org.uk/news/2017/04/blog-the-scandal-of-15-minute-social-care-visits-must-end/

Prime Minister's Office (2011) 'Joint UK, French and German statement on Syria, 18th August', www.gov.uk/government/news/joint-uk-french-and-german-statement-on-syria

Prime Minister's Office (2018) 'Treaty between the government of the United Kingdom of Great Britain and Northern Ireland and the government of the French Republic concerning the reinforcement of cooperation for the coordinated management of their shared border', www.statewatch.org/news/2018/jan/uk-fr-summit-treaty-shared-border-management-1-17.pdf

Rajaram, P.K. and Grundy-Warr, C. (eds) (2007) *Borderscapes: Hidden geographies and politics at territory's edge*, Minneapolis, MN: University of Minnesota Press.

Rayne, T. (2016) 'Why is Britain always at war?', Revolutionary Communist Group, www.revolutionarycommunist.org/capitalist-crisis/4233-wib130216

Rayne, T. (2018) 'Carillion: what is hidden in the ruins', *Fight Racism! Fight Imperialism!*, 262, http://www.revolutionarycommunist.org/britain/economy/5078-cw010218

RCP (Royal College of Physicians) (2012) 'Acute hospital care could be on the brink of collapse, warns RCP', www.rcplondon.ac.uk/news/acute-hospital-care-could-be-brink-collapse-warns-rcp

Redden, J. (2011) 'Poverty in the news', *Information, Communication & Society*, 14(6): 820–49.

Reeve, K., Cole, I., Batty, E., Foden, M., Green, S. and Pattison, B. (2016) *Home: No less will do – Homeless people's access to the private rented sector*, Sheffield: Sheffield Hallam University and Crisis.

Refugee Action (2017) 'Safe but alone: the role of English language in allowing refugees to overcome loneliness', http://www.refugee-action.org.uk/wp-content/uploads/2017/10/Safe-but-Alone-final.pdf

Reid, L. (1990) *Poll tax: Paying to be poor*, London: Revolutionary Communist Group.

Reisigl, M. and Wodak, R. (2001) *Discourse and discrimination: Rhetorics of racism and antisemitism*, London: Routledge.

Renton, D. (2007) *Colour blind? Race and migration in North East England since 1945*, Sunderland: University of Sunderland Press.

Richmond, A.H. (2002) 'Globalization: implications for immigrants and refugees', *Ethnic and Racial Studies*, 25(5): 707–27.

RLA (Residential Landlords Association) (2017) 'Right to rent headline findings: January 2017 survey', https://news.rla.org.uk/wp-content/uploads/2017/05/RLA-Right-to-Rent-Research-Briefing-January-2017.pdf

Rogaly, B. (2009) 'Spaces of work and everyday life: labour geographies and the agency of unorganised temporary migrant workers', *Geography Compass*, 3: 1975–87.

Rosen, R. and Crafter, S. (2018) 'Media representations of separated child migrants: from Dubs to doubt', *Migration and Society*, 1(1).

Rowlands, M. (2013) 'A duty to inform? The outsourcing of state surveillance responsibilities to the British public', *Statewatch Journal*, 23(2), http://database.statewatch.org/article.asp?aid=33251

RSA (Royal Society for the encouragement of Arts, Manufactures and Commerce) (2018) 'Good work for a thriving economy', Food, Farming and Countryside Commission, https://medium.com/the-rsa-food-farming-countryside-commission/good-work-for-a-thriving-economy-64218899466e

Said, E. (2003) *Orientalism*, London: Penguin.

Sales, R. (2002) 'The deserving and the undeserving? Refugees, asylum seekers and welfare in Britain', *Critical Social Policy*, 22(3): 456–78.

Santa Ana, O. (2013) *Juan in a hundred: The representation of Latinos on network news*, Austin, TX: University of Texas Press.

Sassen, S. (2014) *Expulsions: Brutality and complexity in the global economy*, Cambridge, MA: Belknap.

Savage, M., Devine, F., Cunningham, N., Taylor, M., Li, Y., Hjellbrekke, J., Roux, B.L., Friedman, S. and Miles, A. (2013) 'A new model of social class? Findings from the BBC's Great British Class Survey experiment', *Sociology*, 47(2): 219–50.

Schierup, C.-U. and Castles, S. (2011) 'Migration, minorities, and welfare states', in N. Phillips (ed) *Migration in the global political economy*, Boulder, CO: Lynne Rienner Publishers, pp 15–40.

Schuster, L. (2003) *The use and abuse of political asylum*, London: Frank Cass.

Seelke, C.R. and Finklea, K. (2017) 'U.S.–Mexican security cooperation: the Mérida Initiative and beyond', Congressional Research Service, https://fas.org/sgp/crs/row/R41349.pdf

Selby, K. and Cowdery, R. (1995) *How to study television*, Basingstoke: Palgrave MacMillan.

Shafique, A. (2018) *Addressing economic insecurity*, London: RSA and NCE.

Shah, B., Murphy, J. and Ogden, J. (2016) 'Everyday nationhood on the web: an analysis of discourses surrounding Romanian and Bulgarian migration to the UK using Twitter data', paper presented at the British Sociological Association Annual Conference, Birmingham.

Shelter (2016) 'Survey of private landlords', https://england.shelter.org.uk/__data/assets/pdf_file/0004/1236820/Landlord_survey_18_Feb_publish.pdf

Shelter (2017) 'Shut out: the barriers low-income households face in private renting', https://england.shelter.org.uk/__data/assets/pdf_file/0004/1391701/2017_06_-_Shut_out_the_barriers_low_income_households_face_in_pivate_renting.pdf

Silverman, S.J. (2011) *Immigration detention in the UK*, Oxford: The Migration Observatory.

Sivanandan, A. (1991) *A different hunger: Writings on black resistance*, London: Pluto.

Skeggs, B. and Wood, H. (2011) 'Introduction: real class', in H. Wood and B. Skeggs (eds) *Reality television and class*, London: Palgrave and BFI, pp 1–32.

Skills for Care (2017) 'The state of the adult social care sector and workforce in England, September 2017', www.skillsforcare.org.uk/Documents/NMDS-SC-and-intelligence/NMDS-SC/Analysis-pages/State-of-17/State-of-the-adult-social-care-sector-and-workforce-2017.pdf

Smith, C. (2006) 'The double indeterminacy of labour power: labour effort and labour mobility', *Work, Employment and Society*, 20(2): 389–402.

Smith, J. (2016) *Imperialism in the twenty-first century: Globalization, super-exploitation, and capitalism's final crisis*, New York, NY: Monthly Review Press.

Sohoni, D. and Mendez, J.B. (2014) 'Defining immigrant newcomers in new destinations: symbolic boundaries in Williamsburg, Virginia', *Ethnic and Racial Studies*, 37(3): 496–516.

Sporton, D. (2013) '"They control my life": the role of local recruitment agencies in East European migration to the UK', *Population, Space and Place*, 19(5): 443–58.

Stanciu, M. and Jawad, A.-D. (2013) 'Public health services in Romania in terms of European policies', *Journal of Community Positive Practices*, 13(1): 26–44.

Standing, G. (2011) *The precariat: The new dangerous class*, London: Bloomsbury Academic.

Steinhilper, E. and Gruijters, R.J. (2018) 'A contested crisis: policy narratives and empirical evidence on border deaths in the Mediterranean', *Sociology*, 52(3): 515–33.

Stenning, A. and Dawley, S. (2009) 'Poles to Newcastle: grounding new migrant flows in peripheral regions', *European Urban and Regional Studies*, 16(3): 273–94.

Stevenson, G. (1978) 'Social relations of production and consumption in the human service occupations', *International Journal of Health Services*, 8(3): 453–63.

Strauss, K. (2015) 'Social reproduction and migrant domestic labour in Canada and the UK: towards a multi-dimensional concept of subordination', in L. Waite, G. Craig, H. Lewis and K. Skrivankova (eds) *Vulnerability, exploitation and migrants: Insecure work in a globalised economy*, Basingstoke: Palgrave MacMillan, pp 59–71.

Strauss, K. and Meehan, K. (2015) 'Introduction: new frontiers in life's work', in K. Meehan and K. Strauss (eds) *Precarious worlds: Contested geographies of social reproduction*, Athens, GA: University of Georgia Press, pp 1–22.

Strikwerda, C. and Guerin-Gonzales, C. (1998) 'Labor, migration and politics', in C. Guerin-Gonzales and C. Strikwerda (eds) *The politics of immigrant workers: Labor activism and migration in the world economy since 1830* (2nd edn), New York, NY: Holmes and Meier, pp 3–78.

Sturgess, G.L. (2017) *Just another paperclip? Rethinking the market for complex public services*, London: Business Services Association.

Sumino, T. (2014) 'Does immigration erode the multicultural welfare state? A cross-national multilevel analysis in 19 OECD member states', *Ethnic and Migration Studies*, 40(3): 436–55.

Tinson, A. (2015) 'The rise of sanctioning in Great Britain', New Policy Institute, www.npi.org.uk/publications/social-security-and-welfare-reform/rise-sanctioning-great-britain/

Tomaney, J. and Ward, N. (2001) *A region in transition: North East England at the millennium*, Farnham: Ashgate.

Tomlinson, J. (1991) *Cultural imperialism: A critical introduction*, London: Pinter.

Trimikliniotis, N., Parsanoglou, D. and Tsianos, V.S. (2016) 'Mobile commons and/in precarious spaces: mapping migrant struggles and social resistance', *Critical Sociology*, 42(7/8): 1035–49.

Tripp, C. (2007) *A history of Iraq* (3rd edn), Cambridge: Cambridge University Press.

TUC (Trades Union Congress) (2015) 'Outsourcing public services', Trades Union Congress and New Economics Foundation, www.tuc.org.uk/sites/default/files/TUC%20and%20NEF%20 Outsourcing%20Public%20Services.pdf

Tyler, I. (2013) *Revolting subjects: Social abjection and resistance in neoliberal Britain*, London: Zed.

United Nations Statistics Division (2013) 'Principles and recommendations for a vital statistics system, revision 3', http://unstats.un.org/unsd/demographic/sconcerns/migration/migrmethods.htm#B

Urry, J. (2007) *Mobilities*, Cambridge: Polity.

Vickers, T. (2012) *Refugees, capitalism and the British state: Implications for social workers, volunteers and activists*, Farnham: Ashgate.

Vickers, T. (2014) 'Developing an independent anti-racist model for asylum rights organising in England', *Ethnic and Racial Studies*, 37(8): 1427–47.

Vickers, T. (2015) 'The contribution of UK asylum policy 1999–2010 to conditions for the exploitation of migrant labour', in L. Waite, G. Craig, H. Lewis and K. Skrivankova (eds) *Vulnerability, exploitation and migrants: Insecure work in a globalised economy*, London: Palgrave MacMillan, pp 101–14.

Vickers, T. (2016) 'Opportunities and limitations for collective resistance arising from volunteering by asylum seekers and refugees in Northern England', *Critical Sociology*, 42(3): 437–54.

Vickers, T., Clayton, J., Davison, H., Hudson, L., Cañadas, M., Biddle, P., Lilley, S., Fletcher, G. and Chantkowski, M. (2016) '"New migrants" in the North East workforce: final report', Nottingham Trent University, http://irep.ntu.ac.uk/id/eprint/29159/

Virdee, S. (2014) *Racism, class and the racialized outsider*, Basingstoke: Palgrave MacMillan.

Vitali, S., Glattfelder, J. and Battiston, S. (2011) 'The network of global corporate control', *PLoS ONE*, 6(10): e25995.

Waite, L. (2009) 'A place and space for a critical geography of precarity?', *Geography Compass*, 3(1): 412–33.

Warburton, C. (2016) 'Union calls for action over migrant worker construction deaths', www.healthandsafetyatwork.com/migrant-workers/ucatt-hse-migrant-worker-deaths

Watkins, J., Wulaningsih, W., Zhou, C.D., Marshall, D.C., Sylianteng, G.D.C., Rosa, P.G.D., Miguel, V.A., Raine, R., King, L.P. and Maruthappu, M. (2017) 'Effects of health and social care spending constraints on mortality in England: a time trend analysis', *BMJ Open*, 7(e017722).

Watt, P. (2016) 'A nomadic war machine in the metropolis', *City*, 20(22): 297–320.

Watt, P. and Minton, A. (2016) 'London's housing crisis and its activisms', *City*, 20(2): 204–21.

Wayne, M. (2003) *Marxism and media studies: Key concepts and contemporary trends*, London: Pluto.

Webber, F. (2012) *Borderline justice: The fight for refugee and migrant rights*, London: Pluto.

Weiner, C. (2017) 'The market cannot "fix" the housing crisis', Revolutionary Communist Group, www.revolutionarycommunist.org/britain/housing-and-welfare/4633-0517-housing-crisis

Wemyss, G. (2015) 'Everyday bordering and raids every day: the invisible empire and metropolitan borderscapes', in C. Brambilla, J. Laine, J.W. Scott and G. Bocchi (eds) *Borderscaping: Imaginations and practices of border making*, Farnham: Ashgate, pp 187–95.

Whitfield, D. (2012) *In place of austerity: Reconstructing the economy, state and public services*, Nottingham: Spokesman.

Wilkinson, M. and Craig, G. (2011) 'Wilful negligence: migration policy, migrants' work and the absence of social protection in the UK', in E. Carmel, A. Cerami and T. Papadopoulos (eds) *Migration and welfare in the new Europe: Social protection and the challenges of integration*, Bristol: The Policy Press, pp 177–94.

Wilkinson, M., Craig, G. and Gaus, A. (2009) *Turning the tide: How to best protect workers employed by gangmasters, five years after Morecambe Bay*, Oxford: Oxfam.

Wilks, S. (2013) *The political power of the business corporation*, Cheltenham: Edward Elgar.

Williams, F. (1995) 'Race/ethnicity, gender, and class in welfare states: a framework for comparative analysis', *Social Politics*, 2(2): 127–59.

Williams, M., Palmer, S. and Clapton, G. (1979) 'Racism, imperialism and the working class', *Revolutionary Communist*, 9: 8–43.

Wills, J., Datta, K., Evans, Y., Herbert, J., May, J. and McIlwaine, C. (2010) *Global cities at work: New migrant divisions of labour*, London: Pluto.

World Bank (2018) 'Migration and remittances: recent developments and outlook', http://www.knomad.org/sites/default/files/2018-04/Migration%20and%20Development%20Brief%2029.pdf

Wright, S. (2002) *Storming heaven: Class composition and struggle in Italian autonomist Marxism*, London: Pluto Press.

Yaffe, D. (1972) 'The Marxian theory of crisis, capital and the state', *Bulletin of the Conference of Socialist Economists*, Winter: 5–58.

Yaffe, D. (2006) 'Britain: parasitic and decaying capitalism', *Fight Racism! Fight Imperialism!*, 194, http://www.revolutionarycommunist.org/index.php/britain/1042-britain-parasitic-and-decaying-capitalism-frfi-194-dec-2006-jan-2007

Yaffe, D. and Bullock, P. (1979) 'Inflation, the crisis and the post-war boom', *Revolutionary Communist*, 3/4: 5–45.

Yaffe, H. (2009) *Che Guevara: The economics of revolution*, Basingstoke: Palgrave MacMillan.

Yaffe, H. (2019) *We are Cuba! How a revolutionary people have survived in a post-Soviet world*, New Haven, CT: Yale University Press.

Yates, T., Crane, R. and Burnett, A. (2007) 'Rights and the reality of healthcare charging in the United Kingdom', *Medicine, Conflict and Survival*, 23(4): 297–304.

Young, R.J.C. (2001) *Postcolonialism: An historical introduction*, Malden, MA: Blackwell.

Index

Note: Page numbers in *italic* refer to figures.